SWEDEN
THE UNTOLD STORY

CLAUDIA WALLIN

SWEDEN
THE UNTOLD STORY

Translated by Laurie Anne Carpenter

In one of the least corrupt countries in the world, politicians use public transport, do their own laundry and are treated just like everyone else

W PUBLISHERS

To my father, Jú,
eternally present in our hearts.

CONTENTS

ACKNOWLEDGMENTS

To Mats Knutson, for the invaluable conversations. To Paulo Roberto Varejão, Joe Frans and Claes Jernaeus, for the endless hours of support. To Anna Aspegren and Maria Skuldt, of the Riksdag (Swedish Parliament), for the helpfulness in answering my unending questions. To Eduardo Mack and Sofia Polhammer, for the valuable input. To all of those who agreed to be interviewed, for your support in making this book possible.

To Felix, Alex and Max, our little Vikings, for their loving affection.

>And above all to my husband,
>Ulf Wallin,
>for all the reasons in the world.

YOUR EXCELLENCIES, ILLUSTRIOUS LADIES AND GENTLEMEN,

I BRING URGENT NEWS from a distant kingdom. It is imperative to forewarn you, Your Excellencies, that in this strange land the inhabitants have created a country where the most honorable representatives of the people are treated — I kid you not — like ordinary people. Rampant foolery! Some may say that the stories I will recount here are mere fairy-tale hallucinations, for in this wealthy kingdom called Sweden there is a king, a queen and princesses. But do not be fooled! The inhabitants of this nation have taken away all of the king's power, in the name of a democracy that proclaims a freaky 'equality for all', and what I shall disclose to you are things that I have witnessed with these very eyes that the earth will one day swallow.

In these faraway provinces, the very distinguished members of Parliament, government ministers and mayors travel by train or bus to work, in their daily grind to alleviate the miseries of their people. By bus, Your Eminences! And there are many castles throughout the four corners of this prosperous kingdom, but the venerable representatives of the people have to make do with itsy-bitsy offices and pitiful housing in one-room accommodations with shared laundry facilities, unworthy of the illustrious protectors of the rights of the citizens and of democracy.

Such humiliation imposed on the noble guardians of the public coffers could be, perhaps, an effect of the bizarre seasonal variations of this abnormal land on the mental faculties of the people who survive in it. At the furthermost boundaries of this realm, the sun never sets during summer, and in the winter only darkness reigns. Your Lordships can surely imagine, without a lively description on my part, the abominable impact of these phenomena on the brain function of the subversive citizens of this land.

The misinformed will say that there are more moose and reindeer than human beings in these frozen provinces, but this is untrue. The men and women of this land, previously inhabited by brave Viking warriors who fought tooth and nail for the public money, now comprise a population of nearly ten million. And this kingdom is surrounded by other rich dominions known collectively as the Nordic countries, where there are also past and present princes and kings and castles, but where the august representatives of the people live as all subjects live. And I have also witnessed this: in one of the neighboring lands, known as the kingdom of the Norwegians, what many eminent representatives of the people enjoy for lunch are soggy sandwiches they take from the pockets of their suits when hunger beckons.

Altogether, the inhabitants of these godforsaken lands of Northern Europe amount more than 26 million people, determined to wrest any and all privileges from the glorious representatives whom they elect.

Caution is advised, noble friends. Little is heard about this kingdom called Sweden, for there are many who confuse its name with that of Switzerland, the land of fine chocolates and of splendid banks, as Your Lordships certainly know. But beware: news is spreading about the egalitarian kingdom of the Swedes, where no one is more equal than others.

Stockholm, January 6, 2013

INTRODUCTION

SUDDENLY, THE DOOR OPENS. Shocking scenes are set to follow, and it is best to warn you in advance: these scenes are unsuitable for anyone suffering from a weak heart, delusions of grandeur or megalomaniac tendencies.

From behind the door an employee appears, brandishing a coffee cup and humming in a Machiavellian tone. He has just entered the room where an important international meeting is taking place in Rosenbad, the seat of the Swedish government.

"Someone forgot to put their cup in the dishwasher," he announces accusingly, to the astonishment of the foreign delegation sitting around the conference table. They exchange glances, and look on in bewilderment.

"Oh, look! It says 'Fredrik' on the cup," comments the employee, feigning surprise. "Maybe it's your cup, Fredrik?"

The Fredrik in question, looking disconcertedly at

his accuser, is Fredrick Reinfeldt, the prime minister of Sweden.

"The dishwasher was full," murmurs the prime minister, mortified by the flagrant transgression that is impossible to deny.

"You'll just have to empty the machine, Fredrik," replies the employee, adding with sarcasm: "Your mother doesn't work here, Mr. Prime Minister."

Fredrik Reinfeldt rises from his chair and addresses the guests.

"Excuse me, but I need to take care of this," he says, before leaving the room with cup in hand.

The scene described above certainly stunned some of the millions of viewers who watched it in May of 2013. Broadcasters in 39 countries showed it during the opening sequence of Eurovision, the popular European song contest hosted by Sweden on that particular occasion. In Swedish fashion, it carried on a tradition of opening the song contest with a presentation of the customs and values of the host country. In the sketch about the prime minister's cup, the Swedes highlighted the egalitarian nature of their country, which — like the other Scandinavian and Nordic countries in general — repudiates and abominates the existence of any perceived gulf between those governing and those being governed.

Now, some will assume that the sketch was nothing more than a delusional chimera, a fanciful farce designed to entertain the Eurovision audience. Yet the Swedes would beg to disagree.

The scene involving the cup was not unusual:

once during an informal conversation with Roberta Alenius, the prime minister's press secretary, she told me that Fredrik Reinfeldt never left his office, at the end of the day, without first putting his coffee cup in the dishwasher.

At that point, I had already realized that Sweden was not an ordinary country. Not just because of the images of drunken moose staggering along the road after eating fermented apples during autumn or because of the huge lumps of ice I would see plunge from the tops of buildings in the winter. Not even because of the incalculable number of men seen on the streets pushing baby buggies, exercising the full rights of their paternity leave.

What most caught my attention in this unique country, my home for the last ten years, was the absence of any neurosis in the relations between the people and those in power. In other words, this is a nation that treats its government officials and political representatives as ordinary citizens. A country without "Excellencies" and other formal titles of address. A society in which a political mandate does not confer a title of instant nobility to those elected to serve the public, nor bestow upon them the right to privileges and flattery which in so many countries are granted to exotic royal courts of commoners maintained by commoners who are further down in the social pyramid. A place where politicians' wives don't go shopping in official parliamentary cars, paid for with the tax money collected from the very chauffeurs who carry their bags. For, in Sweden, politicians in general are not granted official cars, chauffeurs or private secretaries. They do not travel by private jet or on first-class flights. They do not overnight in luxury hotels or receive extravagant special allowances. No luxuries, no privileges.

The story of this book began on a cold night in Sweden, and it must be said that "cold night" is a redundant term in this icy northern European country. It was 9 p.m. and I was watching Aktuellt, the flagship news program of SVT, the national public TV broadcaster. Having just finished the Swedish language course at the University of Stockholm, I was once again trying out my understanding of the language of the ancient Vikings.

"Did you hear that?" I asked my husband, Ulf. The program featured an interview with Prime Minister Fredrik Reinfeldt by Mats Knutson, one of the country's most respected political journalists.

"The reporter just called the prime minister 'Fredrik'," I said.

"So what?" responded my husband, clearly a Swede. Not "Mr. Reinfeldt," not "Prime Minister." Just Fredrik, a citizen. With all due respect.

From that cold night on, through conversations with Mats Knutson, Swedish politicians, political scientists, lawyers, journalists, judges and people on the street, I began to grasp the logic of the level playing field that exists between the Swedish public and the politicians that represent them. Not only because of the Swedish aversion to the use of formal modes of address in discourse with the authorities, but mainly because of the remarkable sense of equality that prevails here among the population, by both those governing and those governed.

This is a society that abolished the use of formal pronouns in the 1960s, and where everyone is called simply "you." Because, according to the Swedish system of values, nobody is above anybody else. Not even politicians, who should live in conditions similar to the reality of the people who elect them. Not even judges, who, bereft of benefits or special privileges, do not have their lunches bought for them with taxpayers' money with scandalous food allowances linked to their high salaries.

Those in authority must be held accountable, and all information must be freely available to the public: Swedish openness is reflected in the very transparency of the political power, which is monitored by means of the oldest transparency law in the world — a law that makes political corruption at national level a relatively rare phenomenon in the country.

The outcome of those first conversations and interviews in my new home country was a series of news reports I produced for the Brazilian Television. The series was titled "Sweden: A Country of Politicians without Perks and Privileges." Shared globally via the feverish speed of the Internet, the TV reports triggered responses in countries such as Portugal, Spain, Colombia, Mexico, Venezuela and India, from which messages arrived and continue to arrive in search of more information about the reality of the Swedish system. It was in response to these inquiries that I wrote this book, based on the research for the TV series and on interviews conducted in Sweden throughout 2013.

So what kind of country is this?

The Kingdom of Sweden (*Konungariket Sverige*, in Swedish), founded around 1200, is one of the oldest kingdoms in the world. The Royal Palace dominates the magnificent panorama of its capital, Stockholm, a city spread out over 14 islands surrounded by the waters of the Baltic Sea and Lake Mälaren. The kingdom's monarch, however, has long lost his power over this extreme and progressive nation, which has become a paragon in promoting the ideals of equality, justice and social solidarity.

Long gone are the days of the legendary Vikings that inhabited this land, crossing treacherous seas to pillage, burn and terrorize foreign lands. They were blond barbarians, in the worst sense of the word. But they were also great traders and explorers. And they had a custom that was uncommon for the time: they made their decisions in a group, by consensus. They would gather in assemblies called *ting*, which were established throughout what is today called Sweden and other Nordic lands. Those assemblies were like embryonic parliaments, created by a free people who claimed to have no leaders: they were all equal.

In the Sweden of the Middle Ages, another uncommon scene could be observed: peasants were represented amongst the nobility, the clergy, and the bourgeoisie gathered in the Parliament. This was a unique phenomenon in Europe at that time. The profound democratic tradition and the visceral sentiment of equality among the people, which molded Swedish society throughout the centuries, would gradually transform the country into a model of social justice.

At the outset, however, there was hunger. Until halfway through the 19th century, Sweden was one of the most impoverished countries in Europe, with a backward agricultural economy. However, the face of the country would evolve: among the key factors driving change were substantial investments in education, infrastructure, and technology. In the 20th century, formerly underdeveloped and poverty-stricken Sweden rebuilt itself into one of the world's wealthiest and most sophisticated industrial nations.

Thus the foundations were laid for the construction of an extensive and generous welfare state, financed by one of the highest tax rates on the planet and designed to protect its citizens from 'the cradle to the grave'. An organized and harmonious people joined together to rectify income disparity and standard of living inequalities, in a quest to create a new, more humane society.

In 1936, American journalist Marquis Childs, author of the celebrated book *Sweden: The Middle Way*, suggested that the Swedes had discovered a virtuous middle ground between the extremes of capitalism and socialism. The golden times of this Swedish paragon, guided by Social Democratic leadership, would last until the 1970s.

"The deeply held Swedish belief, transcending ideological differences, is that the ills of a free society can be cured, that injustice is intolerable," wrote Childs. The changing times brought challenges to the pioneering Swedish formula, which was based on a vigorous market economy fused with an extensive welfare state.

Yet just as cracks open in the ground and in the frozen seas of this land at the end of each winter, at this point it must be said that this is not, evidently, a society without faults. It is a country with its fair share of problems and contradictions, failures and triumphs, with staunch supporters and fierce critics of the course taken by the kingdom. Deficiencies in the country's integration policies generate a mass of disadvantaged immigrants, inequality grows, and the famous welfare state becomes less generous. Furthermore, as its Nordic neighbors will attest, Sweden is not the only country that rejects political privileges and perks.

Yet it is vital to know that there is a place, here in the latitudes touching the Arctic Circle, where the fundamental exercise of politics is conducted predominantly with integrity, absence of anachronistic privileges, and respect for the taxpayers' money. A country where members of parliament earn, on average, approximately twice as much as elementary schoolteachers. Where sound management policies continuously monitor the efficient use of public funds and bolster confidence in public institutions. Where a society that demands respect scrutinizes those in government and punishes any transgressions. A transparent society in which corruption has become the exception, not the rule. A country where behavior has been transformed.

The Swedes wish for more — more transparency, and fewer politicians who are out of touch with the realities of ordinary people's lives. And the government's sense of self-criticism persists, as seen in the words of Swedish prime minister Göran Persson's address to a student audience in 2002:

"I do not lead the most brilliant government in the world. The cabinet of ministers is no model of intellectual elite, nor are we particularly beautiful either." *(Inifrån — makten, myglet, politiken Thomas Bodström, Norstedts, 2011).*

Joakim Holm, a Swedish citizen: "I'm the one who pays the politicians."

CHAPTER I

NO LUXURIES OR PRIVILEGES

"THERE WILL BE UNBEARABLE hardships," warns an eminent foreign politician to a Swede at the moment his calling to enter Swedish politics becomes an unstoppable yearning: no cheering entourages of useless aides, no special expense accounts or allowances for employing relatives and parasites. No nose jobs covered by 5-star private health plans. No salaries for municipal councilors. Miserable apartments for members of Parliament that resemble two-star hotel rooms. If such an ordeal seems insufferable, it might be useful to invoke Mímir, the Norse God venerated for the infinite wisdom of his mighty head — which, despite having been chopped off in a battle, continues to offer unsurpassed advice.

Sweden does not offer its politicians a life of luxury: in this essentially egalitarian society, the political classes are not granted the privileged status of a pampered elite, nor are they entitled to the prerogatives of a nobility entrenched in power. Without official cars or private drivers, Swedish politicians travel in crowded buses and trains, just like the citizens they represent. Without any right to parliamentary immunity, they do not enjoy preferential legal treatment and can be tried like any other citizen before impartial judges, who themselves are not above the law.

Without salaries for life, Swedish members of Parliament do not receive a well-deserved retirement pension after spending just a few years working for the good of the people. With no private secretaries at the door or private bathrooms and breakfast bars, their bare-bones parliamentary offices are spartan and tiny like a public clerk's office. Without allowances available for renting offices in their constituencies, Swedish MPs work from their own homes, or even in a public library, when they are in their local areas.

"It's OK, but it could be better," grumbles the taxi driver who takes me from Arlanda airport to the center of Stockholm, the capital of Sweden. He complains with indignation, as do many others, about the take-home pay of a member of the Riksdag (Swedish Parliament): horror of horrors, it is approximately two times more than what an elementary school teacher earns on average. According to the Swedish driver's logic, this is an indefensible privilege which should be in an accelerated process of extinction.

No need to consult with Mímir's head to figure out that this is a society that knows who's the boss.

"I'm the one who pays the politicians," says Joakim Holm, a Swedish citizen. "And I see no reason to give them a life of luxury."

"Politicians are elected to work for me and all the other citizens who pay taxes. No one here thinks politicians are a superior class with any rights to privileges," says another Swede, Mikael Forslund.

At the municipal level, any desire to work in politics could be seen, outside of Sweden, as a case for requiring psychological assessment: after all, Swedish councilors do not even earn a salary, nor do they have the right to an office — they work from home. Are they out of their minds?

What the Swedish political model demonstrates is that the straitjackets may be better suited to fit the anesthetized crowds in other latitudes, who gaze witlessly at the fascinating spectacle of the daily abuse of power. Sweden's experience subverts the unhinged concept that politicians should be accorded reverential treatment worthy of a higher caste, comprised of ladies and gentlemen who are more illustrious than the average citizen and therefore deserving of an almost divine right to benefits and privileges which those living below the political Olympus could never attain.

I still remember the strange feeling of witnessing an extra-terrestrial phenomenon when I saw the current minister of Foreign Affairs and former Swedish prime minister, Carl Bildt, pushing a shopping trolley in a supermarket in Stockholm. Or the mayor of Stockholm,

Sten Nordin, standing in a queue at a bus stop. Or the Speaker of the Parliament, Per Westerberg, sitting on an underground train.

Free from major social imbalances, Sweden is undoubtedly a safer and less violent country, where politicians and citizens alike don't usually need to travel in bullet-proof cars. But more importantly, this is a society that elects politicians who are more in touch with the day-to-day realities and pains of ordinary citizens. Politicians who generally do not place their personal interests ahead of those of the people, in a society that demonstrates that political power can be exercised within the boundaries of decency.

"In Sweden, politicians live a simple life, in just the same way as other citizens. It's a tradition," says journalist Mats Knutson, host and political commentator for SVT, the national public TV broadcaster.

In the 1970s, Social Democratic Prime Minister Olof Palme lived in his own house in the suburb of Vällinby, and used to drive to work in his old red Fiat.

"It was a Fiat 600, manufactured in the former East Germany," recounts Marten Palme, son of Olof Palme and Economics professor at the University of Stockholm. "My father valued equality and simplicity, and we lived a normal life. Our summer house on the island of Fårö was quite primitive, and it didn't even have running water or electricity," he says.

Palme's predecessor, Tage Erlander, would take the

tram to the seat of Government. Or he would get a lift from his wife, who worked nearby.

The Swedes decided to establish an official residence for the prime minister only after 1986, when Olof Palme was assassinated as he was leaving a cinema without any bodyguards, in a brutal crime that has never been solved. His successor, Social Democrat Ingvar Carlsson, moved reluctantly into the new official residence. It is said that Carlsson, who as deputy prime-minister lived in a small and modest flat in the outskirts of Stockholm — where he still lives today — , felt that it was somewhat inappropriate for a Swedish prime minister to live in a place called a palace. When built in 1884, the wealthy Sager family had christened it Sagerska Palace.

Less attentive tourists in Stockholm pass just a meter from the front door of the Swedish prime minister's house, without realizing it. The official Sagerska residence does not have any outer gates and is situated in Strömgatan, a pedestrian street bordering the Baltic Sea and Lake Mälaren in the vicinity of the Parliament. The 305 square meters of the premier's private quarters occupy the top floor of the 1,195-square-meter residence, which is monitored by two hidden cameras on the outside, and the occasional presence of a Volvo from the Swedish security forces.

Sagerska is a beautiful mansion. But there are no household servants in the residence of Prime Minister Fredrik Reinfeldt.

"The prime minister's private quarters are cleaned once a week. He must pay taxes on his income for this service," says Anna Dahlen, press officer at the Swedish government.

Without provoking any reactions of supernatural astonishment among the public, Fredrik Reinfeldt speaks naturally about cooking, ironing and washing his own clothes, just like the majority of the citizens of this country.

"And why wouldn't he, if we all do it, too?" I hear from several Swedes.

There are those who will conjure up the acrid stench of populist demagogy when they learn that in Sweden the prime minister gives cleaning tips in newspaper articles and advises his fellow citizens to get down on their knees to scrape the dirt off the floor. But the truth is that taking care of household chores is as natural for most Swedes as drinking snaps, the distilled alcohol consumed in immoderate quantities in the country.

In Sweden, as in many other countries of the world, the profession of domestic servant does not exist. Among the most radical Swedes, the zeal for equality and the fear of the resurgence of a social underclass provokes indignant reactions. During an electoral campaign debate in 2006, sparks were flying against the then leader of the Centre Party (*Centerpartiet*), Maud Olofsson, when she defended the introduction of tax rebates to allow the Swedes to hire cleaning professionals to alleviate the problem of working double shifts.

"And who cleans the maid's bathroom?" asked the moderator Göran Rosenberg, in an irritated tone, during the debate held on the Swedish private channel TV4.

"And who paints the painter's house?" retorted Olofsson. "The cleaning lady can also hire help when needed," she argued.

Olofsson's unexpected response was promptly attacked by the then prime minister, Social Democrat Göran Persson.

"I say that each person should take care of their own domestic duties," said the prime minister.

Persson didn't stop there: with undisguised pride, he said that he was capable of ironing a dress shirt in just one minute.

He was then promptly invited to prove the feat live in the studio on a TV program, where an ironing board was set up. The deed, duly timed by the show's host, can be seen on YouTube under the title "Ett Herrans Liv — Göran Persson Sasong 1 Avsnitt 3 del 4/5."[1]

The shenanigans with the iron earned high viewer ratings for the prime minister. But that year, after ten years in office, Persson lost the elections. Maud Olofsson became the deputy prime minister, and many Swedes began hiring occasional cleaning help primarily

---

1 http://www.youtube.com/watch?v=xSAgICGQDg.

from Polish immigrants. But almost everyone continues to wash, cook and iron, just like Göran Persson.

Cabinet ministers do not live in luxury either: elected by the *Financial Times* as the best European Finance Minister of 2011, Anders Borg lives in a 25-square-meter state-owned apartment in Stockholm during the week.

"Swedish politicians are unpretentious," says Borg's press secretary, Peter Larsson.

The minister of Finance's one-bedroom apartment, according to the press secretary, is in a student housing building at the Swedish Defense University (*Försvarshögskolan*). Several members of staff from the Swedish Foreign Affairs ministry also live in the building. At the weekend, Borg lives with his family in his house in the Katrineholm region, south of Stockholm.

With the exception of the prime minister, no Swedish politician has the right to an official residence: not any cabinet ministers, mayors, or even the Speaker of Parliament. Only politicians whose voter base is outside the capital receive a housing allowance to rent accommodation in Stockholm, or to live in state-owned apartments or even state-owned studio apartments, which can be as small as 18 square meters.

This may seem meager for such eminent people, but it actually is much better than it used to be. Up until the end of the 1980s, subsidized apartments for politicians did not even exist in Sweden. All parliamentarians slept on sofa beds, in their own offices. Today, they all have a guaranteed apartment. And this guarantee is inconceivable for many of the Swedes who have to continue to battle for a place to live in central Stockholm.

"Why don't members of Parliament have to put up with the long waiting lists like we do in order to get an apartment?" asks a worker at the childcare nursery in Parliament. Yes, there is childcare provided in Parliament to take care of the representatives' children.

The apartment may be a guaranteed right, but the bed is not. In most of the Parliament's housing units, where a single room serves as both living room and bedroom, there is only a sofa bed.

How did the Swedish politicians' frugal existence originate? In search of an answer, I decide to meet the Swedish journalist Lena Mellin at the headquarters of the *Aftonbladet* newspaper, where she writes one of the most widely-read political columns in the country.

"But they do have privileges," claims Mellin.

"Which ones?" I want to know.

"Members of parliament don't need to pay their telephone bills. They have the right to live rent-free in apartments in the center of Stockholm. They receive a computer to take home, and don't pay for technical assistance. They earn more than the average citizen. And parliamentarians representing areas outside Stockholm can also travel to their constituencies for free at the weekend," she lists. "If an ordinary citizen gets a job in another city, no other employer pays for the weekend trips."

I ask Mellin if these benefits are considered relatively modest in Sweden, compared to the benefits of politicians in other countries.

"Perhaps. Swedish politicians do not live a life of luxury, because we are a society that chose equality among our citizens as a fundamental value. But they do have privileges," she insists.

"But not privileges such as official cars and private chauffeurs?" I say.

"Cars with chauffeurs for politicians? My God, of course not!" replies Mellin, in shock. "Such benefits create unnecessary problems. Like corruption. In order to get one of these privileged political jobs, many wouldn't hesitate to commit illegal acts," she reasons.

I ask how the Swedes would react if the country's politicians decided, in some wild and uncontrolled hallucination, to raise their own wages, to institute lifelong salaries for themselves, to occupy spacious offices with secretaries to serve them coffee, to employ relatives and dozens of private assistants, to travel by private jet, and to have official cars with chauffeurs. All of this paid for with the citizens' money.

"The Swedish society would never tolerate conceding such privileges to their politicians," says Lena Mellin.

"This is one of the few things that could actually cause a revolution here in Sweden."

"HOUSE CLEANING IS AN ART"

"As dust's worst enemy, Prime Minister Fredrik Reinfeldt cleans his house cheerfully and systematically. But not dressed in his suit. When he does a deep clean, he wears special multi-pocket trousers." Aftonbladet, *Swedish newspaper, 12/21/2008*

Prime Minister Reinfeldt: Cleaning his house and offering advice on how to do it.

A CONVERSATION WITH THE PRIME MINISTER

"I want to be an individual among other individuals, and not someone who is treated like an extraordinary person" — Fredrik Reinfeldt

Fredrik Reinfeldt enters the lobby of the Swedish Parliament with the determined steps of a gladiator on his way into an arena of hungry lions. He will face the monthly *Frågestund* ("Question Time"), in which the prime minister is confronted with a 40-minute round of enemy fire in order to answer questions from MPs about the state of Sweden under his leadership.

The discreet coming and going of representatives and journalists increases on the way to the parliamentary debating chamber. We are all theoretically marooned. The Swedish Parliament occupies the entire tiny island of Helgeandsholmen, surrounded on one side by the waters of the Baltic Sea, and on the other by Lake Mälaren. On the horizon visible through the curved glass panels of the lobby, one can see the glow of the gilded dome of the Stadshuset, Stockholm's City Hall. On the opposite shore, in front of Rosenbad, the seat of government, fishermen cast their rods, hoping for herring and salmon.

"You have ten minutes," says the prime minister's press officer, Roberta Alenius, as we stand in the lobby, signaling the start of my interview with Reinfeldt.

Leader of the Moderate Party (*Moderata Samlingspartiet*), Fredrik Reinfeldt became prime minister in 2006 at the age of 41, when an alliance of four center-right parties defeated the coalition led by the Social Democrats.

Standing in the antechamber of the parliamentary plenary, looking at me with an austere countenance, Reinfeldt spoke of this kingdom where politicians occupy the power previously exercised by the monarchy, but do not live like kings or queens.

Do the lifestyles of Swedish politicians, devoid of luxuries or privileges, follow some sort of moral code of conduct?

FREDRIK REINFELDT: I would say yes. Sweden is a

country without the high level of social inequality that we see in other places, and this is an aspect that we value enormously in our society. For this reason, we seek political leaders that are "one of us," and not "above us." This is a basic principle of Swedish social thought, and one that also pleases me. I wish to be an individual among other individuals, and not someone who is treated like an extraordinary person. The sense of equality among people is reflected in the Swedish soul, in the Swedish sentiment of national identity, in what we trust Sweden is as a nation. I would be harshly criticized, as would any other politician, if people thought that I lived a life of luxury, entirely different from the lives of ordinary citizens.

How did this Swedish value system originate?

FREDRIK REINFELDT: Democracy has profound roots in Sweden. Politicians understand that they are not here to become wealthy or make their families rich, nor to make life easier for just a chosen few. I am here to carry out reforms and to make this a better country, in such a way that people will say, "He really is listening to me, he is solving my problems." Otherwise, the voters will give their vote to someone else. I don't see this as a problem. I also enjoy taking care of everyday chores as I used to do before becoming prime minister. The obvious difference is that nowadays I have a security contingent surrounding me. But I continue to take care of my day-to-day activities, just like any citizen.

Is it true that you iron your own shirts in the morning, as do most Swedes?

FREDRIK REINFELDT: Yes. Not every morning, because I usually iron enough shirts during the weekend for the whole week. I do wash and iron my own clothes.

Do you also cook every night?

FREDRIK REINFELDT: Yes, I cook for myself and also for my three children when they are at my house (Fredrik Reinfeldt is divorced from his wife, Filippa Reinfeldt, who is also a politician). There is nothing strange about this, it is what all Swedes do when they come home from work.

You have the reputation of being a cleaning fanatic. Do you still clean your own house?

FREDRIK REINFELDT: I have two children who are allergic to dust. The need to clean the house well has become a matter of health for my children. Occasionally, I bring in a basic cleaning service to my official residence, but I take care of most of the daily cleaning. But I no longer spend as many hours on this as before becoming the prime minister, when I would spend the greater part of Sunday doing a thorough clean.

Why do you consider it so important to do your own cleaning?

FREDRIK REINFELDT: I like doing it; besides, it is what everyone does in Sweden, not just me. Cleaning the house gives me the sensation of having control over my own life and of taking care of the kids, it's good for me. It's relaxing, and I try to make it pleasurable. While cleaning I wear headphones to listen to music or football matches being played by my team, Djurgården. The sensation of walking through the house after it has been cleaned, while the children sleep peacefully, is fantastic.

What is your best cleaning tip?

FREDRIK REINFELDT: Using the back of a worn-out dress shirt is an excellent way to polish mirrors and windows.

What is your favorite chore?

FREDRIK REINFELDT: Washing clothes. I used to prefer cleaning the house. But now I like washing clothes. It gives me the feeling of being ready for anything.

Many people have also seen you queuing at the checkout in the super-market.

FREDRIK REINFELDT: I do my own shopping, like anyone else, although now I'm accompanied by security guards.

How can you do all of this and still have time to lead a country?

FREDRIK REINFELDT: Household chores don't take that much time. I think it is important to be integrated with family life, despite my involvement with this type of political work. It's a question of organization. I dedicate a small portion of my day to household duties, and then I return to reading documents or making any necessary phone calls. It is perfectly possible to integrate your work life with your home life.

What is your opinion regarding governmental systems in which politicians have privileges accorded to a higher class?

FREDRIK REINFELDT: First of all, it is very important to recognize the fact that many of these countries are democracies and thus it is up to those elected by the people to respond to this type of question. But to state the obvious, if I were finance minister of one of these nations and needed to cut spending, I would know where to begin. Because when a politician needs to cut spending, it is very important that he himself sets the example. In our country, people are always aware of the costs of bureaucracy and the political class. There needs to be balance. If politicians wish to keep the trust of their voters, they must remain close to them.

The Prime Minister's Cleaning Tips

Fredrik Reinfeldt began cleaning his house as a teenager. His mother sectioned off the house into cleaning zones, and one of them would be Fredrik's responsibility.

The following tips were listed in an article published in *Aftonbladet* newspaper, subtitled "Meet a master of cleaning — Prime Minister Fredrik Reinfeldt."

Reduce the number of knick-knacks:

"The basic rule is not to have too many things. Decorative items and knick-knacks collect dust and make it harder to clean."

Wear suitable clothing:

Reinfeldt wears a pair of military trousers with several pockets in which to put his scrubbing brush and other cleaning utensils. "Cleaning the house is an art. You need to concentrate to do it well."

Kneel down to scrub:

"You may think it's silly, but I scrub the floor on my hands and knees, especially the kitchen. This method really gets the dirt out. Just mopping the floor doesn't get the job done."

The kitchen is all-important:

Fredrik Reinfeldt dedicates an extra 15 minutes to the kitchen every night. He cleans the stove and the sink, wipes the table, and starts the dishwasher: "That way you start the next day right," he says.

Use the small vacuum nozzle:

"The genuine pleasure of cleaning the house is in the hidden corners. Finding dust under the sofa cushions or in a little corner of the living room is a source of great motivation. The best way to hear the satisfying sound of the dirt being sucked up in the vacuum hose is to use the small vacuum attachment."

Organize your cleaning:

"Behind every successful clean is good planning," suggests the prime minister. Ideally, you would always start with the outer areas of the house. An alternative would be to clean the kitchen and bathroom first, because they require the heaviest cleaning. Each time he cleans the house, Reinfeldt also selects a certain room in which to do an extra thorough clean.

THE MPS' APARTMENTS

Everyone knew that the end of the world was imminent. Dire rumors spread about the dreaded Year 2000 prophecies, and the great cataclysm that would sweep away everything and everyone in bestial fury. But the pragmatic Swedes, aware that this wasn't the first time the world was supposed to end, moved ahead with their plan for that year: to move the last members of Parliament who still lived and slept in their own offices into the newly established state-owned parliamentary apartments. The change had begun in 1989.

On that most feared day, the wolves did not swallow the sun and the moon, and almost all members of parliament with a constituency outside the capital were granted a subsidized apartment. Utterly plain, and devoid of any unspeakable luxuries.

If a Swede of negotiable virtues is motivated by a sudden desire to work for the people, one of these state-owned apartments will certainly not be the stimulus to seduce him, like a charmed snake, to the political life.

Swedish parliamentarians live in modest apartments with a floor area of 45.6 square meters on average. The smallest are 16.6 square meters. Of a total of 197 properties managed by the Swedish Parliament, only eight measure between 70 and 90 square meters, and only 85 have an area above 45.6 square meters.

Some Swedish representatives live in state-owned studio apartments. Yes, there are studio apartments for politicians in Sweden. They are called "overnight rooms" (*övernattningsrum*), they measure on average 18 square meters and are occupied usually — but not exclusively — by members of parliament at the start of their careers. Altogether there are 57 such studio apartments for parliamentarians.

Regardless of size, none of the living quarters allotted to the Swedish MPs is equipped with what would normally be considered basic amenities. There is no washing machine, dishwasher or cable TV paid for with taxpayers' money, nor even a double bed.

None of the occupants of these parliamentary apartments receives their own washing machine from the government coffers. There are communal laundry facilities in the buildings, and the members of Parliament must schedule a time to wash their own clothes. In most of the apartments, there isn't even a separate bedroom: a single open space serves as both living room and bedroom.

One morning during the short and unreliable Swedish summer, I decide to check out the apartment of the Social Democrat lawmaker Luciano Astudillo, born in Chile. He has been in Parliament for six years, as a representative for Malmö in southern Sweden.

I descend via Katarinahissen, the large public elevator built in 1881 to connect the waterfront area of Slussen to the heights of Södermalm, an island in the center of Stockholm. From the top of the platform that houses the elevator, which is not currently in operation but is set to open again in 2019, you are presented with one of the most fascinating views of Stockholm, the point at which the waters of Lake Mälaren meet the Baltic Sea.

After a few minutes, Luciano Astudillo emerges from the exit turnstiles of the Slussen underground station, next to the Katarinahissen. We walk together along Götgatan street, Södermalm's main artery lined with modern bars and cafés, until we reach the street where Astudillo's apartment as a member of Parliament is located.

I follow the Swedish ritual of taking off my shoes before entering any home, and look around me. It consists of a small living room, a small bathroom and a small kitchen with a microwave oven and no dishwasher. A total of just 33 square meters.

"Where is the bedroom?," I ask.

"The living room is the bedroom. When it's time to sleep, I just open the sofa bed," says Astudillo, who arrived in Sweden in 1975, at three years of age, two years after the military coup that overthrew Chilean President Salvador Allende.

While he shows me the apartment, Astudillo remarks that his young daughter, on her occasional visits to Stockholm, shares the sofa bed with him.

"I have been to Chile on several occasions and I know that the situation there in relation to the parliamentarians is totally different," he says.

We go to the basement of the building, where there is a communal laundry facility. There are just two washing machines. Nailed to the wall by the door, is a 'sign-up' sheet where the representatives reserve the day and hour when they can use the machines. Ironing boards are folded in the corner of the facility.

"I have my own ironing board," says Astudillo. "I prefer to iron my clothes in the apartment."

Astudillo cooks his own food and cleans his apartment. He knows that free cleaning in the state-owned apartments only takes place once a year, during Parliament's summer break.

Once the summer break begins, I visit the MP's state-owned studio apartments in the company of the head of the parliamentary housing sector, Marie Stolpe. At the entrance to the Parliament, she welcomes me with an expression that indicates that she cannot understand why there is such an interest in something so banal.

Next to me, with his dizzying height and disquieting accent from the Skåne region in southern Sweden, cameraman Casimir Reuterskiöld comes along to record the footage that will be sent to the newsroom at TV Bandeirantes, in Brazil.

The three of us walk in the direction of the Royal Palace and cross Stallbron, the bridge that connects the island on which the Parliament is located to Gamla Stan, the Old Town of Stockholm. Off the small public square of Mynttorget, we enter the parliamentary annex, Ledamotshuset (House of Representatives), which also houses parliamentary offices. We clear security and take the elevator to the sixth floor. Thirteen of the building's 52 studio apartments are on this floor. The other five are in the parliamentary complex known as Cephalus, in nearby Riddarhustorget square.

Next to each door in the maze of hallways is a plaque identifying the member of Parliament who currently resides there. Eva Olofsson, Tone Tingsgård, Christina Oskarsson, and Allan Widman are just a few of the tenants at the moment. As we walk on, the acronyms of different party names alternate on the plaques: in these democratic hallways, left-wing and conservative representatives, even if they are fierce enemies in the parliamentary debating chamber, become next-door neighbors.

With the proper authorization obtained from the absent MP who is on leave, Marie Stolpe turns the key in one of the doors. It is a tiny 18-square-meter room.

"It's enough space for a parliamentarian to live in the capital during the week," says Marie, while she opens the sofa that converts into a bed at night.

Perhaps with a hint of exaggeration, the size of the studio apartment reminds me of the prison cells I once visited in the very modern Salberga prison in Sala, on the outskirts of Stockholm, where the prisoners — as in all Swedish prisons — also have private bathrooms.

"We can put in extra beds on wheels if needed, as in the case of a visiting relative," says Marie.

In addition to the sofa bed, a table, a small wardrobe, a small eating area with a single burner stove, a mini fridge and a bathroom are enough to fill the space of the parliamentary studio apartment.

Here, even the kitchen is communal. Marie takes us to the spacious collective kitchen that, in addition to modern recycling stations, has an unexpected dishwasher, an item missing from the state-owned apartments.

"But the representatives must wash their pans and keep the area clean," says Marie.

An announcement attached to one of the kitchen cupboards is a call for parliamentary cleanliness: "*Städa Upp!*" ("Leave everything clean!").

Nearby I see a kitchen adapted for MPs with disabilities, who also have specially equipped rooms and bathrooms.

We leave the Ledamotshuset and walk on with Marie Stolpe toward Munkbron, the site of one of Parliament's seven buildings of state-owned apartments. On the waterfront of Lake Mälaren, Munkbron is a street within the Old Town, on the island of Stadsholmen. From there we can see the island of Riddarholmen and the towers of Riddarholmskyrkan, the church where Sweden's ancient monarchs are buried. To the left, we can see another island, Södermalm.

The yellow-toned façade of the building in Munkbron is simple like that of Luciano Astudillo's apartment building in Södermalm. As is the case in most of the buildings in Stockholm, there is no doorman or concierge, and not even an outside intercom. There is just the customary electronic panel where you enter a code to open the main door.

On the ground floor, the apartment measures little more than 16 square meters. In the minuscule kitchen area there is a single burner stove, a microwave oven and a mini fridge. A single bed, a table and a small wardrobe complete the set-up, which, according to Marie, is occupied by a veteran member of Parliament who has served several terms.

On the second floor, the 40-square-meter illuminated apartment leaps two stars forward in comparison with the apartment below. Nevertheless, with the exception of the kitchen, where more than one person at a time can cook, and a few extra meters in the living room, which also doubles as the bedroom, the basic functional model of the Swedish parliamentary accommodation is repeated here.

The visit ends in the basement of the building, where we see the usual communal laundry facility for the politicians and the inescapable notice on the wall requiring the representatives to reserve a time.

There are, no pun intended, representatives who wash their dirty laundry in Parliament: there is also a communal laundry facility there. A case in point is representative Rossana Dinamarca, of the Swedish Left Party (*Vänsterpartiet*).

"Since I usually arrive at my apartment late at night, I wash my clothes during the day in the Parliament's laundry facility. It's easy, you just have to put your clothes in the machine and come back an hour later to get them," says Dinamarca.

MPs can also leave their children between the ages of one and thirteen in the Parliament's childcare center.

"But they must pay for the children's lunches, which cost 20 krona (about US$3)," says Monika Karlsson, an assistant in the childcare center. "On days when there are sessions at night, we stay open till midnight or longer."

The apartments and studio apartments are available only to members of Parliament like Rossana Dinamarca, who have a constituency at least 50 kilometers from the capital. Representatives from Stockholm do not have the right to a state-owned property or a housing allowance. And the Speaker of the Swedish Parliament does not have the right to an official residence.

"The Speaker of the Riksdag (Swedish Parliament) has no special housing privileges. The Speaker's rights are the same as those of the rest of the parliamentarians," says Maria Skuldt, the press secretary for Parliament.

It is up to each political party to decide how they will house their parliamentarians — who gets the larger apartments, and who gets the studio apartments. Parliament covers the cost of maintenance for the properties. But not all of the costs.

"The parliamentarians have a monthly allowance of 100 krona (about US$15) to spend on electricity, and nothing more. If they wish, they can request cleaning services for the apartment, but they have to pay around 300 krona (approximately US$46) for the service," says the head of parliamentary services (*Ledamotsservice*), Anna Aspegren.

Furthermore, the state pays for apartments exclusively for parliamentarians. Spouses of members of Parliament, family members, and partners are denied the benefit to live or even spend the night on a state property without paying. When the family member of a parliamentarian spends any time at the subsidized property, the representative has a time limit of one month to reimburse the state for the nights they have stayed.

And in this society where more than 75% of women are employed, if the spouse of a representative from outside the capital decides to live in a state-owned apartment with her husband, it is her obligation to cover the cost for half the rent.

"Of course, we don't pay for anyone to live for free, except for the parliamentarians whose constituencies are in other regions of the country," says Anna Aspergren.

Parliamentarians have two options for housing in the Swedish capital: the first is to live in one of the state-owned apartments or studio flats. The second is to rent an apartment on their own behalf and charge Parliament for a refund corresponding to the value of the rent. In this case, the maximum rent that Parliament will reimburse is 8,000 krona per month (the equivalent of approximately US$1,200), a relatively low amount considering the housing shortage in central Stockholm.

"But Parliamentarians who live with their spouses in a rented apartment can only request reimbursement of half of the rent, and they must pay for the property's maintenance themselves," explains Anna Aspegren.

A case in point is the leader of the Centre Party (*Centerpartiet*), Annie Lööf, who shares an apartment with her husband in the Swedish capital.

"Annie's husband has to pay his part of the rent, like any other citizen," says Aspegren.

In 2011, the leader of the Social Democratic Party, Håkan Juholt, sidestepped the rules. And he faced the consequences.

THE APARTMENT SCANDAL

"The national anti-corruption unit investigates Juholt"

Juholt: Paying half of his rent with public money cost him his career.

Håkan Juholt had seemed to be the incarnation of the Swedish Social Democrats' long-awaited Messiah. An eloquent speaker with a winning demeanor, Juholt took over the party leadership in March 2011 charged with the task of re-energizing the electorate and bringing the Social Democrats back to power after two consecutive and embarrassing electoral defeats.

Alas, an apartment paid for by the Parliament and occupied by a girlfriend stopped him in his tracks. The revelation that the leader's partner lived with him in the subsidized apartment, without paying her due part of the rent, disrupted his convulsive rise in the opinion polls. It was October, and the case caused Juholt's star to fall slowly and inevitably like the leaves of the autumn trees.

The *Aftonbladet* newspaper broke the news: Håkan Juholt had been "receiving taxpayers' money to pay the full rent of the apartment" that he had shared with his partner, Åsa Lindgren, since 2007. It was an instant scandal. In total, he had received 320,532 Swedish krona (about US$39,185) over four and a half years. Under the strict rules of the Swedish Parliament, Lindgren should have covered half of that cost, about 160,000 krona (approximately US$19,560).

The case ended up with the police. "National Anti-Corruption Unit Investigates Juholt," the media reported in chorus. Once the preliminary investigation was completed, the Anti-Corruption Unit referred the case to the Swedish National Police's Criminal Department (*Riksenheten för Polismål*), as dictated by laws governing suspected crimes involving parliamentarians in Sweden.

Unabashed, Juholt swore innocence and said he didn't know about the rules that compel spouses and family of members of Parliament to pay for the use of subsidized apartments. But he returned, promptly and without complaint, the unwarranted 160,000 Swedish krona he had received. Juholt acted quickly. But it was too late.

"I made the mistake of not learning the rules regarding the use of apartments. I apologize for this. I would like to emphasize that I did not ask for extra money deliberately," Juholt said. According to Parliament's administration, however, one of the Social Democratic Party leader's assistants had been notified about the matter months before.

Håkan Juholt comes from the town of Oskarshamn, 300 kilometers south of Stockholm. After being elected as an MP in 1994, he occupied a subsidized apartment in the center of the capital by himself. In 2007, Håkan moved into the apartment of his girlfriend, Åsa, in the suburb of Västertorp. At that point, he registered her property as his new apartment in the capital, and went on to request compensation for the rent value of 7,225 Swedish krona.

The cost of this apartment in the suburbs was cheaper than that of the apartment Håkan had previously lived in alone in the center of the capital. The cost of the rent in the suburb was also under the 8,000 krona ceiling set by Parliament for housing assistance to parliamentarians.

Using these and other arguments, Juholt appealed to voters by criss-crossing the country for two months on what was called the "apology tour" (*förlåtelseturnén*).

But Håkan Juholt's sin was unforgivable: the leader's partner was living in the apartment at the expense of the taxpayers' money. She should have paid her share of the rent, and not the taxpayer. At this point, the press had also revealed that his girlfriend had accompanied Juholt on an official trip to Belarus — and in this case, under Swedish parliamentary rules, he would be entitled to reimbursement of only half of the hotel expenses.

The following dialogue with Juholt was published in the October 8, 2011 issue of the *Dagens Nyheter* newspaper:

Reporter: How could you surmise that taxpayers should pay the full rent if you share the apartment with your partner?

Håkan Juholt: The issue never crossed my mind. I didn't know that when a parliamentarian shares a subsidized apartment with someone, he should only ask for the reimbursement of half of the rent. I should have known this rule. I wasn't aware of this information, but I should have been.

Reporter: Don't you think it's logical to split the rent with your partner, since she also lives there?

Håkan Juholt: Certainly.

Reporter: Hadn't you reflected on this logic?

Håkan Juholt: No, I hadn't. The apartment I used

to occupy in the center of Stockholm was more expensive. So I hadn't considered it an issue.

Reporter: How do you think this incident will affect voter confidence in you?

Håkan Juholt: This harms the image of politicians as a whole.

The scandal resulted in angry editorials. The liberal daily *Gefle Dagblad* noted that as leader of the Social Democratic Party, Håkan Juholt had a monthly income of 144,000 Swedish krona (about US$17,603).

"With a salary like this, not even Joakim von Anka (the miserly millionaire Uncle Scrooge of Disney fame) would commit fraud just for a few thousand krona notes," the editorial said. Many believed Juholt's claim that he had no knowledge of the apartment's rules of occupancy. Yet they wondered whether voters would forgive him, and whether Juholt would, after all, be a suitable candidate for the post of prime minister of Sweden.

In January 2012, under intense pressure to withdraw from party leadership, Håkan Juholt announced his resignation. He had lasted ten months in office.

"Swedes repudiate anyone in a position of power filling their own pockets," said political scientist Jenny Madestam, speaking to Swedish news agency TT.

The Juholt scandal led Parliament to introduce new rules: today, all members are obliged to declare, on an official form, whether they live alone or with whom they share their apartment in the capital. Previously it was just a voluntary system.

BEFORE THE APARTMENTS

A CONVERSATION WITH MEMBER OF PARLIAMENT EVA FLYBORG

"Sleeping on an office sofa bed wasn't a problem" — Eva Flyborg

In Eva's time, not even the most demented view of paradise could describe the life of a Swedish parliamentarian. Dishes and clothes were washed by hand in the office sink, there were no beds, and apartments for MPs didn't even exist. During the first four years of her tenure, from 1994 to 1998, Eva Flyborg of the Liberal Party (Folkpartiet) slept on a sofa bed in her own office in Parliament.

I arrive in Parliament for an interview with Flyborg on an icy Swedish winter morning, when even the dogs are shivering in their cold-weather coats. In the entrance hall, an official meets me and leads me to the representative's office in the wing of the building reserved for the Liberal Party. I ask him whether he is Eva Flyborg's aide.

"I work part-time, assisting Flyborg and eight other representatives with a variety of services. In Sweden, there are no private assistants for parliamentarians," notes Lars Johansson, the shared assistant.

As Folkpartiet's spokesperson for energy, industry, and trade affairs, Eva Flyborg is an economist and former employee of Swedish automaker Volvo. She was born in 1963 in Otterhällan, in the

Gothenburg region (on the west coast of Sweden), and is also known as founder of the Swedish Parliament's Beatles Fan Club.

In her current 12-square-meters office, without a secretary, mini coffee bar or private bathroom, she described what life was like in the Parliament back in the 1990s.

Representative Eva Flyborg: Two washing machines for 349 representatives

EVA FLYBORG: The office was small, it was about 10 square meters. There was a tiny bathroom, a coffee machine, a toaster, and that was all. We had to wash dishes and clothes in the bathroom sink. In the basement there was a communal laundry facility, which could be used if it wasn't already occupied by one of the other 300+ representatives.

It wasn't a large laundry facility?

EVA FLYBORG: No, not at all. It was a small facility. Two washing machines.

Two washing machines for 349 people?

EVA FLYBORG: Yes, two. Many representatives preferred to wash their clothes in the office bathroom sink or take their clothes home with them to their local constituency and bring them back clean.

And you had to hang dry the clothes in the office?

EVA FLYBORG: Yes. Where else would I dry them? I just had my office. So I hung my clothes on chairs, the computer, or the lamp. In the morning, when they were dry, I would put them away.

Was working and sleeping inside the office in the Parliament building considered normal, or was there a sense of dissatisfaction among MPs?

EVA FLYBORG: No, it was normal. It wasn't seen as a problem.

Representatives didn't complain about the conditions?

EVA FLYBORG: Your life as a representative is different. It's not a normal job, but you know that going into it. I was a Girl Scout when I was young, so it wasn't a problem for me

to sleep on a sofa bed in the office. And Swedes are a very practical people. You do the best you can. If you need to do laundry and you only have the bathroom sink, that's where you do it.

Then why did Parliament decide to create apartments for their representatives in the late 1990s?

EVA FLYBORG: Apartments for members of Parliament were created to comply with fire safety regulations and environmental standards. It was decided that it was too risky to have representatives living, eating, and lighting candles in their offices, among all the documents and books. So they had to remove us from the Parliament buildings. Otherwise, we would still be living in our offices.

Would you still be living there?
EVA FLYBORG: Yes, I would. It

wasn't a big deal. See, my permanent home isn't here in the capital city. My house is in Gothenburg. That's where I live, that's where my family, my car, and my friends are. I only work in Stockholm for part of the week. Up until a few years ago, I would spend from Monday to Friday in the capital because of my parliamentary agenda, and sometimes even at the weekend. On a few occasions I had to stay in Stockholm for as long as an entire month. I currently spend four days a week in the capital.

How do you compare the Swedish system to countries where politicians enjoy privileges such as spacious offices and apartments, chauffeurs, and private secretaries and aides?

EVA FLYBORG: First of all, I don't judge any country. Each society makes its own choices. It does seem to me, however, that certain privileges granted to politicians in some countries seem excessively disproportionate. Perhaps this is a reflection of the view of society in those countries that political representation is an important function, which should therefore carry a high social status. In Sweden, we do not assign any high status to the role of a politician. Maybe that's the difference. And if a representative were called by an honorary title, people would find it ridiculous. We are all the same. No one is above anyone else. With one exception: the Royal Family. But the Royal Family no longer has any power.

What is your current apartment in the capital like?

EVA FLYBORG: Today I live in one of the largest state-owned apartments for parliamentarians, which measures 48 square meters. That's because I've been a representative for many years, and also because my son lived here with me. So it was a set of factors.

Is it a two-bedroom apartment?

EVA FLYBORG: No, just one small room. I shared the room with my son, who is currently studying in Gothenburg.

Did you have to pay for your son to live in the apartment?

EVA FLYBORG: No, because at the time he was below the age of 12. Parliamentarians' children who are older than 12 must pay to live or stay in the apartment. This is usually the case in any hotel, for example, where they charge for children over this age.

Does the apartment have any amenities such as a washing machine or dishwasher?

EVA FLYBORG: No, it doesn't. We have a laundry facility in the basement of the building. They are two washing machines for two buildings, which have a total of about 80 apartments.

Do representatives wash and iron their own clothes?

EVA FLYBORG: Of course, who else should do it? Why should someone else do this for you if you know how to do it? It's also more practical. I can iron my shirts in two minutes. If I were to take them to a dry cleaner's, I would have to spend time and money. I do not have time for that. It's easier for me to do it myself. I make dinner in twenty minutes, and I iron my shirt in two minutes. It's a very efficient system.

As a representative and a mem-

ber of the parliamentary Committee on Industry and Trade, don't you have a private assistant in your office?

EVA FLYBORG: No. I share a part-time assistant with eight other members.

Isn't there even a secretary to help you, say, book a plane ticket so you can attend a meeting or conference?

EVA FLYBORG: No. It's faster and easier for me to do it myself instead of passing on the information to a secretary who will need to get back to me about different flight options, and then call the agency again until we can find the best alternative, according to the needs and constraints of my personal agenda. So it wouldn't be very efficient to pass this on to a secretary, would it?

Not unless you had a private secretary who would organize all your appointments and coordinate your personal agenda.

EVA FLYBORG: Well, that doesn't exist here in Sweden. Representatives don't have private secretaries.

Would it be an excessive privilege to have a private secretary?

EVA FLYBORG: In my opinion, yes. Because it's not fair to the rest of society. It would be unnecessary and an MP does not need it. Privileges tend to transform a representative, and politicians in general, into people who live above the citizens who elect them. This creates distance between the people and their representatives, which in turn generates a sense of distrust on the part of the population toward politicians.

SPARTAN OFFICES

The parliamentary offices of the Swedish representatives measure on average 15 square meters, and are frugally decorated.

"Sofas are in high demand because there aren't enough to go around," says Ömer Oguz, spokesperson for the Social Democratic Party. He points to a small red three-seater sofa, the kind you would find in the Swedish IKEA stores.

We are in the parliamentary annex of Riksdagens Hus, the hub of the Social Democrat representatives. It is an old circular building situated on the Riddarhustorget square, a few steps from Parliament. The central atrium, open to the public, is dominated by the monumental sculpture of a nude woman, christened *Morgon* (Morning) by artist Ivar Johnson. Around the atrium, small passages lead to Myntagatan Street and to the alleys of the Old Town.

In Riksdagens Hus, 15-square-meters offices for the parliamentarians.

From the entrance to the Parliament complex you can see the imposing tower of the Stockholm Cathedral (*Storkyrkan*), where Princess Victoria, heir to the Swedish throne, married her former personal trainer in 2010. But on the inside, the complex is characterized by its austere interior.

Along the vast corridors, each door opens directly into one of the tiny parliamentary offices. The representatives' offices are sparse — no reception area for a secretary, no coffee area nor private bathroom. Each one features a computer set on a light-colored wooden table, matching bookshelves, and a TV. Some offices also have a small round table.

On each floor, an automatic coffeemaker located in the corridor provides for about 25 parliamentarians. Representatives use paper cups and serve themselves. Some take the opportunity to take out their cases of *snus*, the traditional moist, smokeless tobacco used in Scandinavian countries. The *snus* emits a pungent smell, and is proof that there's simply no accounting for taste. It is packed in paper pouches that look like miniature tea bags, and is placed between the cheek and gums. Many say that it is much safer than smoking cigarettes. For those against it, the *snus* is the anteroom of addiction.

Near the coffeemakers are counters with daily newspapers and other publications. They are for the collective use of the parliamentarians. Their parties fund the newspaper and magazine subscriptions since representatives do not have personal budgets for such subscriptions.

"We can take a newspaper to read in our offices, but we have to return it to the counter," says Social Democrat representative Michael Hagberg.

"I don't see any need to buy hundreds of individual subscriptions in order for each member of Parliament to have his or her own newspapers and magazines. We can also read newspapers and other publications in the building's library, and there are libraries in every parliamentary complex," he adds.

In the corridors, there are garbage recycling stations and lockers that hold office supplies for parliamentarians.

The smallest offices are ten square meters. The largest are on average 25 square meters, with some up to 45. The larger ones are reserved for party leaders and the chairpersons of parliamentary committees. There is no vestige of luxury in the 30-square-meter office of the Social Democratic Party leader. His only privilege is the assurance of a sofa.

NO SECRETARIES OR PRIVATE ASSISTANTS

Private secretaries and aides are not part of a parliamentarian's world in Sweden.

"None of the members of Parliament have private secretaries or assistants," says Mats Lindh, an advisor in the parliamentary services department.

In the Swedish system, each political party represented in Parliament receives restricted funding to hire a pool of assistants. This group of employees collectively services all the representatives of each party.

In general, 50,300 krona (approximately US$6,150) covers the salary of one assistant per parliamentarian. Each party is free to distribute the funds however it wishes, in order to set up a team of assistants that best meets its members' needs. But the general rule is that no member has a private assistant: they all share a secretarial pool, which, among other things, prepares political texts and handles press relations.

In the corridors of the Social Democratic Party's parliamentary headquarters, the spokesperson provides the roster for the secretarial pool: 95 officials work together to support the activities of 130 representatives. In all, there are 52 political advisors, 33 political and press support staff, and ten administrative assistants, who are not usually available to MPs for personal tasks.

"Each representative takes care of their own work schedule. They each reserve their own train or plane tickets, for example," says Ömer Oguz.

Nevertheless, the Social Democratic party leader has a total of ten officials in his parliamentary office. And even a secretary in the reception area.

For Swedish political scientist Rune Premförs, maintaining a task force of private advisors for a single parliamentarian is an aberration. Sitting in his office at Stockholm University, he relates that he once visited a friend who worked for an American senator in Washington. He was surprised to discover that the entire office staff served just that one senator.

"Why should all these resources be at the disposal of a single politician, if they could be divided? Political representatives who represent the people should not be granted privileged conditions or preferential treatment," he argues.

It is a valid argument to say that big countries have big problems, and that to solve them, they need more human resources.

"But this does not necessarily mean increasing personal privileges in the form of private advisors," says Premförs. "Parliamentarians need quality information and consultancy services to support their activities and decision-making. In Sweden, one of the fastest-growing departments in the last 20 years has been the RUT (Parliament Research Service), which provides all kinds of research, statistics, and specialized consultancy to all parliamentary parties," says Rune Premförs.

Up until the 1970s, representatives didn't have assistants or even individual offices in Parliament, recalls political scientist Daniel Tarchys.

"Over time, resources have been introduced such as support with assistants and advisors, but these resources have always been aimed at the party as a whole and not at one particular member of Parliament. The party decides how to use them for collective or individual services," says Tarschys.

"This system reflects the parties' strong position in Parliament, and the strong degree of party unity in Sweden," points outs the political scientist.

In the Swedish government, each cabinet minister has a secretary and a staff that varies from two to nine assistants, according to the department of Governmental Administration (*Förvaltningsavdelningen Regerinskansliet*).

Paula Carvalho Olovsson, Parliamentary Advisor

"I don't work as a private assistant for any particular representative."

The daughter of a former Portuguese representative and a Swedish councilor, political scientist Paula Carvalho Olovsson has worked since 2005 as a parliamentary assistant to the Social Democratic party. At the party's parliamentary headquarters, Riksdagens Hus, she explains what it's like to assist all the members of a single party.

Describe your work as a political assistant in Sweden.

PAULA CARVALHO: I don't work as an assistant for any particular member. I work for the group of social democratic parliamentarians as a whole.

There are more than 100 representatives in the party. Can any one of them ask for your help?

PAULA CARVALHO: They don't all ask for help at the same time because we have a well-organized schedule. The assistants are divided into groups specializing in certain subjects. For example, some of my colleagues work exclusively in the area of social or economic affairs, and others specialize in health or criminal issues. Other colleagues work in the parliamentary committees, writing motions in more formal language. My job is mainly to rewrite parliamentary motions in more accessible language so that parliamentarians can use it when they give interviews, make speeches, or meet voters. So there are assistants with specific expertise for the parliamentarians' different areas of activity.

Does the system work well, or would it be better for Swedish members of Parliament to have more assistants?

PAULA CARVALHO: For us, it works very well. And I think we work more efficiently. When you have too many people working in the same area, they often end up doing superfluous things.

You mean having too many assistants is not good?

PAULA CARVALHO: I don't think so. Swedish members of Parliament can also rely on the Parliament Research Service (RUT), which has nonpartisan consultants with expertise in various fields to produce research, projections, and technical consultancy.

Do the Swedish representatives handle their own schedules and make their own travel reservations?

PAULA CARVALHO: Yes, of course. For us, we understand that this is a must.

How do you compare the Swedish system to that of other countries, where representatives have teams of private assistants?

PAULA CARVALHO: For us, these are different worlds. I don't think it's necessary to have so many advisors in one office. It would never happen here. In the first place, Swedes have never accepted it, nor would they ever allow it. There are many in Sweden who believe that Swedish politicians already have too many rights, and that they earn too much. People here do not like politicians to have things that normal people do not have. Swedish politicians must be like ordinary citizens. And here in Sweden we do not have corruption, like they do for instance in Italy.

THE WAGES: MPs EARN TWICE AS MUCH AS ELEMENTARY SCHOOLTEACHER'S

In order to live in a country with one of the highest costs of living in the world and where citizens pay one of the planet's highest rates of income tax, a member of the Swedish Parliament earns about US$7,000 monthly (2013). In comparison, after taxes are deducted an MP earns approximately twice as much as a Swedish elementary school teacher does.

In Swedish krona, a representative's salary is 58,300 per month. An elementary schoolteacher earns on average 26,500 krona (about US$3,240). In the Swedish progressive income tax system, however, a member of Parliament pays higher taxes on his or her higher salary. After taxes, an MP's net salary is approximately 35,200 krona (about US$4,300). An elementary schoolteacher pays lower taxes and receives on average a net salary of about 18,300 krona (about US$2,240). In other words, approximately half of what a member of Parliament receives.

The gross monthly wages of a Swedish member of parliament are comparable to those of a medical doctor in the public health system, who receives on average 54,900 krona (about US$6,710). According to data supplied in 2013 by Statistics Sweden (*Statistiska Centralbyrån*), the average salary of a Swedish citizen is 35,800 krona (about US$4,375). A nurse earns 32,200 krona (about US$3,940). A police officer earns on average 30,500 krona (US$3,730), and a judge earns on average 45,100 krona (about US$5,515).

With about 35,000 krona in their pockets, Swedish representatives would be considered reasonably affluent, and indeed it is appropriate that they should feel adequately recompensated. After all, extra benefits such as lavish meals allowances, formal-clothing allowances, gratuities, Christmas bonus salary, other bonuses, representation allowances and similar add-ons will definitely not be adding any zeros to their bank accounts.

If their voter bases are outside the capital, the Swedish MPs can request what is called a *traktament*, a cost of living allowance for weekdays during which they work in Stockholm. The daily rate, paid only to parliamentarians whose permanent address is outside the capital, is 110 Swedish krona (about US$13.45).

A quick glance at typical Stockholm prices gives you an idea of what can be bought in the capital with 110 krona in your wallet: a cup of coffee and three or four *bullar* (a traditional Swedish cinnamon bun), or a soft drink and pizza, or two packs of cigarettes, or a plate of traditional *köttbullar*, Swedish meatballs served with lingonberry sauce and mashed potatoes. In small popular restaurants that serve lunch in the city, a meal on the executive lunch menu costs about 90 Swedish krona (about US$11).

Nevertheless, for a large proportion of the citizens who pay the MPs' salaries through their taxes, parliamentarians' salaries are still too high.

"Why should a representative earn more than a teacher?" asks Monika Karlsson, a worker in Parliament's childcare center. Or, as the taxi driver on the way from the Arlanda airport said: "It's fine, but it could be better."

In an enlightened moment, representatives of the Left Party (*Vänsterpartiet*, the former Communist Party) used the same reasoning as Karlsson. They concluded that the salaries of Swedish representatives crossed the line between common sense and the unacceptable. They decided to take action.

At the January 2012 party convention, it was decided that all Left Party representatives would be required to allocate a part of their salaries to fund party activities. As from that date, after they receive their monthly salary of 58,300 krona, they keep only 27,500 (about US$3,360).

"For the Left Party, a guiding principle is that no one should get rich working in public service. A politician should not receive a salary much higher than that of an average worker," wrote the party leader in the city of Norrköping (in eastern Sweden), in an article on the opinion page of the *Norrköpings Tidningar* newspaper.

"We are in politics to promote changes in society, not to get rich and promote our careers [...]. We hope that other political parties will have the courage to follow our example," wrote Niclas Lundström, Linda Snecker and Per Gawelund in *Norrköpings Tidningar* on January 14, 2012.

If a salary cut triggers ulcers in some Left Party members, it's important to realize that, until 1957, members of the Swedish Parliament were not even paid. The decision to introduce salaries for parliamentarians was made, according to the Parliament's archives, after it was concluded that no citizen should be "barred from becoming a parliamentarian for economic reasons." Yet "wages should not be so high as to become economically attractive."

"Until recently, Swedish representatives were provided for by members of their party, not by the state. Then an official salary was introduced, but only for the months of the year in which Parliament held sessions," says Daniel Tarschys, former representative and current professor of Political Science at Stockholm University.

"It was a low salary," remembers Tarschys. "When I was elected to Parliament in 1976, the two months of annual parliamentary recess were not paid, because it was assumed that during this period representatives would return to their regular full-time jobs. Since the parliamentary salary was so low, public servants and employees from private companies who held employment in parallel to their jobs in Parliament often received a small stipend from their employers."

According to parliamentary records, representatives began receiving year-round monthly salaries for holding a full-time political office only as of 1984.

"At the time, a representative's compensation corresponded to the average wages of a public servant. This amount increased gradually, and today is the equivalent to a senior level public servant, but not at the highest level of the hierarchy," observes Tarschys.

Parliamentary representatives earn more than the

average Swedish citizen, but less than most European Union parliamentarians. Swedish Government ministers receive 118,000 krona per month (about US$14,425). The Speaker of the *Riksdag* (Parliament) earns the same salary as the prime minister: 148,000 krona per month (approximately US$18,100), the equivalent of about 70% of what the prime minister of Great Britain earns, and approximately half of the salary of the president of the United States.

Some believe that low salaries do not attract the brightest minds to a career in politics. For others, a low salary also runs the risk of turning a political career into a playground for the rich. Swedish diplomat and politician Hans Blix preaches a middle road: a "reasonably good" salary for political representatives.

"Balance is essential. The salary should be neither too much, nor too little. If you pay high salaries and offer political immunity, a political career will attract the wrong type of person. If you pay too little, it could discourage capable people from entering politics. It is important that politicians comprehend that they are public servants and that it is public money that sustains them," says Blix.

Many people thoroughly disagree with the idea that higher salaries attract better-qualified politicians:

"I have never seen, anywhere in the world, a political system that attracts the brightest minds to a career in politics," says Rune Premförs, Stockholm University professor and political scientist.

SALARIES: WHEN PARLIAMENTARIANS CANNOT GIVE THEMSELVES PAY RISES

The singular privilege of raising one's own salary is a mere pipe dream for Swedish parliamentarians, just as it is for the global masses of salaried workers.

In Sweden, pay rises for members of Parliament are determined by an independent committee called *Riksdagens Arvodesnämd*. This committee is comprised of a president — who is usually a retired judge — and two public representatives, normally former civil servants or journalists.

Recent public representatives include a former spokesperson of former Social Democrat Prime Minister Olof Palme and a former editor-in-chief of the conservative *Svenska Dagbladet* newspaper, as well as former public servants from different regions of the country.

"There are no members of Parliament among us. We are an autonomous committee, with independence guaranteed by the constitution. The administrative office of Parliament cannot dictate any guidelines for us," says the current chairman of the committee, Johan Hirschfeldt.

As former chairman of the Stockholm Appellate Court, Hirschfeldt explains that the committee meets once a year in September after the parliamentary recess of the European summer.

"That does not mean that members of Parliament get salary increases every year," he notes.

To assess whether or not members will receive a salary increase, Hirschfeldt reports that the committee reviews the economic circumstances of Swedish society as a whole, including inflation and wage-variation rates in both the public and private sectors:

"The next time we come together, we will review the overall circumstances, and perhaps decide to give the parliamentarians an increase of 1 or 1.5 percent. Or perhaps no increase will be given."

The administrative office of Parliament appoints the committee. Political reporter and commentator Lena Hennel of *Svenska Dagbladet* reports that the independence of the *Riksdagens Arvodesnämd* members is genuine:

"The committee, which is chaired by a judge, is in fact autonomous. In the Swedish context, where judges are strongly independent, the *Riksdagens Arvodesnämd* is a solid structure to handle the question of parliamentary remuneration," says Hennel,

co-author of a 2013 biography of Stefan Löfven, leader of the Social Democratic party. "We've never had scandals in this area," she adds.

The committee's decision is sovereign: it cannot be contested, and is not submitted to a vote in Parliament.

"Parliamentarians have no decision-making power in the process. And I never know whether they are satisfied with the salary or not, because no parliamentarian has ever phoned to ask for more or to complain," says committee chairman Hirschfeldt.

Another independent committee, the *Statsrådsarvodesnämden*, rules on salary increases for ministers and the Prime Minister. The names of the three members of the committee — which also includes a retired judge — are set forth by the Parliamentary Constitution Committee and put to a vote in Parliament.

NO LIFELONG PENSIONS

Any Swedish citizen of average intelligence understands the reasons why parliamentarians are not entitled to the exotic right to lifelong pensions after serving just two or three terms. Swedish parliamentarians are not offered a pension, but rather a "guaranteed income" (*inkomstgaranti*) for a limited time. According to Swedish law:

"The purpose of the benefit (*inkomstgaranti*) is to provide financial security to the parliamentarian during the time of transition after the end of his activities in Parliament. This benefit is not intended to ensure permanent income for the former member of Parliament."

Former Social Democratic MP Joe Frans, who served four years in office from 2002 to 2006, would have been entitled to one year's pension when he left Parliament.

"However, I started working at another job shortly after leaving Parliament," says Frans. "I reported my new job to the authorities, and the payment of my pension as a former representative was suspended."

In Joe Frans's day, a representative who served for less than six years was entitled to receive parliamentary pension for a maximum of one year. For those who served over six years, the pension was paid for up to two years (for members under the age of 40), five years (for those under the age of 50), or until the representative reached 65 years of age (for those who were 50 or older).

It was fine, but it could be better.

In 2011, Swedish public television decided to investigate parliamentary pensions, and revealed that millions of Swedish krona were being paid to former politicians who were still young enough to get a new job.

Two years later, in their resolve to do away with any remnants of Christian generosity that the system still held, the Swedes decided to toughen the rules.

Under the new rules, the general principle is that every representative elected as of 2014 needs to work for at least eight years in Parliament (two legislative terms) in order to be entitled to a pension equivalent to 85% of the salary (49.555 Swedish krona, equivalent to about US$6,060), for a maximum period of two years. And to receive a pension for more than a year, the former representative must prove that he is actively looking for a new way to earn a living.

"It's important to understand that the system has tough rules in place. They have to prove that they are aggressively looking for a new job. Otherwise, the benefit is cut," said Johan Hirschfeldt, chairman of the committee that regulates wages and parliamentary pensions (*Riksdagens Arvodesnämd*). If the parliamentarian begins serving another mandate or political position, the benefit is also suspended.

But these new parliamentary pension rules were still the subject of much criticism. For a considerable number of Swedes, the system remains perverse:

"It's a mockery" wrote journalist Lena Mellin in her

political column in *Aftonbladet* newspaper. "The repulsive differences between the benefits for parliamentarians and ordinary citizens remain. If you and I lose our jobs, we will be entitled to a social benefit of a maximum of 14,960 krona per month (about US$1,830). But an unemployed political representative can receive almost 50.000 krona per month (US$6,115). Moreover, the representative can get the benefit for two years, whereas, for the average citizen without children under 18, the law provides for only one year."

To add to Lena's outrage, there are possible exceptions to the rule for MPs who have reached the age of 57 years when they leave Parliament. In their case, a reduced pension (45% of the salary) can be paid for a period of up to eight years — in other words, until they reach the minimum age to begin receiving Swedish state social security retirement income, calculated according to years of contribution.

"Of course, a 57-year-old representative should look for another job when leaving Parliament, and they even have refresher courses at their disposal. If they fail to get a job, each year they can request an extension of the benefit but that would immediately reduce the amount of the pension to 45% of the previous salary," says Hirschfeldt.

An SVT news program featured a comment by the public employment agency (*Arbetsförmedlingen*): "Instead of receiving a pension, politicians should go to one of our agencies to try to get a job, as the rest of people do."

Members of Parliament elected as of 2014 and who work less than eight years in Parliament will be granted the benefit only for a period ranging from three months to one year. The days are also numbered for pension plans for widows or widowers of parliamentarians.

"In our country, the pension system is based on the premise that both husband and wife work, and that, therefore, each one is only entitled to his or her own retirement plan based on time of service. That is, women are not entitled to their husband's pension when he dies. But there are still some benefits in the system. If an MP dies, their spouse is still entitled to receive the parliamentary pension for two years, provided the representative had worked for at least eight years in Parliament," says the chairman of the committee for parliamentary salaries and pensions.

As of 2014, the rules state that the pension plan for the Speaker of Parliament must adhere to the same criteria as for the other parliamentarians, with no additional benefits or extras.

In the Swedish government, ministers are entitled to receive full pension for a maximum of one year. If, however, a minister is 50 or older upon leaving office, and has worked for at least six years, they have more rights: after the first year receiving the full benefit, they may receive a reduced pension until they reach the age of 65. From that age on, they will only be entitled to public retirement pension for length of service, at the amount of 14.687 krona a month, or about US$1,800.

Ministers who are 50 and above and who have

worked for at least six years in office are entitled to receive about 45 percent of their salary (of 118,000 krona per month, or US$14,425) until they turn 65. For those who remain in the function for 12 years, the percentage is higher: approximately 60% of their salary.

"Nonetheless, it is expected that these rules may change, since the possibility of a minister or the Prime Minister obtaining a pension until age 65 is a matter of great debate in Sweden," says Elisabet Reimers, a representative of the *Statsrådsarvodesnämden*, the agency responsible for the remuneration of politicians at the governmental level.

Reimers adds: "At the present time, the pension is automatically canceled if the former minister takes up another political position. And if the former minister gets another job, the pension amount is reduced, depending on the amount of his new salary, or is canceled."

The same rules apply to the post of Prime Minister. If the current prime minister, Fredrik Reinfeldt, loses the 2014 elections at the age of 49, he will only be entitled to a one-year pension. But if he wins the election and is 50 or older when he leaves office, he will be entitled to receive a pension of about 46 percent of his salary (of 148,000 krona, or US$18,100), until age 65.

"Should Reinfeldt serve 12 years as prime minister, he will be entitled to a pension of about 54% of his salary," says Rose-Marie Hallen of the *Statens tjänstepensionsverk.*

It's a privilege that irritates the Swedes and has given rise to a national debate. This was especially evident after the Prime Minister publicly announced that the Swedes should be prepared to change their "mental attitude" and consider retiring later, at around 75 years of age. The *Aftonbladet* newspaper demanded consistency from the Prime Minister, featuring the headline "Fredrik Reinfeldt can stop working at 50" (February 2, 2012):

Reporter: You can retire at 50. Don't you think it's time to review the government's pension system?

Prime Minister Fredrik Reinfelfdt: Yes, maybe it's time. But I must say I do not plan on retiring anytime soon, and I don't know any politicians who are considering it. I hope to work as long as possible.

Should he change his mind, Reinfeldt will leave office without any life-long extra benefits paid by taxpayers: according to a government spokesperson, the rules for granting pensions to former prime ministers do not include free benefits such as chauffeur-driven cars, secretaries, assistants, or security guards.

NO PRIVATE CHAUFFEURS

No Swedish political representative has the right to a chauffeur-driven car at his or her disposal. Those who live in the suburbs of the capital face the same commute as the so-called ordinary workers, swaying on trains or in underground carriages on their way to the office. If the winter cold is not inclement, the fittest representatives go by bike. And most of the MPs living in apartments closer to Parliament walk to work, braving Stockholm's long winters and the inevitable slipping and sliding on its frozen ground.

The temptations of comfortably driving to work in their own cars are offset by three good arguments: the Swedish concern about environmental pollution, the high price of parking and the *trängselskatt*, the toll collected from all those people who insist on going by car into the center of Stockholm.

"The Speaker of the Parliament also takes the underground to work," says Maria Skuldt of the parliamentary press office.

The Speaker and parliamentarians alike are entitled to receive an annual card to travel for free on public transport. For reasons Swedish voters do not comprehend, during long distance travel the members of Parliament can choose to travel in silent first-class train carriages.

There are only a few official cars, and their use is limited. Parliament owns just three cars, all Volvo S80s. These are available only to the Speaker of Parliament and to his three vice-presidents, to be used for official events.

"It's not a taxi service," says René Poedtke from

the administrative branch of Parliament. "Cars are not available to take them home or to work. It is also a matter of look after the environment. We need to use fewer cars."

In Sweden, the only politician who is entitled to a car on a permanent basis is the prime minister. The car belongs to the fleet of the Swedish secret police, the Säpo (*Säkerhetspolisen*). Cabinet ministers may request vehicles "when they have strong reasons for needing one," says one government aide. "For example, when they're going to deliver a speech in a distant suburb."

At Säpo's headquarters, the security services spokesperson says that use of cars can occasionally be offered to ministers, depending on assessments of their safety risk.

"But it is not the ministers who decide. All cars belong to the security services, and thus it is Säpo that assesses which minister may be entitled to transport, and on what occasions."

It is common to see politicians on the underground, or walking on the streets, without bodyguards. But since the assassination of Prime Minister Olof Palme in 1986 and the tragedy that resulted in the death of former foreign minister Anna Lindh — stabbed by a mentally deranged person in a department store in the Swedish capital in 2003 — some ministers have come to rely on Säpo's security guards.

THE VW BEETLE OF THE PRIME MINISTER

"I am on my bicycle, waiting at a traffic light (when the light is red here, nobody moves, even if the streets are deserted). There are just a few vehicles around. A red bus, a sky-blue Volvo, and a white VW Beetle right next to me.

I glance over at the driver of the Beetle and almost fall off my bike from shock. I instantly recognize him: I'll be damned if it's not Prime Minister Olof Palme! There he is: blonde, aquiline nose, and shrewd expression, waiting for the light to change. It turns green, he puts it in first gear and speeds off to the seat of government, all by himself in his Beetle without a driver or bodyguard, like any other citizen on his way to work in the morning.

This experience truly impresses me, as I've grown used to seeing heads of state in long, black limousines, with outriders clearing the way and two or three escort vehicles full of mean-looking security agents, fully alert with their hands on their guns — the customary marriage of power and paranoia.

But in Sweden the prime minister drives a Beetle to work and the king rides his bicycle on the streets."

Excerpt from "Roleta Chilena," by Alfredo Sirkis, 1981

NO FIRST-CLASS TICKETS

There are rarely any scandals worthy of headline news involving Swedish politicians and air travel: members of Parliament are not awarded generous plane-ticket allowances.

To avoid any possible turbulence caused by dealings with dubious travel agencies, parliamentarians reserve air tickets at the travel agency located inside Parliament. The agency is paid directly by the department of parliamentary services (*Ledamotsservice*), which controls the representatives' expenses.

The travel agency that serves representatives has a two-year contract with Parliament, renewable for a maximum of two additional years. Subsequently an official competition takes place to choose a new travel agency to serve Parliament.

Where international travel is concerned, the sky is not the limit. "Representatives are not free to fly as often as they want," says Anna Aspegren, head of the parliamentary services department.

A Swedish representative can spend 50,000 krona (about US$6,115) on international travel per parliamentary term, that is, every four years.

In order to fly, parliamentarians must present detailed reasons for their business trips, which must, as is customary in several countries, be submitted for approval by Parliament's office of the presidency.

When traveling outside the country, representatives receive a daily allowance based on a fixed scale: the daily rate varies from 220 krona (about US$27) to 700 krona (US$86), depending on the country visited. In Brazil the total daily amount for a Swedish representative is 407 krona (BRL 140). In Argentina, the maximum that a Swedish representative can spend per day is US$52; in Bolivia and Paraguay, US$33; in the United States, US$70 (573 krona); in Germany, US$75 (614 krona); in Italy, US$71 (580 krona); in Spain, US$66 (540 krona); in Portugal, US$51 (417 krona); in South Africa, US$39 (319 krona); in China, US$74 (605 krona).

These rates may be partially taxed. And if a representative receives free meals during a conference abroad, the corresponding value is deducted from the daily allowance.

"If they get their lunch for free, I don't pay a full daily allowance," says Anna Aspegren.

According to parliamentary norms: "If a representative receives a free meal during a business trip, the value of the meal should be deducted from the daily allowance, in compliance with the following criteria: breakfast — 20% of the daily allowance, lunch — 35%, dinner — 35%."

Another regulation specifies that Parliament will cover lodging only for the parliamentarian. If he or she splits the room with another person whose expenses are not covered by Parliament, in these cases Parliament will cover only 75% of the daily rate.

With a travel agency located inside Parliament, there's no room for extravagance.

"And we are not talking about luxury hotels. Parliamentarians stay in regular hotels," Aspegren observes.

In the Swedish government, officials usually travel on commercial airlines.

"According to government regulations, representatives should reserve the most economical flight available, unless there are specific reasons to reserve another flight," states Josef Salih, of the governmental department of information (Information Rosenbad).

There are only three small Gulfstream planes available for official travel by the prime minister, the foreign relations minister, and the royal family. Occasionally, if available, other ministers may use these planes, which are operated by the Swedish Air Force.

"The Air Force charges the government for the use of the planes," says Salih. A fleet consists of two Gulfstream model G4 planes, with a capacity for 12 passengers, and a Gulfstream G550, with 16 seats.

"If needed, the Executive Squad can also solicit the support of one more aircraft, a SAAB 240 which seats 31 passengers," says the spokesperson of the Swedish Air Force executive squad, Lieutenant Johan Abrahamsson.

The 349 members of the Swedish Parliament fly only on commercial flights. The air force jets are not available to MPs, governors or mayors.

THE PARLIAMENTARIAN'S TRAVEL GUIDE

Upon being elected to office, each Swedish member of Parliament receives a 35-page booklet titled "Travel Policy" (*Reseregler*). Some recommendations for the representative:

• You should choose the most economical means of travel: train, car, or plane.

• Cars should be rented from Parliament's travel agency, using the rental companies with which Parliament has contracts, in order to obtain more favorable rates. As a general rule, a mid-size car must be rented. In special cases, such as the transport of several people, a larger car can be rented. It is not permissible to rent special or luxury cars due to cost and environmental protection considerations.

• If a member of Parliament uses their own vehicle, the shortest possible route must be chosen unless there are special reasons for taking a longer route.

• Parliament pays 2.65 krona (about $ 0.32 dollars) per kilometer driven by the representative in their own car, but of this total, the representative must pay tax on 0.80 krona cents. If the representative travels by motorcycle, the refund is 0.40 krona cents per kilometer.

• Members of Parliament should only use taxis when there is no other alternative public transport available, or if there are special reasons for doing so.

Green Party representative Mikaela Valtersson ended up in the headlines when she took a taxi instead of the train.

Those who break the rules suffer the wrath of both media and electorate. In 2011, the Swedish newspaper *Expressen* exposed the audacity of one member of Parliament in its headline: "Mikaela Valtersson (Green Party, Miljöpartiet) took a taxi instead of the train."

Mikaela Valtersson stepped across the limits of imprudence: she committed the folly of spending taxpayers' money on traveling by taxi, instead of taking the train. According to *Expressen*, an investigation of the representative's expenses showed that she had taken 43 taxis over a period of six months, "at a cost of 17,000 krona (about US$ 2,080) of taxpayers' money, despite living near a train station." The newspaper reported that many taxi journeys were made late at night from Parliament or from Stockholm's central train station to the representative's house. Others took place in the morning. Valtersson argued that it was an exceptionally busy period, during which she worked day and night on budget issues.

"I had to work late into the night, when there was little or no train service. It was such a strenuous period that I felt compelled to take a cab to work," said Valtersson, a representative of the party which most forcefully defends the use of public transport.

"I would never take a taxi instead of a train, under normal circumstances," said Valtersson, who later lost the internal election for leadership of the Swedish Green Party. The party does not have a president, but two spokespersons — always a man and a woman.

NO PRIVATE OFFICES IN REGIONAL VOTER BASES

Swedish lawmakers do not receive any special funds for their activities in their electoral bases: there are no allowances for office rent, food, furniture and equipment rental, office material, cable TV, or subscriptions to periodicals.

When they are in their home regions, parliamentarians use the party's local headquarters, or the public library, to work and hold meetings.

"Many MPs use their own homes," says Anna Aspegren, head of the department that controls the representatives' expenses.

In certain cases, a representative may request an income tax deduction for expenses directly linked to the exercise of their parliamentary mandate, but a reimbursement is not guaranteed.

"Recently, an MP bought a digital camera and asked for a tax rebate, claiming that she needed to buy the camera in order to post photographs of her work as a parliamentarian on the Internet. But the *Skatteverket* (Swedish Tax Authority) denied her request," says Ömer Oguz, the Social Democrats' press secretary.

I asked Anna Aspegren if parliamentarians have any sort of benefit when they are in their local constituencies.

"No way."

So how do these intrepid Swedish parliamentarians get their work done in their local political bases? I call Parliament in search of Rossana Dinamarca, a combative member of the Left Party (*Vänsterpartiet*). Dinamarca is a familiar face in debates regularly aired by Swedish TV, featuring politicians and citizens and focusing on different issues in Swedish life.

The switchboard operator says that she is out of the office, and follows the usual protocol: without asking for my identity, she offers to connect the call directly to Dinamarca's mobile phone. The representative herself answers the phone.

Born in 1974 in Chile, Dinamarca was eight months old when she arrived in Sweden, where her parents took refuge after the 1973 military coup against the government of President Salvador Allende. She has served as a member of Parliament since 2002, representing the region of Västra Götaland, in the Southwest of Sweden.

Rossana Dinamarca doesn't have her own office and shares an assistant with other party representatives.

Where do you work when you are in your constituency?

I work from home. I have a laptop and a mobile phone, which Parliament provides to all representatives. I use the local party headquarters and the public library to meet with other party members. None of the representatives has their own office in the party headquarters, but everyone can use the facilities to hold meetings. We also meet in local cafés.

Do you have a food allowance when you are working in your local constituency?

No. I earn a good salary and I can pay perfectly well for my food or a coffee and *bullar* (Swedish cinnamon rolls).

Is there funding for office supplies?

No, it's not that expensive to buy paper and other supplies. I can buy my own paper with my salary. But when I need to print large quantities or prepare something specific, I can do this in Parliament, where I work during the greater part of the week.

Do you have an assistant at your disposal?

I share a parliamentary assistant with other colleagues when I am in the capital. Assistants do not have transport or paid accommodation to travel to other regions, but that isn't a problem. If I need anything when I'm in my own constituency, I just call our assistant in the capital.

How do you interact with voters and citizens in general?

We organize meetings and events in various cities in the region. But mostly we talk to voters by visiting schools, health centers, factories, and other places of work, to discuss their problems, to become familiar with their living and working conditions, to seek improvements and to inform them about the activities that I and my party colleagues develop in Parliament. It is the most efficient way.

Do you have transport at your disposal to visit these places?

No. I use my own car. I inform the parliamentary authorities how many miles I've traveled, and I'm reimbursed for fuel costs. I also have an annual card for free use of public transport such as trains, buses and the underground. Parliament also pays for hotel accommodation when I need it.

Do you have access to funds for cable TV or other benefits when you work from home in your area?

No, I pay for my own cable TV. I live in an apartment that I rent with my own salary. I know all my neighbors, who are just ordinary citizens facing common difficulties. Historically, Swedish politicians have always been close to their voters. We live like everybody else. I cook my own food, and take care of the house and children. I have two children, four and eight years old. People in Sweden would never accept special privileges for politicians. Politics depends to a large extent on the degree of trust people have in the system.

NO PARLIAMENTARY FUNDS FOR CONSULTANCIES OR PUBLICITY

Swedish members of Parliament are not entitled to special parliamentary funds for hiring consultants, research services or technical work, nor for publicizing their parliamentary achievements.

When they need research and analysis to support their policy decisions, Swedish representatives often use the Research Services of the Parliament (RUT — *Riksdagens utredningstjänst*), instead of squandering public money on dubious private consultants. RUT is a parliamentary department that brings together economists, political scientists, lawyers and experts from various fields — all who serve members of Parliament from all parties.

"The most important element is that RUT is non-

Prime Minister Olof Palme and his family in their suburban home in the 1970s.

partisan. Our team is comprised of technicians and professionals without any political affiliation, a factor which confers greater legitimacy to the work done here," says Robin Travis, RUT's head of the section for Law and Politics.

All of RUT's team members are civil servants who work full-time in Parliament. They remain in their jobs regardless of election results.

"I also am a civil servant, and my immediate superior is the administrative director of Parliament. The actual President of Parliament has no say in how I do my job," Travis points out.

These specialized consultants are available to representatives for tasks such as customized research, financial and legal advice, data related to regional

Palme driving his old Fiat on his way to work.

and international statistics, and analysis of the consequences of implementing reforms and modifications.

"All of the work is done confidentially, until the content has been made public by the representatives or the parliamentary committees that requested it," says Robin Travis.

Representative Rossana Dinamarca regularly uses the RUT services.

"I use a lot of RUT's consultants and specialists. We often need extensive research and consultation, and RUT is an indispensable tool. Especially for a small party like ours, which does not have large numbers of political advisors," says Dinamarca.

Neither Dinamarca nor any other representative

Elected as Europe's best minister of finance, Borg lives in a 25-square-meter apartment.

receives funds to publicize their parliamentary activities. Yet she remarks that this would be an unnecessary resource: "We publicize our activities by participating in debates, visiting workplaces, writing articles and using social media, which is an excellent way to keep in close contact with people. We also have press advisors in the group of assistants who serve the party in Parliament."

Swedish voters can read about parliamentarians' activities online. On the official Swedish Parliament page, each individual representative's page has a section called *Sagt och gjort* ("Said and Done"). There you can find copies of all motions presented by the representative, videos of speeches he or she has given, interpellations, and other parliamentary activities.

A CONVERSATION WITH MEMBER OF PARLIAMENT KENT HÄRSTEDT

"We don't have superfluous luxuries. We need to use taxpayers' money wisely, if we want their respect. There are unemployed people and other problems in our country, so public funds should be used in the smartest way possible" — Kent Häsrtedt

Representative Härstedt: washing and ironing his own shirts every week.

Social Democrat representative Kent Härstedt is a survivor, in the most tragic sense of the word. He was afraid and the night was cold on that September 28, 1994, when the ferry Estonia began to sink into the raging Baltic Sea with 989 people on board. Gigantic waves had broken the locks of the ferry's bow ramp. Within minutes, the voyage would become a living hell.

In the bar of the enormous ship, bottles flew across the room like missiles, and passengers were thrown against the floor and walls. Several people had broken arms and legs. Many were bleeding, dying. In panic, scores of passengers threw themselves off the deck onto the ship's hull, as the ship tilted steeply. Others tried desperately to grasp onto lifeboats that were splitting apart. The deck was full of life jackets. But in the blind struggle for survival, some even dragged the life jackets off other fellow terrified passengers of the Estonia, which was en route from Tallinn, Estonia, to Stockholm.

Kent Härstedt knew he must jump into the icy cold, raging sea. The waves were as high as seven meters and many would die from hypothermia, with the temperature of the surface water at 10°C. He leapt into the water and struggled to make his way aboard an overturned lifeboat. Before rescuers could arrive, many of those on the lifeboat with Härstedt had died. Only six remained alive.

Nineteen years after the tragedy, I meet Härstedt in his ten-square-meter office in Parliament. I ask him how he was able to be among the 137 survivors of one of the worst maritime disasters of post-war Europe, and his face contorts with the memory.

"When people started dying, we began gathering their bodies on top of us. I lay there under the dead bodies so that they would protect me from the cold and keep me warm. I don't know how many dead people were on top of me. The waves were really high and the sea struck the boat over and over," recounts Härstedt, who was 29 at the time. In total, 852 people lost their lives.

Since 1998, when he was elected as an MP for the Skåne region, he has continued to survive the typical routine of a Swedish representative.

Do you consider yourself privileged by becoming a politician?

KENT HÄRSTEDT: It depends on how you define privilege. I have the right to a mobile phone, an office in Parliament with cable TV, an apartment in the capital, and access to specialist consultants that work for all of the representatives in Parliament's research service. I do everything else, from writing speeches, articles, and parliamentary motions to reserving airline tickets on my own. I do not have a secretary, assistant, or private advisor. I share an assistant with three other representatives.

Many Swedes consider it a privilege for representatives to earn a salary that is much higher than that of a teacher, for example.

KENT HÄRSTEDT: I understand how they feel, because a representative's salary is above the average salary of many workers. But our work is quite intense, and we also have many expenses. For representatives from other regions, it is much more expensive to live in two cities, even though the apartments in the capital are subsidized. But we do not have superfluous luxuries such as those in other countries. I can't imagine having a private secretary, or even a chauffeur-driven car.

Why?

KENT HÄRSTEDT: We need to use taxpayers' money wisely if we want their respect. There are unemployed people and other problems in our country, so I think that public funds should be used in the smartest way possible. We live like normal people. Ingvar Carlsson (former Swedish prime minister) was always at the bus stop when I left work. Last week, I saw him at the same stop. You always see high-profile politicians walking the streets. They all live normal lives.

Do Swedish citizens respect their politicians?

KENT HÄRSTEDT: In general, people believe we are trustworthy and honest individuals. They may not approve of everything that we do and decide, but in general the voters believe that we have integrity. That's why it is important that we as representatives do not have a different standard of living to the citizens that we represent. We wish to live as nearly as possible to the same conditions as they do, although we have a different life — we travel, draft laws, and have certain privileges.

Which privileges?

KENT HÄRSTEDT: As a representative, you have the opportunity to meet important people and to influence the future of the country, and I consider that a privilege. But I believe there are some aspects that could be improved in Sweden. I don't think we need a lot of assistants; it's an excessive luxury. However, I would like a full-time political advisor working with me to help draft bills, motions, speeches, and articles. I would rather have this privilege in my professional life than any benefits in my private life, such as a larger apartment or a chauffeur. In my world, having an assistant would be a dream. But having one advisor would be sufficient.

Can representatives recommend relatives for positions such as assistants or party advisors for your office?

KENT HÄRSTEDT: There isn't a specific law that prohibits this, but I have never seen it happen here.

As a representative, are you entitled to a healthcare plan?

KENT HÄRSTEDT: We don't have a special healthcare plan. There is just the public health system that all citizens have a right to.

Could you describe your daily routine as a representative?

KENT HÄRSTEDT: I live in southern Sweden. Every Tuesday I drive my car to the airport and get a flight to Stockholm and then take a train to Parliament. I work in the capital until Thursday night or Friday afternoon, and I dedicate the rest of my time to working in my local constituency. Once a week, I iron my shirts and hang them in my closet, so that I have enough clothes for the week. I wash my clothes in the apartment or in the community laundry facilities in Parliament. Since I don't have a cleaning lady, I also clean my apartment. At night, I cook or buy something to eat at home.

In Parliament, is there a restaurant with subsidized prices for representatives?

KENT HÄRSTEDT: No, no. And the daily allowance that representatives from other regions receive to live in the capital is 110 Swedish krona (about US$13,50) doesn't really cover the daily expenses. I just paid 90 krona for my lunch, which is an average price for a simple meal. I have to pay for breakfast and dinner out of my own pocket with the salary I receive as a representative.

Like other representatives, you work at home when you are in your constituency. Do you have any assistance there?

KENT HÄRSTEDT: Parliament provides each representative with a computer for their office in the capital, and a laptop that can be used when we work in our local constituency.

How do you cover the costs of office supplies when you are in your hometown?

KENT HÄRSTEDT: I buy them myself. Paper, pens, folders, and other small things. More complex items can be obtained at my office in the capital, where I work most of the week. We also have an official stationery and postal service in Parliament itself. But if I happen to be in my home region and need to post something, I buy a stamp. It's not expensive.

Where do you hold meetings?

KENT HÄRSTEDT: Usually I use the local party headquarters or the public library. In the public libraries of three cities — Stockholm, Gothenburg and Malmo — there are special rooms reserved for Parliament, so that representatives can hold meetings. In the other cities, we use library cafés. No representative has their own office in the local party headquarters, but we can use the facilities and meeting rooms there. It is also common for us to meet with voters in local cafés.

Do you have some sort of food allowance for this type of expenditure?

KENT HÄRSTEDT: No, no.

Swedish representatives do not have budgets for publicizing their parliamentary activities. How do you inform your voters regarding your work?

KENT HÄRSTEDT: In all modern societies today, social media is an extremely efficient means of communication. I use Facebook, for example, to keep my voters up to date on my activities all day long. They know exactly how I spend my time, what I am doing, and with whom I am meeting. They know, for example, that I am in this interview with you right now. It's on my Facebook.

You slept on a sofa bed in your own office from 1998 to 2002 and were one of the last parliamentary representatives to move into an apartment. What was it like sleeping in your office?

KENT HÄRSTEDT: It could sometimes be annoying, because I would wake up and the first thing I would see was my desk and computer. But it wasn't such a big deal. At night, we would all say goodnight to each other in the hallway, them lock our office doors to go to sleep. The office was about ten, maybe twelve square meters. There was a small bathroom with a shower, where I would also wash my clothes. It was what everyone did. Today, none of the offices have private bathrooms.

What is your current subsidized apartment like?

KENT HÄRSTEDT: It's a 35-square-meter apartment, with one room that serves as both a living room and bedroom. I have a small kitchen in the living area and a bathroom. There are communal laundry facilities in the building, but I decided to buy my own washing machine that I installed in the kitchen. I also wash clothes in the laundry facilities located in Parliament because I have found it to be practical.

What would you say to a foreign member of Parliament that has access to privileges that don't exist in Sweden?

KENT HÄRSTEDT: Think about those who are paying your bills and expenses, and try to be sensible and conscious of the way you spend the taxpayers' money.

Mona Sahlin and her US$900 Louis Vuitton: Repentance after criticism by the media for her perceived extravagance.

MONA SAHLIN'S HANDBAG

In 2010, the leader of the Social Democratic Party, Mona Sahlin, faced the wrath of the press for appearing in an official photo holding a Louis Vuitton purse that cost a total of 6,000 Swedish krona (about US$735): Sahlin had violated the Swedish creed of equality, which vilifies any perceived difference between elected leaders and voters. The Social Democrat leader should not carry a bag that costs half the salary of so many workers, decried the newspapers. Besieged by her critics, Sahlin argued that she had received the bag as a gift from a friend on her 50th birthday. But the bag was a burden too heavy to bear: Mona ended up auctioning the bag and donating the proceeds to a charity.

A CONVERSATION WITH HANS BLIX

FORMER HEAD OF THE UNITED NATIONS' MONITORING, VERIFICATION AND INSPECTION COMMISSION IN IRAQ AND FORMER SWEDISH MINISTER OF FOREIGN AFFAIRS

"No one has ever called me Your Excellency" — Hans Blix

Just three blocks from the Social Democratic Party head-quarters in central Stockholm, Man in the Moon is a bustling focal point for beer guzzlers and foodies alike. Greenhorn and long-established politicians circulate through the lounge of this rowdy gastropub, alongside a clientele comprised of illustrious unknowns and the occasional lunatic. More than once, I saw Prime Minister Fredrik Reinfeldt there. But what always holds my gaze is the dignified image of Hans Blix, dining discreetly beside his wife. On Fridays, I walk almost instinctively through the room in search of the presence of Blix, who also happens to live nearby.

Former Swedish Minister of Foreign Affairs and erstwhile head of the International Atomic Energy Agency (IAEA), Hans Blix is best known for the reality shock he tried to apply to the world when acting as the head of weapons inspections for the United Nations in Iraq.

In the run-up to the 2003 US-led war against Iraq, international news stations repeatedly showed the improbable image of this Swedish diplomat, who confronted the most powerful country on the planet by reporting that UN inspectors had found no evidence whatsoever of prohibited weapons programs in

Iraq, and that more time was needed to carry out inspections. After the invasion, Blix accused the US and British governments of dramatizing the threat of weapons of mass destruction in Iraq, in order to strengthen the case for the war against the government of Saddam Hussein. Ultimately, no stockpiles of weapons of mass destruction were ever found in Iraq.

It is exactly 10 a.m. when I ring the doorbell of Blix's apartment in Stockholm, this punctual city where being late can affect the liver of its inhabitants and destroy friendships. It is Blix himself who answers the door, makes coffee and arranges the fresh croissants on a tray. As if he were just anyone, some might say.

Hans Blix was born in 1928 in the city of Uppsala, the setting of Ingmar Berg-man's Fanny and Alexander. The large living room of his 170-square-meter apartment is covered in Persian rugs.

"I am addicted to rugs," Blix confesses. After taking up all the space on the floor, he then began hanging them on the walls. There are also colorful ceramic sets and a miniature tree decorated with semiprecious stones, souvenirs from his four trips to Brazil.

In Sweden, representatives, ministers, mayors, governors, the Prime Minister, and authorities in general are addressed as just "you," and not "Your Excellency," as they are in some countries. How should I address you?

HANS BLIX: No one has ever called me "Your Excellency." Beginning in the 1960s, we abolished formal pronouns in Sweden and now everybody calls each other *Du* ("You"). People don't

Blix (between Tony Blair and George W. Bush): changing tires and vacuuming.

want to treat politicians as a kind of elite group, which lives on another echelon, far removed from the problems of ordinary citizens.

What is your opinion about the political system of countries where politicians are considered to be an elite class?

HANS BLIX: If I lived in such a country, I would vote for parties that were committed to reducing the level of privileges for politicians. When politicians have special privileges, these benefits end up distancing them from the people they are there to represent. Voters should write and tell their politicians the following: "If Your Excellency does not do a good job for us as a representative of the people, we will not vote for Your Excellency in the next election."

During your time as cabinet minister, did you have any privileges,

such as a food allowance or subsidized apartment?

HANS BLIX: No, I have always lived in this apartment, which I have rented since 1968. Actually, my rent is higher than my retirement pension as a former government employee. The rent is almost 17,000 krona (about US$ 2,080), and my pension income, after almost 20 years as a government employee, is 13,000 krona (about US$1,590). If it weren't for the pension I receive as a former United Nations employee, I wouldn't be able to afford living in this neighborhood.

Your government retirement pay is relatively low.

HANS BLIX: Yes, because I left public service in Sweden in 1991, and my retirement pay is calculated on the basis of the salary that I received at the time. But I am not complaining. I have everything that I need. I also have a car, and after waiting for nearly 20 years, I finally got a parking space in the building, which I have to pay extra for.

As minister of Foreign Affairs, did you have the right to a chauffeur-driven car?

HANS BLIX: I never had an official car or a driver to take me to work. I remember once being on the pavement in front of the building where I live, changing the tires on my car. You know, here in Sweden we have to change our tires every year; we have summer tires and winter tires, to drive on the snow and ice. I was rolling my winter tires from the garage to the pavement to change them and someone on the street asked me, "You do that yourself?" I said, "Who else should be doing it?" Ministers have never had the right to an official car with a driver. The Swedish security services maintains a pool of cars. If I needed to go to a meeting at some embassy, I could have a car driven by a driver from the security services. But they never took me back and forth from home to work.

What changed in your life when you became the Swedish foreign minister?

HANS BLIX: Not much, except for the volume of work that I needed to take home. And here in Sweden, we share the household chores. Since we had children at the time and there were not as many childcare centers as there are today, we had to hire an *au pair*, since my wife also worked. I still cook frequently, and my wife takes care of washing the clothes, which is not my favorite job. I also vacuum the house, and occasionally we have a cleaning lady come to help clean.

Were your expenses controlled?

HANS BLIX: Early on, in 1948, I joined the youth movement of the *Folkpartiet* (Liberal Party), and so I know very well how cautious you must be as a public representative and with how you spend taxpayers' money. As a minister, you know exactly how much you can spend on political dinners and which restaurants are acceptable. I don't remember what the maximum limit was, but it wasn't extravagant and absolutely did not include champagne. Ministers must also make sure that their staff are careful to act with total integrity.

What are the flaws in the Swedish system?

HANS BLIX: It's not all a bed of roses. On the local level, small scandals have occurred. And sometimes, Swedish representatives abuse the system. Recently the press discovered that a representative (Peter Persson, of the Social

Democratic party), flew from Stockholm to his home area, and then took a taxi from the airport to his summer home 70 kilometers away. Not only did he take a taxi instead of taking a bus, he also charged Parliament for the journey. This is unacceptable.

What degree of corruption would you say exists in Swedish politics?

HANS BLIX: In the 18th century, we had a certain level of corruption, and over time it decreased. Corruption is a deformity. In fact, it is actual thievery. It is stealing from the taxpayers. In Sweden we pay one of the highest income-tax rates in the world; thus, we do not want to be robbed. This requires widespread governmental transparency, strong anti-corruption institutions, and an agile press. An extremely important factor has been a free press. When the press is free, it can expose any corruption. People do not like to see powerful people stealing their money. For example, when the press makes it known that state authorities spent a certain amount on dinners or workshops for their employees, the newspaper headlines say, "Your tax money is paying for public servants' dinners." These cases are denounced, and this helps to minimize and prevent abuses. This is why most of the Swedish governmental agencies are clean.

What future do you see for countries like Brazil?

HANS BLIX: In my opinion, the country's primary mission in this process is to lift the masses out of poverty, through better schools, better opportunities, and better quality of life in general. I think that, as in Sweden, the population's access to quality education and better quality of life will result in people who are more aware of their circumstances and more demanding of their politicians.

AT THE STOCKHOLM CITY HALL
AND MUNICIPAL COUNCIL HEADQUARTERS

In Sweden, mayors do not have the right to an official residence. City council members do not receive a salary, and do not even have the right to an office: they work from home.

The Blue Room: Grandeur reserved only for the annual Nobel Prize banquet.

In the majestic headquarters of the Stockholm City Hall (*Stadshuset*), on the banks of the Riddarfjärden Bay, the grandeur is of epic proportions. But for just one day of the year. Every December 10, on the anniversary of the death of Swedish chemist and industrialist Alfred Nobel, Swedish royalty presides there, amidst fanfare and trumpets, over the lavish banquet held in honor of the Nobel Prize winners.

The celebration is as colossal as the feeling of remorse that struck Nobel, years after he had invented the deadly dynamite in 1867. In 1888, when Alfred Nobel's brother Ludwig died, a French newspaper erroneously announced the death of Alfred Nobel: *Le marchand de la mort est mort* ("The merchant of death is dead"). Thus Alfred had the unique opportunity of reading his own obituary.

"Dr. Alfred Nobel, who made his fortune by finding a way to kill the most amount of people in the shortest time possible, died yesterday," said the text of the misleading obituary.

"The story of the newspaper's mistake announcing Alfred Nobel's death is terrible, but true," said Annika Pontikis, of the Nobel Foundation.

The words of the obituary hit Nobel as hard as a stick of dynamite. Totally alive, he who had been planning to donate his wealth to scientific research decided he didn't want to go down in history as the father of dynamite.

In his will, to the despair of his family and friends, the Swedish inventor donated almost all of his incalculable fortune to establish an annual award for those who, in different fields of knowledge, would contribute to the development of humanity. The award was established in 1901. Since 1930, the Stockholm City Hall (*Stadshuset*) has hosted the Nobel Prize banquet with impeccable pomp and circumstance.

The event takes place in the imposing Blue Hall (*Blå Hallen*), which oddly enough is not blue: at the last minute, Swedish architect Ragnar Östberg thought it was better not to paint over the original red bricks. The mandatory attire is black-tie. White-gloved waiters place

6,730 pieces of porcelain, 5,384 glasses and 9,422 pieces of cutlery on tables for the 1,300 banquet guests. San Remo, the Italian Riviera town where Alfred Nobel lived his last years and died in 1896, sends more than 20,000 flowers each year to decorate the hall.

Everything is perfectly synchronized with the entrance of the royal procession into the Blue Room. From the high steps that lead to the hall, more than 200 waiters make a sweeping entrance as they descend toward the tables with their enormous platters and copious amounts of delicacies, which on one occasion included 2,692 pigeon breasts, 475 lobster tails, and 45 pounds of delicately smoked salmon. The banquet ends with a gala ball in the dazzling Golden Hall of the *Stadshuset*, where the Royal Family, Swedish politicians, Nobel laureates, and guests swirl around the walls covered in 18 million mosaic pieces made of gold and glass.

But once the party is over and the politicians are back at City Hall, the circumstances are quite different. In Sweden, mayors are not entitled to an official residence. City council members do not receive a salary, and do not even have the right to an office: they work from home.

It's a Saturday morning when cameraman Casimir Reuterskiöld and I type the address of Social Democrat Councilor Karin Hanqvist into the car's GPS, in order to record a news story. The building is located near Bromma Airport, close to an upscale Stockholm neighborhood.

We walk into a modest two-bedroom apartment. On

a table in the open-concept kitchen is the computer that Hanqvist has on loan from the City Hall to work from home as a councilor. In order to serve as a councilor, she earns a monthly stipend of 1,533 krona (about US$190). She says that she earns her actual salary as a childcare center worker — "a normal job, like most other council members have":

"We are ordinary citizens, elected to represent ordinary citizens. And ordinary citizens work in regular jobs," says Hanqvist for the camera.

There are a total of 101 council members in the Stockholm City Council, elected in proportional representation elections held every four years, in parallel with the general elections for Parliament and the county council (*Landstingsfullmäktige*).

Stockholm's City Hall and Council: Behind these walls there are no perks or privileges for the council members.

Council meetings take place sporadically, as is common in most countries. Realizing that the job of council members is not full-time, the Swedes inventively decided it didn't make sense to pay them regular salaries.

"In Sweden, the job of a council member is considered volunteer work," says Hanna Brogren, Director of Communication for Stockholm City Hall.

At municipal assemblies throughout Sweden, 97% of politicians receive no salary.

"We have a law that allows city council members to miss a few hours of work, when necessary, to dedicate themselves to political activity. In these cases, the city council reimburses council members for the hours that their employers deduct from their salaries," explains Brogren.

Like Karin Hanqvist, Swedish city council members have regular full-time jobs, parallel to their political activities in City Hall — with the exceptions of retirees or students who are elected as council members. Deputy city council members receive 867 krona per month for their work. In addition to the monthly stipend of 1,533 krona, council members earn an additional 980 krona (about US$120) per session held in the House.

"If a council member participates only in a part of the session, we only pay half the value of the additional amount," says Ida Strid, of the Stockholm City Hall administration.

It was fine, but it could be better.

The Swedes felt there was still some fat that could be trimmed off the expenses: at present, council members no longer have the right to take computers out on loan, even though they were diligently returned to the city council at the end of the term.

"Nowadays most people have their own computers and mobiles, and several council members use an iPad during meetings," says Strid. "So a more modern solution seemed to be to just give council members a contribution of 200 krona per month (about US$25) toward the cost of technical assistance for their own computers," states Strid.

Council members do not receive mobile phones, nor are their phone bills paid by the city council.

"Councilors are not entitled to mobile phones, nor are they compensated for any phone calls. Only the mayor and deputy mayors have mobile phones that are paid for by City Hall," notes Ida Strid.

I ask her if the council members receive any benefits, such as a travel allowance.

"No. But if a council meeting extends beyond ten at night, they can take a cab home. Also, they are entitled to free parking on nights when there is a council meeting in session," she says.

"Any other benefits?"

"Yes. Councilors receive free copies of the Parliament's newspaper, the *Riksdag & Departement,* and the publication of the county employers' association, *Dagenssamhälle,*" says Ida Strid.

Only a handful of politicians receive a salary to work full-time in City Hall. The president of the assembly and the two vice presidents receive, respectively, 69,030 krona and 34,515 krona per month. The City Hall is led by a woman, Margareta Björk, and most of the council members are also women.

In the City Hall, the list of salaried employees includes the mayor and the 11 deputy mayors. The salary of Stockholm's mayor is 116,800 krona monthly (about US$14,280). Deputy mayors receive 94,400 krona (about US$11,540) if they have been in office for less than four years, or 106,400 krona (about US$13,010) if they have been in the position for a longer period. The salaries of the mayor and deputy mayors are linked to increases in the salaries of government ministers.

A small group of people from different political parties also receives special compensation for part-time or full-time activities, such as participation in the municipal council.

"In addition to the council members, who receive a gratuity allowance, only 23 politicians receive remuneration for partial or full-time work in City Hall and the Stockholm City Council," says Ida Strid.

In Sweden, the mayor is, in fact, the politician who holds the position of *finansborgarråd* (the municipal commissioner for finance). In the Swedish system, council members elect the mayor, deputy mayors, and the municipal council (*Kommunstirelse*), the city's decision-making body.

Since most council members work full-time in regular jobs, they rely on some assistance to research all aspects of city council decisions: it is up to the Executive City Council to provide council members with a compilation of all the facts and proposals surrounding a certain issue, so that they can make an informed decision.

Seven of the 11 deputy mayors are members of the parties that hold the majority in City Hall, and four are from the opposition. The mayor and each of the seven deputy mayors from the major parties are responsible for leading departments with specific responsibilities for each area of the municipality's activities, such as education, urban planning, environment, and culture.

Altogether the mayor and the eleven vice-mayors form the Council of Mayors, and prepare questions to considered by the Executive Town Council. The Council is responsible for ensuring that all policy decisions are implemented, monitored, and evaluated. Consisting of 13 members from governing and opposition parties, this Council is assisted in its functions by two administrative bodies. The mayor chairs both the Council of Mayors and the Executive City Council.

Full transparency is the standard: the ordinances, documents, motions, and decisions of the City Council and Municipal Executive Council are posted on the Internet. Stockholm residents can register on the site to automatically receive, via email, minutes of meetings and agendas of committee activities.

The Councils also employ auditors to oversee the finances and operations of the entire municipality. Their reports are also posted on the Internet.

With approximately 860,000 inhabitants, Stockholm is the largest of the 290 Swedish municipalities. Close to two million people live in the greater Stockholm region.

A CONVERSATION WITH CITY COUNCILOR CHRISTINA ELFFÖRS-SJÖDIN

"Being a city councilor is a volunteer job which can easily be carried out during free time" — Christina Elffors-Sjödin

The striking interior of Stockholm's City Hall is a curious explosion of contrasts. Three colossal golden candelabras dominate the chamber's aristocratic hall, which is decorated with deep-red rugs and framed by curtains of the same tone. The solid wood galleries and the president's podium, crowned by a curtain of draped red fabric, complete the hall's palatial air. But when you look straight up at the vertigo-inducing heights of the hall, it is the symbolism of the Viking era that steals the scene.

The chamber's ceiling is made to look like a Viking ship facing downwards. It is said that in order to avoid inconvenient attacks after landing on unknown shores, the Swedes' ancestors would gather beneath the cover of their upturned boats in order to plan their plundering in peace. Their intentions were not always noble. But the Vikings went down in history as a people who always made their decisions together, for better or worse.

Through the Viking ship's hull, one can see the painting of a blue sky: a reminder that all decisions made in the chamber are transparent and must "fly" towards the people. In other words, all chamber sessions are to be open to the public.

Through a door in the main council chamber, council member Christina Elfförs-Sjödin leads me to the meeting room. She apologizes for not having her own office or coffee to offer, and explains what it's like to work simultaneously as the head of a childcare center and as a Moderate Party council member.

How do you feel about the fact that you have worked as a council member since 2006 without receiving a salary?
CHRISTINA ELFFÖRS-SJÖDIN: I'm fine with it, because I don't think we should have paid city councilors.

Why not?
CHRISTINA ELFFÖRS-SJÖDIN: Because we are just exercising our citizenship, in an activity that does not require a full-time commitment, and thus we should not be paid for it. If we paid salaries to councilors, many might take the job here to make money or have a career, instead of being committed to changing things for the better. And I don't think that being a city councilor should be a job.

What is it like to be a city councilor?
CHRISTINA ELFFÖRS-SJÖDIN: It's a volunteer job that can be easily done in your spare time. We receive a small gratuity, a very modest amount, which is actually sufficient. To make a living I work as the director in a full-time childcare center.

Why shouldn't a city councilor work full time and receive a salary, like the members of the Swedish Parliament?
CHRISTINA ELFFÖRS-SJÖDIN: Because Parliament members work much more than I do. They represent the entire country. I only represent Stockholm, and the workload doesn't justify full-time paid work.

The council members who occupy these seats in the chamber receive no salary.

You do not have an office or assistants, and you work from home. Do you have any type of assistance for your work as a council member?

CHRISTINA ELFFÖRS-SJÖDIN: The support I have comes from two of my party's employees, whose function is to assist all my party's 38 council members.

What kind of support do these two employees provide?

CHRISTINA ELFFÖRS-SJÖDIN: Mainly in the areas of media and press relations. If I need any specific information, or a consultation with the mayor regarding some important issue, these two provide assistance and background material.

You don't receive a travel allowance. How do you pay for your commutes in the city as a council member?

CHRISTINA ELFFÖRS-SJÖDIN: Well, it's for these kinds of expenses that we receive a small monthly payment of 1,533 krona (about US$187) from the City Hall. But since I need to work in the daycare every day, I use my own funds to buy a card that entitles me to use public transport.

What kind of transportation do you use to travel to the council headquarters?

CHRISTINA ELFFÖRS-SJÖDIN: Train. I live in the suburbs, and I take the train to the Stockholm Central Station and from there I walk about ten minutes to the *Stadshuset* building. Council members are entitled to take a taxi when the sessions in the chamber end after 10 p.m. But if the session ends even ten minutes before that time, we cannot take a taxi.

Since you don't have the right to a mobile phone, do you pay from your own pocket to make work-related calls?

CHRISTINA ELFFÖRS-SJÖDIN: I use my own mobile phone. Everyone in Sweden has a mobile phone. And it does not cost that much to make extra calls.

How much time per week do you dedicate to your activities as a council member?

CHRISTINA ELFFÖRS-SJÖDIN: On average, five hours a week. Reading documents and proposals is the most time-consuming task. I also take the time to respond to the many emails I get from voters, with questions and requests on various issues.

Can you describe your job as a city councilor?

CHRISTINA ELFFÖRS-SJÖDIN: Chamber sessions are held every three weeks, between 4 p.m. and 10 p.m. I write my own speeches, make visits to associations, meet with voters, and read a considerable number of documents and proposals. As my party holds the majority in the House, only the opposition council members present motions. My party's proposals, which are presented during the election campaign after deliberations with different segments of society, are drafted outright by the mayor's office. For example, during the campaign we promised to build a thousand houses in Stockholm per year. When elected, the mayor and deputy mayors communicate with community sectors to determine where housing is to be built. The councilors then vote on specific aspects of these and other issues.

So a city councilor doesn't need to work full time?
CHRISTINA ELFFÖRS-SJÖDIN: Absolutely not. Five hours a week is enough.

You have a family, you work full time as a childcare center director, and you work as a council member. How do you manage to keep it all in balance?
CHRISTINA ELFFÖRS-SJÖDIN: I have a very understanding husband, who is not involved in politics (laughs). It was more complicated when my daughter was young and I served as a district councilor, which took between 25 and 30 percent of my time. But now my daughter is older, and the work of a council member is not as intense as that of a district councilor.

Do you have help with your housework?
CHRISTINA ELFFÖRS-SJÖDIN: Yes, a cleaning lady, once a month.

What led you to enter politics?
CHRISTINA ELFFÖRS-SJÖDIN: I wanted to have a Montessori school for my daughter, but at the time there were none. So I decided to start the school myself, through a cooperative of parents. In order to

receive government subsidies to set up the school, I contacted several council members. From there, the idea snowballed.

Once the interview is over, we leave the City Hall building and face the unrelenting cold March air as we walk together along bustling Vasagatan Street. Once we reach the Stockholm Central Station, Christina says goodbye and takes the train to the suburb where she lives.

In contrast to Elfförs-Sjödin's experience, easily integrating work, family, and household chores with political activity at the municipal level, some city councilors do find it challenging. In February 2013, a report from *Sveriges Radio* (Swedish Radio) showed that women and

young people were the most likely to withdraw from politics at the local level. One of those interviewed in the report was 27-year-old nurse Louise Wiberg, who had a small child and another on the way when she became a Centre Party council member in the southwestern town of Vara.

"I used to work at a nursing home during the day, and attended political meetings on Monday evenings and Tuesdays. For me, it is important to participate in political life and in the decisions that determine how our society should be. But there came a point where it was no longer possible to balance political life with work, home, and children," Wiberg told the Swedish radio station.

IN REGIONAL ASSEMBLIES, 94% OF POLITICIANS ARE NOT PAID A SALARY

At the regional level, political representation in Sweden is also considered an extra activity to be pursued in parallel to the paid employment from which every politician must draw his or her own livelihood.

Sweden, a unitary state, is divided into 290 municipalities (*kommuner*) and 20 counties (*landsting*). In all its municipal and regional assemblies, there are no exceptions to the rule: council members and regional representatives do not receive salaries and are not entitled to an office, a secretary, assistants, or chauffeur-driven cars.

Just as in the municipalities, only the presidents and the committees of the Regional Assemblies (*Landstingsfullmäktige*) receive remuneration to work as part-time or full-time politicians. Regional representatives are paid only a small gratuity.

"In the Regional Assemblies, 94% of politicians do not receive wages," says Bo Per Larsson, manager of the Swedish Association of Local Authorities and Regions (*Sveriges Kommuner och Landsting*).

"Typically, politicians at the local and regional levels, work every day in regular jobs, unless they are retirees or students," says Larsson.

Despite this rule, there is an exception to the austere tone of Swedish standards: the historic and largely ceremonial position of the county governors, or *landshövdingar*. They live in official residences, receive salaries, and have chauffeur-driven cars at their disposal, albeit only when they participate in official events. However, this is not actually a political position: governors, generally from different sectors of Swedish society, or former politicians, are public servants appointed by the central government to represent the executive authority in the counties.

"It's a 400-year old tradition," explains Björn Eriksson, former governor of the county of *Östergötland* (in southeast Sweden) and former Commissioner of the Swedish National Police (*Rikspolisstirelsen*).

"Up until 1860, the *landshövdingar* were the king's representatives to the counties, and to this day His Majesty King Carl Gustaf XVI stays in the governors' residences when traveling around the country," adds Eriksson, who became the national coordinator of operations against sports-related crimes.

The position of *landshövdingar* was introduced in 1634, when Sweden was divided into counties. Until 1958, so-called governors still officially held the pompous title of *Kunglig Majestäts befallningshavande*, His Majesty's official representatives. And in some counties, such as Östergötland, they still live in real castles.

One of Sweden's most controversial personalities, former governor Björn Eriksson lived until 2009 at Linköping Castle, a 1,900-square-meter building dating from the 12th century. He would organize numerous official events in the county of Östergötland, as well as unofficial events such as theatre performances in which he participated occasionally as an actor and sometimes served coffee to the guests.

"A staff maintains and cleans the castle, which also houses a museum of the Middle Ages, which is open to the public. During my time there, we also had a cook, but only for official occasions. In my normal daily life, I have always cooked my own food," says Eriksson.

"Do I think that the position will one day be abolished? I don't think so. Tradition plays an important role here. But if some *landshövding* uses his position for personal gain, such as using a chauffeur-driven car for anything but official events, it could be the end of the system," he says.

Anders Knape, president of the Swedish Association of Local Authorities and Regions, strongly believes the tradition will carry on.

"Tradition maintains that the *landshövdingar* are a symbol of the country. They have strong support from local people, who also appreciate the tradition of official residences and the protocols of the position. When the county governor says he would rather live in his own apartment, people oppose the idea. But not all counties have castles for governors," says Knape.

The county governors preside over the regional administrative councils (*Länsstirelssen*), which represent the Swedish executive authority throughout its regions. Their task is to ensure that county citizens are benefiting from the central government's decisions, and also to inform the executive authority about the regions' needs. But their executive power is restricted: the Regional Assembly is the highest decision-making body of the *landsting* (counties), whose main responsibility is to manage public health services.

"For historical reasons, county governors participate in ceremonial events, in various contexts. Thus the position possesses a mostly symbolic aspect, although the governors do have some administrative powers in areas such as the protection of animals and the distribution of European Union resources to local farmers. But these governors in Sweden are not true governors in the sense that is most common in other countries. They are civil servants, not politicians," says the president of the association.

According to Statistics Sweden (*Statistiska Centralbyrån*), the county governor's average salary is 62,600 krona per month (approximately US$7,650), which is approximately 5,000 krona (about US$611) more than average monthly salary for a medical doctor in Sweden. Governors are usually appointed for six-year terms, which may be extended if the holder has not reached the age of retirement.

"No, no, no!"

— Jon Johnsson, deputy mayor of one of Stockholm's districts, on whether the position entitles him to a salary, secretary, assistants, or official car.

Like a Swedish politician would do, I decide to take the train to the suburb of Skärholmen in order to meet with the local deputy mayor. In order to manage its counties and municipalities, Sweden adopts, as do other Nordic countries, a highly decentralized system. The municipality of Stockholm is divided into 14 districts, responsible for municipal services in their respective geographical areas. The largest part of the municipal budget — 75% — is passed on directly to these districts. Each district has a District Council (*Stadsdelsnämden*) formed by politicians from different parties, who are appointed by the Stockholm City Council.

Deputy Mayor Jon Johnsson, who in the Swedish no-

menclature holds the position of president of the Skärholmen District Council, has scheduled the interview for late
Thursday afternoon. It would have to be at the end of an
afternoon, because that's when he ends his day as principal
of a primary school. And it would have to be on a Thursday
because it's the only day of the week when he can use a
room in the district's public administration building, which
is normally occupied by a public official.

As I board the train, I receive a text message: the deputy
mayor is letting me know that he is on a bus, stuck in the
rush-hour traffic jam, and apologizes in advance because he
believes he will be ten minutes late. I take advantage of the
time to walk around the Skärholmen neighborhood, home
to a high concentration of immigrants. In the public sports
gym, several residents swim, play sports and work out in the
clean and well-maintained facilities.

Skärholmen has 34,000 inhabitants and an enviable
budget: each year City Hall allots the district 986 million
krona, equivalent to about 97 million euros. But there is
no luxury for the president of the District Council.

The borrowed room Jon Johnsson uses measures
ten square meters. When I open the door, Johnsson offers me a glass of tap water, which in Sweden is fit to
drink. He tells me he found it fascinating to live in Brazil
in 1981, when his father worked for Swedish-owned Ericsson in both Rio de Janeiro and Campinas.

"I remember we had a cleaning lady there once a
week. But my mother used to clean the house the day
before she arrived, because she didn't think anyone
should have to clean up our mess," says Johnsson.

With a burst of uncontrollable laughter, he answers my question as to whether his position as president of the District Council entitles him to a salary, secretary, assistants, or an even a chauffeur-driven car.

"No, no, no!" replies Johnsson, who has held the position since 2006. He says that he goes by bus every day to work, and uses funds from his salary as a school principal to buy the annual card entitling him to use public transport. He says he also pays for his own food.

"There is nothing Swedish voters hate more than politicians who try to take personal advantage of their political positions. I do not wish to be rude, but I think that systems that grant certain benefits to politicians are dangerous. Because they end up turning politicians into a sort of higher class, and they soon forget how ordinary citizens live. And if politicians don't have the same living conditions as their constituents, they won't know what needs to be changed," Johnsson reasons.

"If I lived in a palace and was used to chauffeur-driven cars, I would definitely forget what it is right or what needs to be reformed in society. Besides, I have no desire to live better than other people," he adds.

Johnsson supervises the activities of the 26 Skärholmen district councilors, who meet twice a month — always at the end of the day, after work, from 6 p.m. to 8 p.m. During the first meeting of the month, the Council makes decisions about different issues such as the distribution of funds to primary schools. The meeting, which is open to the public, is held in the auditorium of the Skärholmen public administration headquarters.

"All citizens interested in participating in the decisions are welcome, and the first hour of the meeting is always reserved for the public, who can voice their opinions and ask questions," says Jon Johnsson.

The second meeting of the month is held with the local public administration authorities, which implement the Council's resolutions.

"Of course, I'm also invited by different local groups to meetings and discussions, which usually happen at night. There are usually two or three such meetings per week. I also spend a lot of time answering emails and phone calls from people wanting information on various subjects."

Like city council members, district council representatives receive only an allowance for their political work. Of the 26 directors, eleven take part on the board as deputies and receive the equivalent of 150 euros per month, plus 45 euros for a monthly meeting. Thirteen advisers, who are responsible for a greater amount of political activity, receive an allowance of 350 euros per month and participate in monthly meetings and visits to childcare centers and other public institutions.

Twice a month, the Council's vice president has to take unpaid leave from work to participate in political activities, but receives compensation equivalent to about US$864 a month. As president, Johnsson works on the board once a week on a full-time basis, as well as participating in additional visits and meetings. In total he receives 10,000 krona (approximately US$1,225) a month for his allowance from City Hall and the reimbursement for the days that are discounted by his employer. As a school principal, his salary is 37,000 krona (approximately US$4,525) a month.

"Of course, there are people who enter politics with

a career in mind, and there are several prestigious political positions in our country. Ministers and members of Parliament earn good salaries. But most local politicians, about 40,000 citizens, do not get paid salaries. I think this is due to our long tradition in Sweden: political representatives of ordinary citizens should be ordinary citizens," says Johnsson.

According to him, the motivation to engage in local politics without a salary comes down to the opportunity to participate in decisions that determine the course of the local community.

"I've learned a lot, too. I have met with several religious leaders and learned about their religions, I have learned how to build houses and how different social problems can be solved. But I'm not interested in a political career. My work as a teacher is rewarding, and I am satisfied with the job that pays my bills."

Johnsson lives in a rented apartment, and washes his clothes in the building's communal laundry facilities.

"My neighbors in the building are low-income people, most of them immigrants, and many are unemployed. And there is one thing that immigrants have difficulty understanding: in Sweden, politicians are forbidden to demand favors or interfere with the work of the public administration. Some immigrants who are not entitled to receive certain benefits assume that I can just give an order to the public administration and say, 'Grant this benefit to that person.' But if I did that, I would be reported to City Hall for interference in the work of a government agency. My task is to determine the amount of resources that should be spent on granting social benefits, and the rules that should be applied.

But it is up to the public administration to decide how to handle each individual case."

Johnsson is referring to a fundamental principle of the Swedish system: political bodies define general budgets and guidelines for the implementation of public policies, but it is up to government agencies to fulfill the vigorous and sovereign role of implementing those public policies.

Each year, the City Hall sends funds to Jon Johnsson's District Council and provides directions about how the resources should be allocated in accordance with the decisions reached by the City Council. The District Council, in turn, decides how specifically to distribute resources; for example, among schools and local institutions.

"But I cannot tell a schoolmaster, for example, that he must approve this or that student, or how he should proceed." The Council has the power to decide, for example, what goals we want our students to reach, and whether schools should implement Chinese language classes. We are not allowed, however, to dictate what methods schools should use to achieve those goals. Each public authority has the right to decide independently how to do its job," emphasizes the President of the Council.

"Therefore, Swedish politicians simply cannot promise, 'If you vote for me, I will give you a prosthetic leg, or this or that," he adds.

Bribery attempts, according to Johnsson, are rare.

"I recently received a request for permission to build a church in our area, from the Romanian Orthodox Church. They offered me a bottle of excellent wine. But accepting it would have been a crime."

A CONVERSATION WITH THE MAYOR OF STOCKHOLM

"I am not entitled to a luxurious official residence and I don't ride around in a chauffeur-driven car. Politicians do not ride in limousines here"
— Sten Nordin

A cold air mass is engulfing the entire country, announces Swedish Radio on that March morning when the snow lashes against the windows. As if this regular wintry occurrence were even newsworthy, I ponder, as I leave for my interview with Mayor Sten Nordin. The streets are covered with layers of hardened ice, and I consider putting on anti-slip ice grips over my shoes, the kind of grips that Swedes, out of vanity or embarrassment, write off as an accessory for the elderly. But once again, pride wins out over common sense.

Mayor Sten Nordin is probably arriving at bus stop number 3, in Hantverkargatan street, near the City Hall. I've seen him there before, glancing randomly at the electronic panel that indicates, with Swedish precision, in how many minutes the bus will be arriving. Cameraman Casimir Reuterskiöld, who lives in the neighborhood of Kungsholmen, often sees the mayor in the same bus queue at the end of the day, often carrying a shopping bag from the Konsum supermarket.

On the way to City Hall, some pavements are cordoned off for the workmen, who are tossing huge lumps of ice off the roofs of city buildings. This work goes on all winter, to prevent cases of injury or death to pedestrians from large chunks of ice falling from the tops of buildings.

As I approach the waters of Lake Mälaren, I see the golden dome of the Stockholm City

Every day Mayor Sten Nordin either goes by bus or walks to his office.

Hall with its three crowns, the traditional symbol of Sweden. I glance briefly at the stretch of bay where a police car crashed through the frozen surface of the bay a week ago following a fatal maneuver, killing the policeman.

The gigantic City Hall building, erected in the early 20th century using more than eight million bricks, is in the style of an Italian renaissance palace. I continue on to my meeting with the mayor through the so-called Council Corridor. There, above the portals of the political offices, I see marble busts representing workers who helped construct the building: Oscar Asker, a carpenter; E. Törnblad, a mason; Johan Ludvig Malmström, a logger, and four other co-workers.

Walking beside me, spokesman Aaron Korewa leads me to a meeting room at the end of the hall, and apologizes that the interview cannot be held in the mayor's office. I ask why, and he says, "The office is just too small." Minutes later, Mayor Sten Nordin (Moderate Party) appears in the corridor, walking towards us.

What do the marble busts of ordinary workers represent?

STEN NORDIN: This is an important symbol for us. At the time of the City Hall's construction, 80 years ago, the idea was to portray the ordinary citizens shoulder to shoulder with the politicians who were going to work here. This reflects the strong belief, here in Sweden, that politicians and citizens should be equal. There should not be great differences between the living conditions of a politician and a citizen.

You are often seen in the bus queue, at the end of the day, carrying a grocery bag.
STEN NORDIN: Of course.

You're not entitled to a chauffeur-driven car?
STEN NORDIN: I have a car for use in events, or on occasions when there is a security risk. But I come to work by bus and sometimes on foot, as most of Stockholm's residents do.

As mayor, you don't have the right to an official residence. Do you have any benefits, such as a travel or food allowance?
STEN NORDIN: No. I only have my salary, that's all. Once a week, the deputy mayors and I meet for lunch. We order meals from the restaurant located here in the building, and the City Hall reimburses us for the amount we pay for this weekly lunch. But we are obliged to report the value of the meal to the *Skatteverket* (Swedish Tax Authority), and we have to pay tax on the amount. I have, of course, an allowance for special occasions, such as for when I receive visitors from abroad.

You receive an above-average salary. Do you also have the right to a

Sten Nordin
STOCKHOLMS FINANSBORGARRÅD OCH KOMMUNSTYRELSENS ORDFÖRANDE

Nordin's advertising campaign. According to Nordin, lifetime pensions are a privilege that must be put to an end.

lifelong pension when you leave your position as mayor?

STEN NORDIN: Yes.

Do you consider this a privilege?

STEN NORDIN: Yes, indeed this is a privilege that has been much debated, and so the rules will be changed. And I think they should be changed. Currently, if a mayor is less than fifty years old when he leaves office, he receives a pension for a maximum of two years. But if he is fifty years old or older, he is entitled to a pension for life. And we think fifty years of age is too early for a person to retire.

Why shouldn't most local politicians be paid?

STEN NORDIN: It is important for us not to have many full-time politicians at the local level, for we believe that local offices should be strongly linked to ordinary citizens and be run by ordinary citizens. This is the concept of our local democracy. A local politician must have his or her own job, and devote several hours a week to political activities. We think this is very good for democracy, and for this reason we do not want many paid positions.

How does the system work?

STEN NORDIN: The City Council establishes the goals for the work to be carried out in the municipality, and the Executive Municipal Council, which is elected by the councilors, compile different propositions. These proposals are then presented to the councilors, who vote and decide which will be approved.

Before being voted on by councilors, the issues are discussed in several committees. Some decisions are made directly by the Council. In other words, if the City Council is the "Parliament" of Stockholm, the Executive City Council, presided over by the mayor, is the city government. When a political decision is passed, the city's business and administrative bodies — which are run by committees appointed by the House — carry out the implementation.

How many assistants do you have in your office?

STEN NORDIN: Fifteen people. I have political advisors, two press aides, and a secretary. Most of my team is made up of political advisors,

because we are responsible for drafting policy proposals for the City Council.

What do you think about the political systems of countries where mayors are entitled to official residences and all local politicians receive full-time salaries, have multiple advisors, a secretary, and a private driver?

STEN NORDIN: This would not be our way of conducting local politics, as it would create a huge gap between politicians and ordinary citizens. Citizens need to believe, and have concrete reasons to believe, that I understand the situation in which ordinary people live, because I live in similar conditions. Of course I receive an above-average salary, but I am not entitled to a luxurious residence and I don't ride around in a chauffeur-driven car. Politicians do not ride in limousines around here. If they had so many benefits, they would distance themselves from the citizens they represent. I am a citizen among other citizens.

A JUDICIAL SYSTEM WITHOUT LUXURIES

"I do not eat lunch at the expense of taxpayers" — Göran Lambertz, Sweden's Supreme Court justice

Every day, Göran Lambertz puts on his suit and tie, gets on his bike and pedals fifteen minutes to the train station. He locks his bike in the station's huge bicycle storage area, boards a train and travels 40 minutes to his place of employment — the highest level of Sweden's judicial branch. He is one of sixteen justices of the Swedish Supreme Court.

I meet Lambertz on an April morning at his house in bucolic Uppsala, a university town 70 kilometers from Stockholm. It's a surprisingly modest home. There are two bicycles in the small garden. The front door opens to a narrow living room, decorated with simple '70s-style furniture. Above the sofa is a colorful modernist painting, contrasting with the otherwise soberly decorated room. To one side is a large bookshelf. A wooden staircase at the back of the room leads up to the second floor. Each floor measures about 60 square meters. Beside the staircase is a tiny hallway leading to a minuscule kitchen, where the judge is preparing coffee.

Like all Swedish justices and judges, Göran Lambertz does not have access to an official chauffeur-driven car or a private secretary. Without a housing allowance, they all pay their housing costs out of their own pockets. Like the country's politicians, Swedish magistrates have neither special immunity nor privileged courts; they can be tried and punished like any other citizen. Their salaries range from approximately US$6,000-12,000 — but they do not have the right to receive any extra benefits, such as Christmas bonus salary or other bonuses, gratuities, health-risk premiums, bonuses, rewards, 5-star private healthcare plans, representation funds, childcare allowances, travel allowances or food allowances.

"I do not eat lunch at the expense of taxpayers," says Lambertz in the kitchen, as he sips his coffee.

Intrigued by my interest in filming him on his way to work at the Supreme Court, the judge prepares to be recorded. He arranges the dishes in the dishwasher, says goodbye to his wife, and grabs his bicycle. As he pedals, his long beige-colored overcoat flies in the wind like a courtroom robe.

The shortest path to the train station crosses a forest near the house, in a suburb far from central Uppsala. Neither the light rain that has begun to fall nor the cameraman's brisk instructions seem to bother the judge.

"Go up and ride back down again," yells the cameraman to Lambertz, from the top of one of the forest hills. The sequence featuring the judge pedaling through the woods is repeated four times, and shows the magistrate is in good physical shape. Lambertz is not even out of breath as he reaches the station's public bike park, and quickly walks toward the platform.

"I cannot miss the train that is leaving now," he says.

A former Law professor at the University of Uppsala and a former Chancellor of Justice (Government's Ombudsman), Göran Lambertz led one of the divisions

Lambertz, of the Supreme Court: Swedish judges do not accept gifts, such as cruises or resort vacations.

of the ministry of justice before becoming a Supreme Court justice in 2009. Controversial and eloquent, he is one of the country's most well known magistrates.

In the old mansion that houses the Supreme Court, near the Stockholm Royal Palace, Lambertz leads us up the majestic central marble staircase. Large oil paintings on the walls of the building depict noble court representatives from the distant past, a time when there were servants and privileges. Judge Göran Lambertz has no secretary or private assistants in his small office. There is no luxury.

"Luxuries paid for by taxpayers' money are immoral and unethical," says the magistrate in the interview given in his office.

What is a Swedish judge's salary, including extra benefits?

GÖRAN LAMBERTZ: Swedish judges earn between 5,000 euros (about US$6,225) and a maximum of 10,000 euros (about US$12,450), which is the salary for Supreme Court justices. This is a good salary, and it allows you to live well. It is sufficient. There are no extra benefits.

Do Swedish judges receive any perks such as bonuses, gratuities, representation funds, travel and food allowances, or private healthcare?

GÖRAN LAMBERTZ: No. I do not eat lunch at the expense of the taxpayers. All judges pay for their own meals. None of us have the right to chauffeur-driven cars or to private healthcare plans. We just use the public healthcare services, like all the rest of the citizens.

I noticed that you don't have a private secretary. Do you have any personal assistants?

GÖRAN LAMBERTZ: We don't have private secretaries, but we do have a pool of assistants that work for all sixteen Supreme Court magistrates. There are more than 30 young law professionals who assist the judges in all aspects related to legal cases. We also have a pool of about fifteen administrative assistants that are available to all of us. Thus none of the judges have personal secretaries or assistants to provide exclusive assistance to them. Instead, all of these professionals work on specific cases that are tried by the Court.

What do you think of systems in other countries, in which politicians and judges have privileges such as extra bonuses and even private jets at their disposal?

GÖRAN LAMBERTZ: I cannot understand why anyone would want to have such privileges. We only live once, and I believe life should be lived with high ethical standards. I can't understand someone attempting to benefit from public funds. Luxuries paid for with taxpayers' money are immoral and unethical because it is using public funds for your own personal benefit.

Can Swedish judges accept gifts, such as cruises or resort vacations?

GÖRAN LAMBERTZ: This simply does not happen. Actually, just yesterday I received a gift from a group of law students. They came for a visit to the Supreme Court, and as they were leaving they gave me a packet of biscuits and a jar of jam. This was the only present I received all year. But nobody would offer a judge things like money or alcoholic beverages. This just doesn't happen. At Christmas time, a bank, for example, could perhaps offer gifts to public authorities or offices. But this doesn't happen in the courts. Sometimes, maybe, a bank or a law firm might send boxes of chocolate to some court as a Christmas gift, but never an individual gift for a particular judge.

Have there been any cases of Swedish judges involved in bribery or rigging sentences?

GÖRAN LAMBERTZ: I have never in my life heard about a corruption case involving Swedish judges. A clean judicial system is essential. For if the system isn't above suspicion, there can be no justice. Judges should provide an example of honesty for all politicians, and for society as a whole. If the judges are not above reproach, all of society is disrupted. If judges are corrupt, then all members of society can also be corrupt. A judicial system that loses the respect of the population can unleash chaos throughout society.

What does Sweden do to prevent corruption in the judicial system?
GÖRAN LAMBERTZ: Actually, not much. The reason is that Sweden has a long tradition of people, in general, not being corrupt. If someone offered to bribe a judge, or if a judge asked for a bribe, it would set off a huge scandal in the country. But it just doesn't happen.

What's the explanation for this?
GÖRAN LAMBERTZ: Perhaps the explanation is that Swedish society promotes honesty first and foremost, and exposes dishonesty whenever it is discovered. We are an open society, and the media will always denounce corrupt behavior. Dishonest acts are not kept in the dark. This is the essence of the system. Everyone knows that if inappropriate behavior is discovered it will be denounced. The police and the media will find out. And the judges would never dare act inappropriately. I don't think any Swedish judge would ever accept a bribe. It is so forbidden that it is unthinkable. It's too far removed from our traditions. And if an illegal act is committed, it will be reported to the police. So even if some judge considered committing an illegal act, he or she wouldn't do it. They would be afraid of being turned over to the police.

What is the level of transparency in the Swedish judicial system? Could I, for example, examine judges' expenses and access official court documents?

GÖRAN LAMBERTZ: Yes. Any citizen can come here and check on court expenses and the judges' earnings. Lawsuits and proceedings in progress are open to the public. Judges' expenses can also be checked, although there is little to check. Judges rarely use public funds, and they do not have benefits such as expense accounts. Swedish judges earn their salaries, and that's all that they cost the state. Exceptions are rare trips for conferences, during which travel and hotel expenses are covered. Judges' private bank accounts can only be verified if a judge is suspected of a crime. But everything else is open, except for cases in which the court protects the identity of a person, such as victims of rape, for example.

Any citizen can go to the Supreme Court and check on an official case document?

GÖRAN LAMBERTZ: Yes. Any citizen can come here and ask to see the documents of a legal proceeding. A court employee will provide the requested files, which can be read in a room equipped for these requests. Copies of the files may also be requested. There is nothing to hide. The basic idea is that everything that is decided in the country's courts is open to public access. The Swedish judicial system is not perfect, but it is not impenetrable.

Who audits the judges and the courts?

GÖRAN LAMBERTZ: There isn't a specific government agency for this, but entities such as the Parliamentary Ombudsman and the Chancellor of Justice have the power to inspect the way in which the courts deal with different cases, how much money they spend, and if they operate in an efficient manner. They cannot interfere in the trials themselves, but they can control the court's spending and efficiency. Journalists also check our salaries and the income we receive from any other sources. For example, income from when we work on legislative and disciplinary committees, and in other functions where a judge can act. Many people think that judges earn too much, and this generates criticism.

What do you think it will take for other countries to become less corrupt?

GÖRAN LAMBERTZ: Politicians must assume their responsibility before society and their duty to set a good example, so that citizens can trust them. Thus they will be doing their part to create an honest society. If you are a judge, you most certainly have the duty to be honest and to promote honesty, in addition to being prepared to have your work and activities continually scrutinized. Many countries need leaders who constantly promote honesty, and who set a good example. Leaders who show that they are not seeking wealth for themselves, who never accept bribes and who officially censure dishonorable acts. A serious anti-corruption movement needs to be formed, with zero tolerance for corruption. Everyone must begin at square one, and have zero tolerance for dishonesty. And all those who hold positions of power must set a good example.

CHAPTER II

TRANSPARENCY: WHO WATCHES THE WATCHMEN?

"Sunlight is said to be the best of disinfectants."
— Louis Brandeis

SCRUTINIZING THE POWERS THAT BE is an idea that dates back to the days when citizens walked in togas along the streets of Rome. Crooks and rogues sprang up like mushrooms among the ruling elite of the day, and the vices and luxuries of Roman senators bled the public coffers dry. These were, in short, times in which foxes were appointed to watch over the chicken coops. The starving masses fended off their hunger and despair with the food distributed by the rulers during the circuses and gladiatorial games held in the Empire's amphitheaters. Throughout ancient Rome, the shrewd politics of bread and circuses (*panis et circensis*) subdued the unruly proletariat. It was at this point that the satirical poet Juvenal asked: *Quis custodiet ipsos custodes?* ("Who watches the watchmen?")

Sweden began guarding the guardians of power over 200 years ago. In 1766, the country created the world's first transparency law: a vigilant population and a free press should keep an eye on those in power and their acolytes. Public access to official government documents became a constitutional right for all citizens, enshrined in a special chapter of the Swedish Freedom of the Press Act, which would be enacted a quarter of a century before the proclamation of the freedom of the press by the French revolutionaries.

One of the advocates of the Swedish transparency law, Anders Nordencrantz, defended ending secrecy of government matters with the following words:

"I have not here concerned myself with whatever a dignitary of the state has done or wants to do, but only with the evil he is able to do, with the support of the laws, if he wants to do it. And that is not at all how the laws of a free people should be constituted."

The Swedish Constitution states: "Every citizen shall be entitled to have free access to official documents." The Swedish transparency law sweeps across all levels of power, providing citizens with broad access to information from institutions and individuals who make decisions on their behalf.

Known as the Principle of Public Access to Official Documents (*Offentlighetsprincipen*), this law reduces the gap between the government leaders and those they govern, and curtails opportunities for corruption. In other words, it makes stealing less convenient.

In Swedish society it's possible to trace the expenditure of ministers, representatives, and judges; to read the prime minister's official emails and correspondence; to check the expenses of the national police commissioner or the commander-in-chief of the Armed Forces; to verify government authorities' income tax data; to keep abreast with how public agencies are spending tax money; and to monitor the actions, motions, and official decisions made by any of the kingdom's authorities.

According to the Swedish Constitution, the fundamental basis of the transparency law is that openness is the rule and secrecy, the exception. The overwhelming majority of official documents must be accessible by the public. The exceptions to the rule are listed in the so-called Law of Secrecy, which makes it possible to classify as "secret" documents related to issues such as national security or international relations, tax policy, the investigation of crimes or individual privacy, such as a person's medical records. A document can be kept secret for a period of two to 70 years.

If government officials or any authority refuse to allow access to official documents, they can be challenged in court — even if the documents are classified as confidential. In 2004, the government classified as confidential the list of dead and missing Swedes in the tsunami tragedy that struck Southeast Asia, killing more than 230,000 people. The alleged reason was to avoid exposing the identification of the homes of the missing Swedes, in case they might be broken into and robbed. But a higher court overturned the government's decision and the names were released.

In the event of legal proceedings concerning the opening of documents, the law is clear: the burden of proof for the right to access such information is not the responsibility of those requesting the information. The government officials denying access to the information must justify, before the law, why a document should not be provided.

"Access to official documents is an essential citizen's right, and it is the system's main mechanism for stopping corruption and the misuse of taxpayers' money," says Göran Lambertz, one of Sweden's sixteen Supreme Court justices.

Certain boundaries, however, are unassailable.

"If, for example, the Swedish Ministry of Defense sends correspondence to the Brazilian authorities regarding a possible sale of the Swedish Gripen fighter jets to Brazil, that information may be public, but depending on the nature of such communication, there is a possibility that it could be considered classified," Lambertz observes.

I call *Skatteverket*, the Swedish Tax Authority, to verify just how much secrecy surrounds Sweden's leader, Fredrik Reinfeldt. The tax official confirms that I can obtain the prime minister's income tax declaration. Five days later, a duplicate copy of Reinfeldt's statement is in my mailbox with the following message: "Attached to this letter is the document that anyone can request from *Skatteverket*, displaying Prime Minister Fredrik Reinfeldt's income tax statement."

The government provides a special service for those who wish to obtain official information, but have special needs, such as speech or memory difficulties. The system is called Teletal, in which trained employees intermediate between such citizens and the public authorities. A citizen with a speech impairment, for example, can call Teletal and request help. The employee then calls the government agency that the citizen wishes to communicate with, facilitates the three-way conversation, and even annotates the information received, if the person has difficulty in writing.

The transparency rules require Swedish ministers and representatives to disclose their private stock market investments, in order to prevent conflicts of interest. The list of the politicians' stock portfolios is published and updated regularly.

According to the logic of Swedish transparency rules, the authorities's decisions must be open and accessible so that citizens can easily choose the information they wish to obtain, without having to depend on the media. And in order to ensure diversity of opinion in society, the Swedish government has provided generous subsidies to all the country's small, medium, and large newspapers since the 1970s.

The watchdogs of the transparency apparatus are the Ombudsman of Parliament and the Government. These two centuries-old institutions oversee compliance with the law regarding access to information held by public agencies. They receive complaints from the public and prosecute or reprimand any government officials who violate the rules of transparency. The system of control also includes independent audits of the accounts of all public companies funded with taxpayers' money in reports that can be accessed via the Internet. The annual financial reports of political parties are also audited by private companies, such as Price Waterhouse Coopers, one of the global audit giants, and are also available on the official websites of the parties.

The idea is to ensure an open society for all, with access

to information about what happens behind the doors of government. The pioneering Swedish model of transparency has become a benchmark for other democracies, and is considered by many to be the most open system in the world. But it is not perfect, as nothing ever is.

"As Max Weber once said, bureaucracy is secretive by nature," says Swedish political scientist Rune Premförs, while slowly sipping his coffee in his small Stockholm University office. "Make no mistake: government officials will always try to avoid having their actions made public."

Even in Sweden, obstructions to the law of transparency occur. Despite these enduring times of peace in the country, certain sections of the Swedish government seem to admire an old maxim by former British prime minister Winston Churchill: "In war-time, truth is so precious that she should always be attended by a bodyguard of lies."

In 2012, someone lied when they denied the government's knowledge of the involvement of a Swedish military agency in an agreement to build a weapons factory in Saudi Arabia. The secret agreement was revealed by public radio station *Sveriges Radio*, which then discovered that the email attesting to the government's knowledge of the transaction had been omitted from official records. The email was eventually discovered in the official records of the Swedish military agency. Officially, military exports to Saudi Arabia are not banned in Sweden. But the secrecy surrounding the talks, far from public scrutiny, sparked a wave of criticism that culminated in the resignation of the Defense minister, Sten Tolgfors.

Government blunders on the path to transparency, such

as Tolgfors's disastrous episode, drive Swedish journalists to the brink of insanity. The volume of their criticism of government officials varies by the decibel. Yet despite their indignation, reporters and political scientists recognize that the age-old Swedish law of transparency, which has inspired many nations to lift their veils of secrecy, still makes Sweden one of the most open countries in the world.

But it is necessary to watch over the watchmen, say the Swedes. And it's a daily war:

"No transparency law has any value without a vigilant population," says political scientist Rune Premförs.

For political scientist Premförs, govern-ments will always avoid making their actions public

TRANSPARENCY IN GOVERNMENT

In a country that hasn't been to war since 1814, it makes sense that there would be a road called Peace Street. The discreet Fredsgatan traverses the heart of the government in the Swedish capital, extending to the offices of the Foreign Ministry and halfway through unveils a view of the grand arcade of Parliament. At the end of the street leading to the stellar beauty of Lake Mälaren, the Swedish flag flutters over Rosenbad, the seat of government. Located on the opposite side of the street, the government's Central Registry is open to the public.

In the main lobby, the government official shows the list of daily correspondence and the Prime Minister's official emails, which can be read by anyone. No identification is needed, and no reason for any information search needs to be given. Not all information is open to the public. But according to the law, what is available must be provided quickly.

"We have orders to process requests as quickly as possible," says staff member Patrik Jakobsson.

The official document archive is gigantic. Bearing the hardly succinct title *Regeringskansliets Arkivsupport och forskarsal*, the government's Registry keeps information about government ministers, the prime minister and the actions of the executive power. The archive is constantly updated to allow access to government documents and decisions made by various ministries. To obtain a document quickly, at the moment it is completed, the ministry in question can be contacted immediately.

Documents such as Acts of Parliament and government proposals, applications for public funding, government spending details, ministerial reports, balance sheets and financial statements, guidelines for the government's budget, and many other types of documentation produced by the government can be tracked in the Central Registry computer room — with the exception of information classified as secret, according to the Law of Secrecy.

"Documents that are considered confidential, such as certain communications between the prime minister and the heads of foreign states, cannot generally be accessed," says the official.

I ask to verify the most recently submitted accounts for Prime Minister Fredrik Reinfeldt. One of the documents is a receipt for a lunch the prime minister had with the president of the Swedish Central Bank. As required for all Swedish politicians' expenses, the document lists the names of the participants, the location, the reason for the event, and an itemized list of what was consumed: in this case, two executive lunch meals, two servings of *petit fours* and two bottles of Ramlösa mineral water. The bill: 770 krona (about US$94).

Attached is another receipt from the government headquarters' restaurant for coffee and cakes provided by Reinfeldt during a meeting with European Union ambassadors and business managers. The detailed list with the names of 14 Swedish government participants as well as 31 foreign guests comes to 3,440 krona (approximately US$420) for the coffee service, water, and cakes.

I search on one of the computers for a list of the prime minister's and other ministers' most recent private investments, which is published twice a year. Later I receive a copy of the six-page list. Among the prime minister's financial applications, I see that there are certificates from *SEB Choice Latinamerikafond*, the investment fund of Swedish bank SEB (*Skandinaviska Enskilda Banken*) in Latin America.

I leaf through the list of the Prime Minister's daily correspondence, and I see, among other letters, an invitation to a reception hosted by U.S. President Barack Obama. The emails of the day are mainly messages sent by institutions and members of the public, such as one from a man who, in complaining about the taxes applied on pensions in Sweden, warns Reinfeldt: "Retirees are going to throw you out of government in the next elections."

Work emails, such as messages exchanged between Reinfeldt and his ministers, are not open to the public.

"But for the most part, the messages containing an approved official decision are considered official documents, and therefore are public," says the official.

"And if the prime minister is traveling, citizens can read his correspondence even before he does," adds Jakobsson.

The service is free. As in any governmental agen-

At the government's central registry, there is quick access to documents, proposals, and government propositions.

cy, the information can also be requested via phone, email, fax, or post. Also available for access are videos, CDs, and recordings related to specific themes. Copies of official documents are free up to the limit of nine pages. A fee is charged for anything over this ceiling: 2 krona (US$0.25) per page.

The central registry houses all the official documents of the Executive branch dating from 1997. Older documentation is kept in the National Archives of the country. Anyone seeking specific information from the Executive branch can go directly to a ministry: each area of the government has a specific service sector to handle requests for information from citizens about official documents.

I leave the central registry with copies of the prime minister's emails under my arm, and I walk along Fredsgatan for a few blocks, to the agency that oversees the parliamentarians' expenses.

KEEPING AN EYE ON THE PARLIAMENTARIANS' SPENDING

"The journalists are always here," says the clerk with an earnestly courteous smile as she greets me in the small lobby guarded by a uniformed security guard. We walk through the premises of the *Ledamotsservice* (Parliamentary Services), the agency that monitors the expenses and accounts submissions of all members of parliament.

At the end of the corridor, in a room dominated by long shelves, the parliamentarians' expense reports and original invoices are stored. They are large individual files, with the names of each of the 349 members of parliament. There is also a folder with the name of Per Westerberg, the speaker of Parliament and occupant of the country's highest office. In the Swedish hierarchy, the speaker of Parliament is above the prime minister, and below only the king, who by official protocol is the head of state. Unlike other parliamentary democracies, in Sweden it is the president of Parliament, not the head of state, who appoints or exonerates the prime minister.

Any citizen can come here and browse the folders, or ask for information via phone, the Internet, fax, or mail.

"The main reason for our work is to ensure that taxpayers' money is not squandered by parliamentarians," says Anna Aspegren, the head of the department. "They are in Parliament to make efficient use of the taxpayers' money and we wish for these rules to be followed."

Any expense report submitted by the president of Parliament and other parliamentarians are checked to the last detail by the ten employees in this department, says Aspegren.

"If the parliamentarians submit incomplete or inaccurate information about a particular invoice, we call and ask for an explanation," says one of the officials.

But inaccuracies in these reports are rare, according to the head of the department.

"Our perception is that parliamentary members are more concerned with doing the right thing than with cheating. Thus it is very rare to have to argue with them. When we identify some type of discrepancy or inaccuracy, we contact the parliamentarian in question. In most cases, they thank us for pointing out the mistake. Especially since the errors are usually discovered by the journalists who hang around here," notes Anna Aspegren.

Indeed, the *Ledamotsservice* tried to warn the then leader of the Social Democrat party, Håkan Juholt: if in fact he was sharing his apartment with a partner, Juholt could not claim reimbursement for the full rent. His girlfriend would have to pay half the amount to live in the property.

"One of Juholt's aides was notified by our agency, but the request for reimbursement of the full rent continued being submitted. Journalists came here and found out, and Juholt had to face the scandal," recalls Aspegren.

Transaction details

Transaction number:	29065232	Invoice number:	312	**AP/AR ID:**	11106	**Invoice date:**	18.09.2009

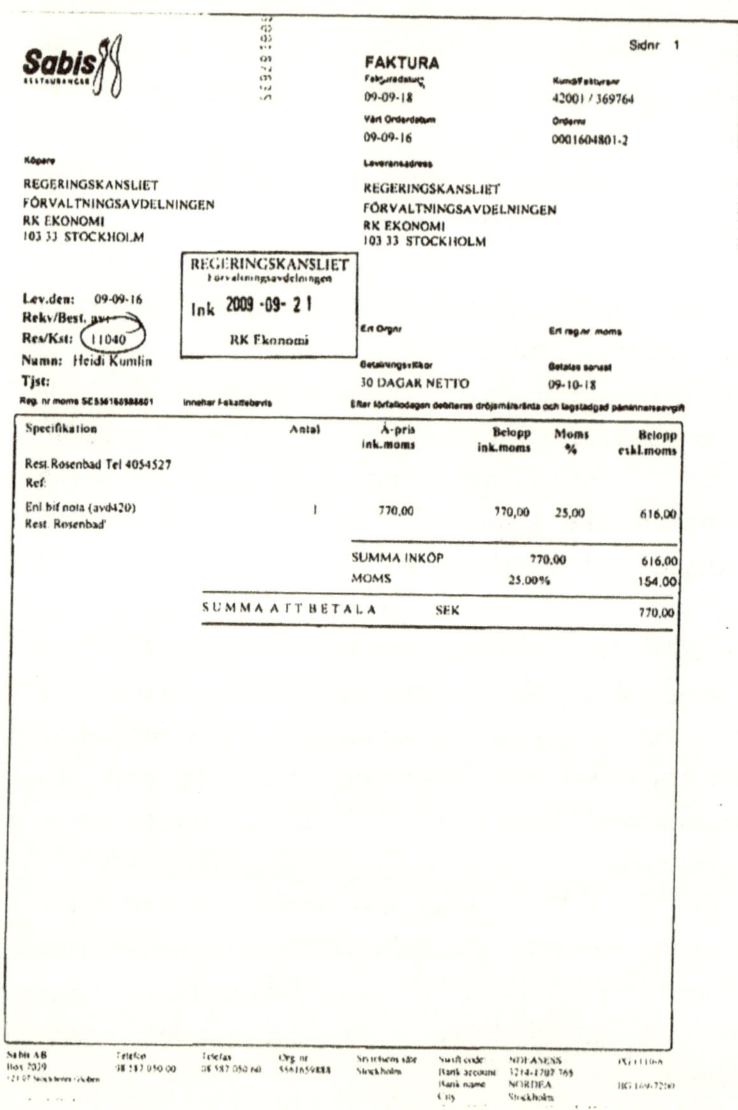

GL Analysis

Trans Type	Valuta	Valutabelopp	Belopp	Konto	Kst	Fin	Vsh	Bet/Anl/Idobj	Intupp/Gobj	Proj/Idobj	Mp	MK
	SEK	-770.00	-770.00	2581	11040			RTA			8888	1
	SEK	-725.00	-725.00	3011	11040					HKN0927	8888	0
	SEK	45.00	45.00	1541	11040						8888	0
	SEK	725.00	725.00	17500001	11040					HKN0927	8888	0
	SEK	725.00	725.00	5531	11040	10010000	799			HKN0927	8888	0

Folders with the deputies' bills and expenses are available in the Parliamentary Services sector.

Yet there are seemingly few opportunities to steal. Swedish parliamentarians do not have, for example, expense accounts to host social gatherings or pay the bills in expensive restaurants.

"No. No way," says Aspegren from her chair. The president of Parliament, however, does have an annual fund at his disposal for expenses such as receptions for foreign visitors and dinners with ambassadors. In 2013, the budget for this fund was 1.12 million krona (about US$146,700).

When traveling abroad, invoices for tickets and hotels are sent directly by the parliamentary travel agency to the *Ledamotsservice*. Before making the payment, the agency staff crosscheck the data received by the agency with the travel report submitted by the representative.

"There is not an excess of invoices, because there are not many things that the representatives are authorized to spend money on. In the case of travel, there is no possibility of forging invoices, since tickets and hotels are booked by Parliament's travel agency," says Aspegren.

When representatives travel within Sweden, they know they should choose "the most economical way of getting to their destination." The guidelines of the representatives' travel manual also require the parliamentarians to consider the likely impact on the environment when they plan the route and means of transport. But no one is questioned about how they apply the rules.

"In principle, parliamentarians are free to decide. We don't give them the third degree. But they must explain to voters why they chose to take a plane, for example. And the voters will, of course, judge them for it," says Aspegren.

"Recently, a representative had to explain to the newspapers why he had taken a plane, when other parliamentarians had gone by train to the same destination. When the representatives waste money and ignore concerns about protecting the environment, people here in Sweden get angry," she adds, noting that members of the public often visit the *Ledamotsservice* or contact the agency in search of information on representatives' spending.

Representative Eva Flyborg, of the Liberal Party (*Folkpartiet*), acknowledges pressure from the media:

"I once took a taxi to a meeting because I was carrying a lot of paperwork and I was a bit late. And the reporters asked me, 'Why did you come by taxi, if all the others came by bus?' The media investigates politicians all the time, and reminds us that we should not be spending taxpayers' money unnecessarily. And that's good," says Flyborg.

According to Anna Aspegren, generally the work of the *Ledamotsservice* goes smoothly, without any friction or disputes with the politicians.

I ask, "Do the rigid controls make the system cleaner, or is it honest because of the high moral standards of most Swedish politicians, who repudiate dishonesty and taking advantage of public funds?"

"I suppose it is both," says Anna Aspegren. "But we are always checking everything. And the representatives must provide evidence of all expenses, with company invoices that are also verified. So there is not much room for dishonesty."

"ALMOST HEAVEN"

"The Swedish transparency system is almost paradise," says Björn Hygstedt, information director of the *Svenska Dagbladet* newspaper. During his career, Hygstedt has removed several government officials from their posts, using the law of transparency and public access to official documents. Among his victims is a senior Swedish military commander who was fired "for using taxpayers' money to throw parties and rent luxury cars," says the journalist. But access to information isn't always fast or guaranteed.

"There are obstructions," says Hygstedt. "The Swedish transparency law is unique in its breadth and openness, but certain authorities are addicted to unnecessary secrecy."

Similar criticism comes from Supreme Court justice Göran Lambertz, who in 2001-2009 held the official position of Chancellor of Justice (Government's Ombudsman), one of the watchmen who ensure compliance with the rules of transparency.

"Sometimes, public servants think that they can keep certain information a secret, and thus the system doesn't always work efficiently," says Lambertz. "But the principle of transparency is a system that, to a great extent, works as it should," he says.

Award-winning journalist Nils Funcke, considered one of the leading experts on the Swedish transparency law, agrees:

"It's an extraordinary system that has been operating for more than 200 years in Sweden and gives citizens plenty of opportunity to scrutinize public authorities. But we expect even more from the system. We want it to be perfect."

According to his assessment, when applying the Swedish transparency law the rule is openness, and secrecy is the exception.

"Most authorities take the principle of public access to official information very seriously, including the courts of law," says the journalist.

I ask Funcke if the Swedish judicial system is completely clean, and once again I am told the same thing I have been told so many times before:

"I've never heard of a corrupt judge in Sweden."

But there are gaps in the overall transparency system, says Nils.

"One of the problems is that many public servants are afraid to make a mistake when releasing information, so they end up adopting excessive caution. In addition, some public authorities do not process the request for information as quickly as they should, while others overuse the stamp of secrecy. There are also heads of public authorities, such as the police, who advise officials against divulging too much information, and this is against the law," he notes.

Nils Funcke keeps his finger on the trigger. In 2006, he was responsible for the resignation of Foreign Minister Laila Freivalds, using the law of transparency.

THE MINISTER AND THE PROPHET

Politically speaking, Laila Freivalds was barely breathing through respirators after her unfortunate decision to go to the theatre at the wrong time on a fatal day. It was December 26, 2004. Ever since the morning, terrifying news had been reaching Sweden, detailing the fury of the tsunami that had hit the coast of Southeast Asia. Badly injured Swedes were dying in hospitals in Thailand. Thousands of people were missing. Panic-stricken at the news of the tragedy, many tried to search for news of missing family members via the Swedish Foreign Ministry's telephone exchange, where the few staff on duty had little or no information to give out on what was a public holiday. While the Foreign Minister was watching the play, a world in shock watched the virtually apocalyptic images of the tragedy.

When the sea receded, more than 230,000 people were dead. Among them, 543 Swedes. Letters and more letters arrived at the Swedish government headquarters, calling for the resignation of Minister Laila Freivalds for her inept performance in the face of one of the deadliest natural disasters in history. Freivalds publicly apologized for having gone to the theatre that evening. And, unlike the more than 500 Swedish victims, she survived the cataclysm. But little more than a year later, her time would come. Although the gigantic waves of the tsunami had not battered Freivalds, that task would be left, emblematically, to the prophet Muhammad.

In September 2005, Danish newspaper *Jyllands-Posten* triggered a wave of protests across the Arab world by publishing twelve cartoons of the Islam's sacred prophet. This time Laila Freivalds kept a closer eye on the news. Danish embassies were set on fire, millions of people took to the streets in Muslim-majority countries, and the International Union of Muslim Scholars incited a total boycott of Danish products. The protests spread as Western newspapers, in the name of freedom of speech, republished the cartoons of the Prophet Muhammad. Flags of Western nations were burned, and enraged crowds attacked several diplomatic missions.

In Sweden, Freivalds would make another unfortunate decision. When the electronic edition of the *SD Kuriren* newspaper published a cartoon of the Prophet Muhammad in February 2006, the Foreign Ministry decided to censor the publication. *SD Kuriren* is the official newspaper of the Swedish far-right party, known sim-

Former minister Freivalds: struck down by the law of transparency after the tsunami.

ply as Swedish Democrats (*Sverigedemokraterna*), which at that time was beginning its disturbing political rise in the country.

Soon after the publication of the cartoon, one of the minister's aides, Stefan Amér, contacted Levonline, the company that owns the server that hosted *SD Kuriren*'s website on the Internet. The Swedish secret police, Säpo, also contacted the company. The next day, Levonline took down *SD Kuriren*, closing the Swedish Democrats' website. This was a breach of the constitutional freedom of the press, and the ministry was showered with criticism. Laila Freivalds pled ignorance: the adviser had acted on his own, without her consent.

"I cannot keep track of everything my employees do," Freivalds said. But she was lying.

"I suspected the minister was not telling the

truth. The issue now was how to prove it," says Nils Funcke, the writer of the story that led to Freivald's downfall.

Funcke contacted the Ombudsman and found that the Government had already demanded an explanation from the Foreign Ministry and the secret police concerning the website's closure.

"According to the law of transparency, official communication between state authorities is to be public," says Funcke.

"I contacted the Ombudsman every day until the Foreign Ministry's reply was sent through to it. I read the statement and saw that in the five words 'after consultation with the minister,' the text confirmed that the ministry's aide had acted on approval of Minister Laila Freivalds," he said.

Freivalds's lie, revealed by the journalist in the publication *Riksdag & Departement*, produced seismic waves across the country.

Freivalds was reported to the Parliamentary Constitution Committee (KU). Days later, the minister's resignation was announced. The official website of the Swedish Democrats went back online after being shut down for six days. And in the 2010 elections, the far-right party won a parliamentary seat for the first time in history, barring the center-right alliance from reaching an absolute majority.

"I used the principle of transparency to gain access to the Ministry of Justice's official communication, and I had no problem obtaining the information as soon as it was issued," says Funcke, who won the Swedish Grand Prize for Journalism that year.

In certain cases, information needs to be extracted by the sword of justice. That is what happened in 2005, when the authorities assumed that plans for the construction of then Prime Minister Göran Persson's new home could be concealed as a state secret.

THE PRIME MINISTER'S SECRET MANSION

The weekend shift had barely begun that Saturday morning in 2005 when the phone rang in the newsroom of public television SVT. It was the prime minister, Social Democrat Göran Persson.

"My house is not a mansion," he asserted down the line.

"SVT's teletext service had just reported that the prime minister had bought a mansion," says Mats Knutson, a political commentator for the channel, during our meeting in the lobby of the Swedish Parliament.

For Persson, the news was catastrophic: buying a mansion is not something a Swedish politician does without being nailed to a cross by the media and the electorate. Especially when it comes to a Social Democrat politician. Persson should have known better. In the 2002 election campaign, he himself had crucified Conservative Party leader Bo Lundgren for buying a more expensive house than the average citizen could afford.

"How can you, who purchased a house for 6 million Swedish krona (about US$733,500), understand the conditions in which ordinary citizens live?" Persson had attacked.

Persson had won that election, but now he himself was in trouble. If the house was indeed a mansion, the prime minister had broken a sworn tradition in Swedish politics, and especially of social democracy: to live simply, and, preferably, in the same way as ordinary people live. That's what Persson's predecessors, such as Olof Palme, had always done. Ingvar Carlsson, another former Swedish premier, lives to this day in a small, modest apartment in Tyresö, a municipality south of Stockholm.

A lively discussion in the media ensued to determine whether Göran Persson's new property was, after all, a house or a mansion. Aerial photographs, sketches, and drawings of the property situated in the region of Södermanland, 160 kilometers from Stockholm, were printed in newspapers and magazines. As I looked through the illustrations, nothing seemed to me to be ostentatiously luxurious: the pictures showed a traditional red-painted farmhouse common in the Swedish countryside. But the size of the land bothered the Swedes: 5,000 square meters, according to the *Aftonbladet* newspaper. Even more troubling was the price of the home: 12.5 million krona (about US$1.53 million).

To make matters worse, Persson had plans to renovate the property and the local authorities had classified the blueprints for the new house as secret documents.

Persson, his wife and the new house: You can't buy a mansion and represent the Labor Party.

Säpo, the secret police, argued that the project should be kept confidential. But the law of transparency was invoked, and an administrative court ordered the authorities to open the documents to public access.

"The court has removed the stamp of secrecy from the building plans, and we can now disclose them," wrote *Aftonbladet*, as it provided the details. Each of the house's two stories would measure 178 square meters. It would have three bedrooms and two bathrooms, plus four fireplaces and a library.

"Göran Persson and his wife will be able to sit in their own library, reading a good book in comfortable armchairs in front of a fireplace. Or they can invite guests for dinner and wine in a large dining room." The article proceeded to provide a meticulous description of the house: "The facade will be made of wood, and the bricks on the roof will receive a special coating."

So it was decided: the house was a mansion. Persson was now walking on thin ice.

"Persson's credibility is threatened by his dream mansion," wrote the *Aftonbladet* newspaper. It polled readers on its website: "Can the Prime Minister build a luxury home and still represent the labor movement?" Three-quarters of respondents answered "no."

Later the press discovered that the prime minister also intended to build extensions to the property.

"Persson's mansion will get even bigger," thundered the *Aftonbladet* again:

"The house that already exists on the property is not enough for the prime minister. Now he is requesting planning permission to build another house, an annex of 54 square meters for guests, and a garage."

The cost of the renovation: 7 million Swedish krona (approximately US$856,000). There was no doubt that the prime minister and his wife had the means to acquire the house. Göran Persson, who had separated from his former wife, had bought the house with his new wife, Anitra Sten, who had been the head of Systembolaget, the powerful company that controls the state alcohol monopoly in Sweden. Torp, the name of the property where the house was located, was the new love nest for Göran and Anitra.

But the problem wasn't just the price or the size of the house.

The issue, according to political commentator Lena Mellin, was in Persson's choice: the prime minister had adopted the lifestyle of the old elites.

"A good job in town. A country mansion, with ample opportunities to invite guests for the weekend. Exactly how the Swedish aristocracy lived, and in certain cases, still lives. Like the British," wrote the columnist.

It was election campaign time, and on SVT, the public TV channel, the debate moderator, Mats Knutson, questioned the prime minister on the issue. Göran Persson rejected Knutson's statistics on increasing economic inequality in Swedish society, and replied that the purchase of a property worth several million krona had not alienated him from the average citizen.

"I know just as much about ordinary citizens as before," said the prime minister.

But there are those who argue that the saga of the Torp mansion was one of the factors in Göran Persson's defeat. He lost the 2006 election to the center-right party alliance.

In addition to losing the election, Göran Persson most likely lost a few more strands of hair over his new house after he was summoned to the police station and interrogated. It was discovered that he had not submitted a health and safety risk assessment plan for the workers on the property — required for any construction work in Sweden.

THE PENALTY FOR THOSE WHO ARE CAUGHT: "THEIR POLITICAL CAREER ENDS"

Despite the inclinations of some authorities to use the stamp of secrecy, as in the episode of Göran Persson's house-mansion, Swedish journalists are almost unanimous in asserting that the benefits of the Swedish transparency law are still significantly greater than its failures.

"The law is an essential tool for monitoring government and preventing corruption in Sweden," says political reporter Mats Knutson.

Political commentator Lena Mellin, of the *Aftonbladet* newspaper, agrees.

"Typically, there are very few obstructions to the transparency system," says Mellin.

According to Knutson, it is possible for a government official to attempt to manipulate or delay public access to information.

"If a document is classified in a public authority's registry as being in the preparation phase, for example, it cannot be read. But from the moment an official decision is made, the document has to be made available, except for cases provided for in the law of secrecy," says the political commentator of the SVT channel, and one of the country's most respected journalists.

By law, all official information must be immediately made available in each government authority's general registry. A document is considered official from

Knutson: "You need to know what to look for and where to investigate."

the time it is finalized by an authority. And the instant a document is sent or received by a government agency, it also becomes automatically official.

"This is the key to the whole system: as soon as a document is received or sent from one public agency to another, it becomes an official document, and therefore open to public scrutiny. In order to monitor the actions of each authority, you just have to check the general registry of a public agency," says political scientist Rune Premförs.

Preliminary drafts or versions of an official decision, for example, are not initially classified as official documents. But once a decision is adopted, the preliminary drafts also become official documents.

"Normally, files containing a formal decision include a large number of preparatory documents, which provide a good overview of the decision-making process — who made the proposals and who decided what. And a government proposal is always made public before it is sent to Parliament," adds Premförs.

It's an ocean of documents, says Mats Knutson. You have to know what to look for, and where to investigate.

"As a reporter, you usually receive a tip-off, and start investigating. It is also possible to monitor government officials through the reports of independent auditors who oversee public agencies," he says.

To navigate this vast sea of public information, one tool widely used by Swedish journalists is Infotorget, one of several Swedish online content providers with information on almost everything and everyone. These providers have a powerful database that brings together agencies such as tax authorities, the traffic department, the national registry of companies, and more. A quick consultation is all that is needed to find out whether a person is in arrears with the tax authorities, what their income is, if they have any debts, if they have failed to pay traffic fines, what properties they own, and if they are members of corporate boards of administration, among other information.

"It just takes one click to find out who has a criminal record," says the *Svenska Dagbladet* information director. "This is one of the first measures taken when the name of a new minister is announced."

With providers like Infotorget, you can check out basic information about any person.

"By Swedish law, however, if a search involves more detailed information about an individual, such as their financial data, we are required to notify this individual about the person who has sought the information, and what kind of information was requested," says Christian Olsson, an Infotorget public relations employee.

The art of watching the watchmen is taught in university classrooms. This information comes from Mikael Grill, one of the leaders of Sweden's Association of Investigative Journalists (*Grävande Journalister*). He has received awards for "grilling" certain authorities. I meet with Grill at SVT headquarters, where he works as a reporter.

"In journalism colleges, we have a specific course on the law of transparency. There are also courses to instruct journalists on how to analyze financial reports and accounting reports," says the journalist.

As soon as he left the university classrooms, Grill began testing the system.

"I went into the office of the municipal authorities in Sundsvall, in northern Sweden, and asked to read the politicians' emails. Although they agreed to my request, they placed an employee next to me at the computer, overseeing the personal emails that could not be read. But in Sweden we can see a government official's email list with the titles of different subjects," he says.

For political scientist Rune Premförs, the Swedish system of transparency is still a point of reference in the world.

"I'm unaware of a more open system," he says.

According to Premförs, keeping the public in the dark about state activities and decisions is not possible in Sweden like it is in other countries in the European Union.

"I've done a lot of research in countries like France and Germany, and the difference in transparency rules is considerable. The European Union basically has a French model of administration. In this model, the notion of transparency is seen as bizarre by the political class. Citizens are not to know what goes on behind the closed doors of the government," Premförs says.

For politicians caught in less-than-honorable circumstances in light of the law of transparency, punishment is often harsh.

"In general, their political careers are over," says Mats Knutson.

In 2006, two ministers went into free fall and disappeared from the political scene, just days after the announcement of the new cabinet. The press discovered, among other unforgivable indiscretions, that they had employed nannies under the table, neglecting to pay the related taxes.

NANNYGATE

"Borelius resigns, abandoning politics and her position as a federal representative."

Maria Borelius lasted eight days in the ministry: she had hired nannies without paying the corresponding taxes.

After a decade of political defeats, their hour had finally come. Renewed by a reconfigured program, the liberal-conservatives of the Moderate Party now presented themselves as the "new workers' party." In the 2006 election, their center-right alliance of four parties would win a historic victory, buoyed in part by an electorate that was apparently convinced that their legendary welfare state, substantially funded by high taxes, would not be thrown down the drain.

Everything seemed new and promising — beginning with Prime Minister Fredrik Reinfeldt himself, who at 41 years of age had become one of the youngest leaders of the country. It was a radiant Reinfeldt who presented, on October 6 of that year, his bold cabinet of ministers. Anders Borg, minister for Economic Affairs, was 38 and sported an earring and ponytail. Appointed as minister for Integration and Gender equality, Nyamko Sabuni, born in Burundi, was the country's first black minister. Two ministers were homosexual, including the minister of Immigration, Tobias Billström, and the minister of Environment, Andreas Carlgren, who was legally married to his partner. And to everyone's surprise, returning to the Swedish political scene as minister of Foreign Affairs, was former Prime Minister Carl Bildt.

The euphoria was intoxicating, but the hangover was set to be colossal. Part of the government cabinet was comprised of newcomers, without enough mileage to know that in Swedish politics, a squeaky-clean resume is a matter of survival. The Swedish press had reported shortly after the announcements that two ministers had employed nannies cash-in-hand without paying the obligatory taxes and social contributions — on what would immediately be christened by the British *Financial Times* as "Nannygate."

Searches in the country's official open archives would also reveal that three ministers had utterly ignored paying the mandatory TV license, the tax that funds the public broadcaster. In just ten days, Reinfeldt's cabinet would suffer two casualties.

The first head that rolled was that of the minister of commerce, Maria Borelius. Under intense media pressure, she admitted that in the 1990s she had employed nannies cash-in-hand without paying due taxes.

"I am the mother of four children, and at the time I was running my own business," Borelius argued, explaining that she could not have handled domestic and professional life without the help of nannies. But then she uttered the fatal phrase: "I did not have the means to pay all the taxes and fees required to have a nanny."

Doubting this information, Social Democrat press secretary Magnus Ljungkvist decided to check it out. As the law of transparency guarantees access to tax department archives, he began researching the income tax returns of Minister Maria Borelius and her husband. He discovered that in the 1990s the Borelius family earned a total of 17 million krona, a sum considerably higher than the average earnings of a Swedish family. Ljungkvist also discovered that Borelius had inherited a house from her father in 1996, worth four million krona.

"You're screwed, Borelius," wrote journalist Lena Mellin in the title of her political column in the Aftonbladet newspaper.

"In the 1990s, Borelius paid her nannies under the table. That was stupid. But even more stupid was to claim that she didn't have the money to pay honestly," criticized Mellin.

"Minister of culture Cecilia Stegö Chilò resigns under pressure."

Minister of Culture Cecília Chilò's downfall was caused by revelations that she had not paid for a public TV license.

Over the following days, the walls closed in on Borelius. Further investigations revealed that the minister's husband had bought their family's summer home in southern Sweden through a company based in the island of Jersey, one of the world's offshore tax havens. The same mechanism had been used to avoid paying taxes on the purchase of an apartment in Cannes, France. And to top it off, it was discovered that in the past two months Borelius had not paid the obligatory TV license for all those who own TV sets in Sweden.

The prime minister called his minister in for one last conversation.

"She herself realized that she could not continue, and we agreed she should resign," Fredrik Reinfeldt told *Sveriges Radio*.

Maria Borelius left her post as minister and also resigned her seat in Parliament as a representative of

Reinfeldt's Moderate Party, the largest political party in the government coalition. She lasted eight days in office, and never again returned to politics.

Two days after Borelius's departure, Reinfeldt's cabinet suffered its second casualty. Culture Minister Cecilia Stegö Chilò had also paid her nannies in cash in order to avoid taxes. But Stegö Chilò's resignation came with an added embarrassment: the press discovered that she had not paid her TV license for the past 16 years. The license fee of about US$200 a year is the main source of funding for Swedish public broadcasters — and it is precisely the Ministry of Culture that oversees compliance with the law's guidelines.

Stegö Chilò's husband tried to save her from national shame. Five days before her appointment to the ministry, as if trying to put wings on a pig, he registered the family TV set with the agency responsible for collecting the television license fee. Stegö Chilò's resignation was inevitable.

"Before I became a minister, I committed transgressions that are unacceptable — not paying for the television license and hiring nannies without paying taxes — but I tried every way possible to correct them," she said on the government's official website. She tried to pay off her debts and settle her bills. But it was too late.

"Since there is no way to resolve the situation in a reasonable time, I see no possibility, through competent and committed work, to repair the damage I have caused the government," she added.

Cecilia Stegö Chilò lasted ten days in office, and also disappeared from the political scene.

But Reinfeldt's nightmare was not yet over. The media were now attacking Immigration Minister Tobias Billström, who had not paid the TV license fee for ten years. In an awkward statement, Billström said, "I chose not to pay, because I thought that SVT (Swedish public TV) wasn't producing good programs. But people become wiser over the years, and I certainly believe that everyone must abide by the laws that are passed."

With the heat turned up, the situation reached the boiling point. Resentful citizens denounced Tobias Billström, Maria Borelius, and Cecilia Stegö Chilò to the police for violating the TV license law. Radiotjänst, the agency responsible for collecting the license fees, filed criminal charges against the three. And when the prime minister questioned the agency's decision, he got a slap on the wrist from Parliament.

"Is it really Radiotjänst's view that any person who presents himself to the government agency, willing to correct his mistake and pay the sum due, should be reported to the police?" Reinfeldt had asked in an interview with the Swedish radio.

He should have kept quiet: in Sweden, a principle called *Ministerstire* (a sort of ministerial code of conduct) forbids ministers and the prime minister from interfering with the decisions of government agencies. Reinfeldt was diligently reported to Parliament's Constitutional Committee (KU).

"In the investigation into Prime Minister Fredrik Reinfeldt's statement concerning Radiotjänst's decision to bring criminal charges against the three ministers, the committee finds that the prime minister, like other citizens, is free to express his views, but the prime minister also has a duty to exercise special caution in certain circumstances. For example, in the case of declarations that could jeopardize the independence that, according to constitutional laws, is guaranteed to the courts and public administration agencies," proclaimed the committee's official communication.

Then onto the scene came a former nanny, who told the *Expressen* newspaper that she had worked at the home of Finance Minister Anders Borg without being officially registered. The minister insisted that the woman had only provided occasional services as a babysitter, but admitted having employed house cleaners without paying taxes.

The case went to the attorney general. According to some reports, the sum paid by Borg to nannies and cleaners hadn't reached the threshold at which the payment of social and employment taxes becomes mandatory. The evidence was insufficient, and two months later the prosecutor dropped the charges.

The minister of Immigration also remained in his post, and the season of resignations was finally closed. And before announcing the replacements for the two ministers who had been burned at the stake, the prime minister took extreme care in vetting them.

"I always paid for my TV license and have never paid a cleaning lady under the table," said the new minister of Commerce, Sten Tolgfors, when presented by Reinfeldt to the Swedish press.

Since Swedes pay one of the highest tax rates in the world in order to fund the country's still generous welfare state, they are ruthless with politicians who step out of line. Swedish journalists often use public access to information from auditors to launch attacks against politicians who commit sins against the State Treasury, as happened with Gudrun Schyman.

CLAUDIA WALLIN

GUDRUN'S SIN

"Headlines of tax fraud and loss of party support were decisive in Gudrun Schyman's resignation."

Gudrun Schyman: "There is no defense for what I have done."

In Swedish politics, the capital sin is to avoid taxes. But Gudrun Schyman, who led the Left Party (*Vänsterpartiet*, formerly the Communist party) for ten years, apparently forgot that paying taxes in Sweden is more inevitable than death. In 2003, following revelations about irregularities in her tax returns, Gudrun was forced to resign — and to reimburse the Treasury's coffers.

In the newspapers, the party leader's tax return was dissected like a frog. Among the irregularities was a trip to Brazil, for which she had not presented sufficient documentation in order to justify a tax credit. Journalists also found that Schyman had requested reimbursement for taxi fares to Arlanda airport, even though members of parliament are entitled to free travel on the train connecting the airport to the capital. Unforgivable.

In total, tax authorities rejected deductions in the amount of 70,787 krona (about US$8,650), which Gudrun had listed in her 2001 returns. "How could you, Gudrun?" questioned the *Expressen* newspaper headline.

"There is no defense for what I did," Gudrun replied in remarks to the press. "I was pressed for time, but it wasn't my intention to deceive (the Treasury)."

Scathing editorials were written about the case, and the *Ekobrottsmyndigheten*, the Swedish Financial Crimes Authority, kicked in. "Gudrun Schyman at risk of arrest," the *Expressen* announced.

The party leader ended up at the police station, where she was subjected to questioning. Throughout the police investigation, Gudrun denied having committed tax fraud. She claimed to have been inattentive with the receipts and the tax return.

In the end, Gudrun had two alternatives. She should either admit guilt for blatant carelessness in completing her tax return, or be sued and brought to court.

"I am just a human being. I choose to admit sheer oversight," she decided.

Gudrun Schyman paid the Treasury the full amount owed and was further ordered to pay a fine equivalent to 50 days' pay of 21,750 krona (about US$2,660).

"Cases such as this one affect citizen confidence in our system," said case prosecutor Sven-Erik Alhem. "The effect is that citizens start to wonder why they should follow the system's rules if they (the politicians) do not. And this is very dangerous."

Gudrun's second conviction would be even harsher

— the rejection by the members of *Vänsterpartiet*, her own party. One Sunday morning, in a hastily called press conference, Gudrun capitulated.

"I believe I could have restored the confidence of our party's electorate. However, in order to do this I would have needed 100% support from party members. This I was not able to obtain," she said, then announced her resignation from the *Vänsterpartiet* leadership.

For her constituents, the leader no longer represented the party's *skattemoral* — the moral duty to pay taxes.

Convinced that a woman's place is in Parliament and not in the kitchen, Gudrun Schyman exited from the Left Party to devote herself to co-founding the Feminist Party (*Feministiskt Initiativet*). In the following years Gudrun, renowned as a female activist, returned to headlines on the strength of her intrepid activism. On one occasion, she proposed levying a tax on all men to cover the costs of domestic violence against women. And before the 2010 general elections, she literally burned 100,000 Swedish krona on a barbecue grill, in a public act of repudiation for gender wage disparity.

"Men receive a penis bonus because they earn 10 to 20 percent more than women," Gudrun complained. But the message did not seduce the electorate, which gave the *Feministiskt Initiativet* only 0.4% of the vote. Or had Gudrun simply lost the voters' confidence?

Not even celebrities escape the tax office's ever-vigilant radar. In the 1970s, police invaded the theatre stage of legendary Swedish director Ingmar Bergman.

SCENES FROM A POLICE INVASION IN INGMAR BERGMAN'S THEATRE

After being arrested in a theatre and accused of tax evasion, film-maker Ingmar Bergman suffered a nervous breakdown.

A blue Volvo pulls up and parks in front of Stockholm's *Kungliga Dramatiska Teatern*, the Royal Dramatic Theatre. It is a winter afternoon on January 30, 1976. Two police officers get out of the car and quickly climb the theatre steps: if the suspicion of tax evasion is an urgent matter, the suspect must be arrested straight away. Immediately. Without waiting for the end of the drama that is playing out on stage.

What follows is something out of a movie script. The police abruptly interrupt the rehearsal, arrest Ingmar Bergman and confiscate his passport so that the director and playwright would remain within the reach of the law. Bergman is then taken to a tax court. Appalled, several actors leave the stage and accompany Bergman to the scene of the investigation.

Following the police's theatrics, the prosecutor said that Bergman was being accused of establishing Persona Films AG — his international film production company — in Switzerland in order to escape paying high taxes in Sweden. If found guilty, Ingmar Bergman would have to pay cumulative retrospective taxes for the years from 1969 to 1974.

To gather further evidence of the alleged fraud, police officers searched and confiscated documents at the homes of Ingmar Bergman and his lawyer. In early February, Bergman was prosecuted for tax evasion.

Persona Films AG was registered in Switzerland in the late 1960s, when Bergman planned to set up an international film production center. The plan, however, was later abandoned, and the company was then used to collect income generated by Bergman films exhibited abroad. When the *Riksbank* (Central Bank of Sweden) indicated that Persona Films was not being used to produce films, the company was closed, and its assets (worth about US$600,000) were sent to Sweden. But in the eyes of tax auditors, Persona Films had been established to avoid paying Swedish taxes, which Bergman should now honor retrospectively.

The charge, which later would be proven to be unsubstantiated, was eventually withdrawn. But the episode had profoundly troubled the director, who was already internationally renowned for films such as Cries and Whispers (1972), Scenes from a Marriage (1973), Persona (1966) and Wild Strawberries (1957).

Days after the police invaded the theatre, Bergman suffered a nervous breakdown and was hospitalized in a deep state of depression. The pressure had been too much for the director, who had so often depicted on-screen his own desolation and the despair of complex human existence.

The rebellious son of a Lutheran pastor, Ingmar Bergman often spoke of his unhappy childhood and his father's severe punishments, including being locked in a dark cupboard. Harry Schein, director of the *Svenska filminstitutet* (Swedish Film Institute), observed that at the time of Bergman's arrest, humiliation was a recurring theme in several of his films. He was a master of existentialist themes and often portrayed the suffering of the troubled artist.

In *The Rite* (1969), a judge promotes the interrogation of three actors who are accused of staging an obscene spectacle. In *The Seventh Seal* (1957), in which Death plays chess with the protagonists, the defeated player makes a final and desperate appeal after losing the game to the adversary who always wins: "Is there no exemption for an actor?"

The stage still held special significance for Bergman. He had begun his career in the theatre, to which he remained faithful throughout his life: "Theatre is the beginning, it is the end, in truth it is everything, whereas cinema belongs to the sphere of prostitution and the slaughterhouse," the director once said.

The episode of Ingmar Bergman's arrest on the stage of the *Kungliga Dramatiska Teatern* provoked protest inside and outside Sweden. Only the *Aftonbladet* newspaper, which at the time belonged to the Swedish labour confederation LO (*Landsorganisationen*), defended the tax auditors: it would be hypocritical to lament Bergman's plight, the paper argued, since other tax evasion suspects had received the same treatment without raising public protest. All citizens should be treated equally, regardless of their names or positions.

On March 23, 1976, the prosecutor withdrew all charges against Ingmar Bergman. But the acknowledgment of the error came too late. Shortly after the prosecutor's statement, the director announced that he was leaving Sweden to go into voluntary exile. He left his assets and possessions behind so that no one would think he was trying to escape further charges from Swedish tax auditors.

Despite Prime Minister Olof Palme's criticisms over how the case had been handled, Bergman swore he would never again work in Sweden. He closed the studio that he maintained on the island of Fårö, in the southeast of the country, and moved to Munich, Germany. But in 1984 the director did return to live in Sweden, where he died peacefully in his sleep in 2007, at the age of 89.

THE AUTHOR OF PIPPI LONGSTOCKING AND THE 102% TAX RATE

Another notorious example of Swedish tax folklore is the case of author Astrid Lindgren, who revolutionized children's literature with the character of Pippi Longstocking. A short time after Ingmar Bergman's case, Lindgren, who also fell into the clutches of the Swedish tax authority, leveled one of the most forceful attacks on the Swedish tax system.

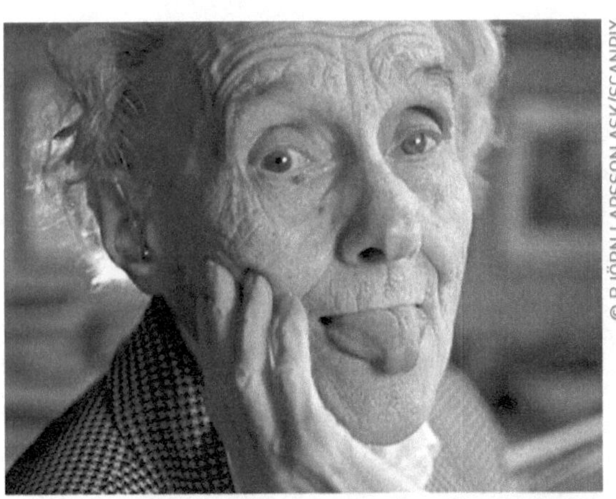

With a 102% tax rate on her income, author Astrid Lindgren mocked the Swedish tax system.

Astrid Lindgren was, as one might imagine, a good fighter. Her Pippi Longstocking would take a bull by the horns, beat up the boys, and send the thieves running. The Swedish author created her character in 1945, at a time when girls wore ribbons in their hair, crocheted, and waited for their prince charming to ride up on his white horse. But strong, libertarian Pippi lived alone, was a veritable feminist in the 1940s, and not only had her own horse but could lift it up above her head.

Swedish publisher Bonnier bitterly regretted rejecting the original manuscripts. "I could not take responsibility for chaos in kindergartens and sugar on the floor," said editor Gerhard Bonnier at the time. Another publisher accepted Pippi Longstocking's story for publication, and it reached bookshops amid widespread criticism. The character's detractors warned of a collapse of public morals.

But the book was an immediate and resounding success. Pippi's story was the first of more than 70 books written by Astrid Lindgren and was translated into more than 70 languages. Lindgren herself would narrate, years later, how Pippi was born:

"In 1941, my seven-year-old daughter, Karin, had pneumonia. Every night, when I sat at the head of her bed, she begged me to tell her a story. One night, completely exhausted, I asked her what she would like to hear, and she replied, 'Tell me a story about Pippi Longstocking.' She had just invented the name on the spur of the moment. I did not ask who Pippi Longstocking was. I just started to tell a story about her. And because she had such an unusual name, she turned out to be an unusual little girl. Pippi proved to be a success with Karin, and then with her friends. I had to tell the story over and over."

A slip on the ice, according to the author, was the reason the stories were turned into books:

"On a snowy night in March of 1944, I was walking in the center of Stockholm. Snow was falling, and I fell on a slippery layer of ice, twisting my ankle. My injury required a long period of rest, and to pass the time, I began to write the Pippi stories."

Lindgren became a celebrity, and began earning money. Paying her due share of Swedish tax share wasn't a problem for her: "I pay my taxes willingly," she said more than once. But the problems she would later have with the tax office would be as surreal as the characters in her stories.

In 1976 Astrid Lindgren discovered that because of a new requirement in the Swedish tax system, as a self-employed writer she would have to pay a 102 percent tax rate on her income. That was when the author decided, with the same sharp tongue of her Pippi, to write a satire criticizing the new tax burden imposed by the Social Democratic party, which had ruled Sweden for more than four decades.

The story, entitled *Pomperipossa in Monismania* (also known as Pomperipossa in the World of Money), was published in March 1976 in the *Expressen* newspaper. It narrated the allegory of Pomperipossa, a children's books writer from a distant country, who — faced with a heavy burden of taxes to pay — begins asking herself whether the wise rulers of the place have begun to lose their minds.

Lindgren wrote: "Pomperipossa truly loved her country, its forests, mountains, lakes, and groves. But not only that: she also loved the people who lived there, and even the wise rulers who governed the country. She believed they were wise, and so she voted for them each time there were elections to choose the wise men who would govern Monismanien. Over the past 40 years they had created an admirable society, in which nobody needed to be poor, and everyone had a piece of the cake called the social welfare. Pomperipossa felt happy for being able to contribute her part to preparing the cake."

But soon the contented Pomperipossa discovers that for the current year she will need to pay a tax rate of 102% on her income. And she begins to wonder how she can deal with the absurdity of that situation.

"If I go to the wise rulers and knock on their door, they may take pity on me and give me a plate of soup once in a while," says the imaginary author, beginning a sequence of ironies that compounds the tragicomic narrative.

The saga of Pomperipossa reached Parliament's debating chamber and sent shock waves through government. The minister of Finance, who had initially refuted the author's arguments, ended up admitting that Astrid Lindgren had pointed out an error that needed to be corrected. And the tax law was indeed amended. But the dispute precipitated by Pomperipossa endured and, in the opinion of some, was one of the factors that determined the defeat of the Social Democrats in the elections that year.

Astrid Lindgren, however, remained faithful to the party during all her life. She died in her home on Dalagatan Street, in Stockholm, in January 2002. Her funeral was held on March 8 — International Women's Day.

THE TRANSPARENCY MANUAL

Under the rules of transparency, each public authority must keep a record of official documents and be prepared to respond to requests for information from Swedish citizens. The Ministry of Justice's manual provides a lesson on transparency for beginners:

"In the newspaper, there is a report on a local Legislative Assembly decision. Mrs. Andersson wants to know more about it, so she goes to the authorities. In a special room equipped with computers, she searches the list of all the documents. The list contains a brief description of each document's content.

Mrs. Andersson finds the document she wishes to read. Without asking for her identity, the municipal official examines her request, searches for the document in the files and delivers it to her. After reading the four-page document, Mrs. Andersson asks for and receives, free of charge, a copy of the document.

If the clerk had concluded that some of the information contained in the requested document is secret, under the Secrecy Act, he would then consult a superior. If the clerk's suspicions are confirmed, Mrs. Andersson would then have received a copy of the document, but with the confidential parts removed.

If all the information contained in the document is considered to be secret, access will be denied. The clerk will then ask Mrs. Andersson if she would like a written document stating that her request has been denied. With this document, Mrs. Andersson could appeal the decision in an administrative court."

In another example from the manual, a journalist, Mr. Lindberg, is interested in obtaining details about a recent Ministry of Justice decision.

"At the Ministry headquarters, he gets a copy of the official decision. Lindberg also requests and receives copies of documents related to the matter sent to the Ministry by the National Police.

The journalist then asks to see the personal notes made by the minister of justice during the government meeting that led up to the decision. The official then informs the journalist that he cannot have access to personal notes, since they do not constitute an official document.

Lindberg is not satisfied, and decides to appeal the decision in the Ministry of Justice. But eventually, his request is denied."

When a government official denies access to a document requested by a citizen, as in the case of Lindberg, the citizen has the right to appeal the decision in an appellate court and, ultimately, in the Swedish Superior Administrative Court. Complaints can also be made to the guardians of the law of transparency: the Ombudsman of Parliament and the government's Ombudsman.

THE SYSTEM'S WATCHDOGS

In 1809, the Swedes were racking their brains with uncommon restiveness: it was no longer possible to postpone the invention of some method to protect the people from the authoritarian arrogance of power. From this mental effervescence an original solution was produced, and the world gained a new word: ombudsman, or representative of the people. The institution of the ombudsman, a singular Swedish invention, would deal with the helplessness of the individual in face of the abuses perpetrated by the authorities and the honorable excellencies in the kingdom.

The idea emerged following the reign of King Gustav III, who had a theatrical demise: the monarch's life ended in 1792 with a bullet in his back, shot by a noble malcontent during a masquerade ball at the Stockholm Opera, which had been founded by the king. Under the new constitution, approved in 1809, the Parliamentary Ombudsman came into play as an independent arbiter with the authority to monitor the acts of public authorities and protect the citizens' rights.

Under the terms of the law, the Ombudsman should be a person "known for his legal knowledge and for his discernible integrity." His mission was to protect the rights of the citizens against the excesses of power. His job was to hear the complaints and demands of the people, overseeing the application of the law by judges and public servants, and carrying out inspections of the public agencies. The first Ombudsman in Parliament was named in 1810, and the same basic principles still apply to this day.

Two hundred years after its creation, the institution of the Ombudsman continues to be a central element of the Swedish apparatus for the protection of the citizen against the abuse of power by the authorities, operating as an independent link between people and power. The eyes and ears of the structure of vigilance over public agencies and courts are the Ombudsman of Justice (*Justitieombudsman*, also known as the Parliamentary Ombudsman, or simply JO), and the Chancellor of Justice (*Justitiekansler*, or JK), who deliberates, in the name of the State, on cases involving compensation claims.

Any citizen has the right to present a complaint or grievance against a public authority — and this right extends even to children and to prisoners who are serving prison sentences, according to the official handbook published by the Parliamentary Ombudsman's office. The gravity of the grievance is irrelevant. An emblematic case involves a father who sent the JO a complaint against a school after a teacher had taken away a laser pen from his son in order to maintain discipline in the classroom. The grievance arose because the teacher had forgotten to return the pen, which remained locked up in the school office without identification. The Ombudsman went into action and the school was forced to return the pen — not to the student, but directly to the police.

"Every citizen has the right to be treated by the authorities in a courteous and impartial manner," says the handbook.

This Swedish invention spread throughout other democracies. The concept of the ombudsman currently exists on all continents, in approximately 140 countries. In Sweden, the institution has grown and spread to other activities: today there is the Children's Ombudsman, who protects the rights and interests of the young; the Press Ombudsman, concerned with ethics in the media; and ombudsmen for Equality, Discrimination, Consumer Rights, and Disabled Rights.

The watchdogs of the law of transparency are the Parliamentary Ombudsman, who reports to Parliament, and the Chancellor of Justice, who acts as the Government's ombudsman. Any state agency's refusal to dispense official information may be investigated by these two institutions, which are comprised of independent jurists who act on their own initiative or in response to grievances from citizens.

Together they monitor the implementation of the law of transparency, and they work to keep all government actions visible for all to see.

A CONVERSATION WITH THE PARLIAMENTARY OMBUDSMAN

"We need to be vigilant. Because a lack of transparency breeds a corrupt state, and a corrupt state is a threat to democracy" — Elisabet Fura

I walk along the avenue of Hamngatan in the accidental company of an unusual group of Hare Krishnas, who play their instruments in woolen gloves and stroll down the street wearing boots and sweaters. As I continue on my way to the Parliamentary Ombudsman's office, a large group of protesters pushing baby buggies is blocking the way.

"No more deaths of women during childbirth," says one of the signs. "A woman's right to her own body," was stamped on the poster stuck to one of the buggies. Incredulous, I stop the protester and ask, "But do these sorts of problems even exist in Sweden?"

"No, no," replies the man, as puzzled by my question as I am with the poster he carries.

"We are here in solidarity with women in countries where these unacceptable problems still occur.

The ever-present Swedish solidarity.

I make my way through the buggies and reach Västra Trädgårdsgatan Street, where the Ombudsman's office is located. Looking for the number of the building, I come across the curious front door of the Finnish Embassy. "Embassy" is printed on a little sign next to one of the doorbells. Underneath it, a second sign indicates access to one of the most sacred of Finnish institutions: the "Sauna." In theory, you can reach the ambassador directly in the hot steam room, with his eucalyptus branch in hand.

Across the street from the Finnish sauna, the Parliamentary Ombudsman (JO) leads a team of 65 people. Attorney Elisabet Fura directs the office in which three other ombudsmen work, and is the head of the institution. Former president of the Swedish Bar Association, Fura previously served on the European Court of Human Rights in Strasbourg, France.

In her role as Ombudsman, Elisabet Fura regularly oversees public authorities, municipalities, police forces, and the country's courts, in addition to enforcing the mandates of the law of transparency. Each autumn the office of the JO submits its annual report to Parliament, which can also be accessed via the Internet on the Ombudsman's official website.

In 2011-2012 the Ombudsman received 326 complaints concerning freedom of expression and obstructions to access to official documents. 100 of these resulted in public condemnations. In 2013,

Ombudsman ELISABET FURA: investigating and being investigated.

one of the main grievances the JO received was directed against the Swedish Minister for Industry, Annie Lööf, for her ministry's delay in releasing information requested by a journalist.

The case went to the Constitutional Committee of Parliament (KU), the agency that scrutinizes the actions of government members. All representatives have the right to report a minister to the committee, which is composed of politicians from the different parties represented in Parliament. Standing before the KU bench, Annie Lööf got an earful from the committee, and then publicly redeemed herself.

The Annie Lööf investigation is one among the hundreds of files held in the Ombudsman's office, where Fura welcomes me.

What is the importance for democracy of a system of transparency?

ELISABET FURA: Monitoring the powers that be is a prerequisite for democracy. Every person who exercises power must be scrutinized and held accountable for their actions. And without transparency, it is impossible to scrutinize power. But it is not enough to just have laws. Citizens and public servants need to be inspired to change their way of thinking, so that an open and democratic society can be established. It is not something that happens overnight; it is a gradual process. The countries of the European Union have been making changes in the right direction, in terms of greater transparency of government actions. But changing people's attitudes takes time because it is difficult to transform an entire culture. In France, for example, the instinctive attitude of a bureaucrat is to say "No, you cannot see this document; you do not have this right." The Swedish attitude is "Yes, you can see this document, but first I need to check if there is any information here that needs to be protected." It is also important to promote trust in the institutions.

What is the Ombudsman's role in this process?

ELISABET FURA: You could say that the Parliamentary Ombudsman exercises particular supervision over Swedish public authorities, whereas the courts handle the normal supervision of the system. Of course, in any area of activity, people make mistakes. But the Parliamentary Ombudsman is not an institution designed to find fault and punish. Our main task is to identify systemic errors and improve the performance of government officials and agencies that provide services for citizens. We are here to see if the government officials and agencies need to refine their performance, and to determine how they can become better.

How does this work in practice?

ELISABET FURA: If, for example, I read in the newspapers that the police are not respecting gay rights, it is my job to investigate and discover the cause of the problem. It may reflect a failure in legislation, or a failure in law enforcement, or it may also be that our police officers are not being sufficiently educated to deal with human rights issues. In this case, our mission would be to assist authorities in improving the performance of their duties, and to ensure that officials abide by the law. It is our responsibility to ensure that public authorities treat all citizens with impartiality and objectivity, and that they respect the law regarding access to official documents.

What are the pitfalls to be avoided when enforcing the transparency law?

ELISABET FURA: Throughout the world, including in some established democracies, governments tend to say that transparency is important, but that at this particular moment we need to close our eyes for a moment because the decisions we are going to make are so serious and important that we cannot be as transparent as we would like to be." This occurs, for example, in times of economic crisis, such as right now. But this position is totally erroneous, because without the ability to oversee government decisions, people lose confidence in the government. And when the government announces its difficult economic decisions, even though there is not enough money to do all the good things that need to be done, citizens do not respect these decisions, since they do not understand how they were made. It is unhealthy to adopt an attitude that transparency is only beneficial when the sun is shining and things are going well. For this gives government officials a false sense of security.

The decisions of the Parliamentary Ombudsman's office have no legal power, and therefore public authorities have no formal duty to comply with its orders. What is the real impact of your work?

ELISABET FURA: There are two important aspects. First, the role of the media is extremely important, so we strive to maintain a high level of service to journalists. They have immediate access to everything here, and as soon as someone files a complaint they can keep track of our daily journals and records, and they do in fact watch everything. We also allow journalists to review the emails we send and receive.

Do journalists have access even to the emails that you exchange with ministers and public authorities?

ELISABET FURA: Yes, they have access to basically everything, except for a few points specifically defined in the law of secrecy. Thus the media plays an important role in terms of the impact of the Ombudsman's decisions. In addition, there is the power of persuasion contained in these decisions. We always strive to maintain a high level of quality in our investigations in order to produce well-documented decisions. So when we complete an investigation and decide to censure a particular public official, that official will most likely abide by the decision and make the necessary course of changes and corrections.

Do public authorities actually comply with the Ombudsman's decisions, even without being legally bound to do so?

ELISABET FURA: Yes, yes. It's a cultural matter. Public authorities frequently use reports produced by the Ombudsman to improve their internal rules and procedures. The institution of the ombudsman is more than 200 years old in this country, and the officials take our democracy seriously. Recently, we censured the Ministry of Industry. We found that ministry employees were not respecting the Constitution because a journalist had waited for several weeks for some requested information, and had not been treated impartially. The minister and even the prime minister himself had to explain themselves before the Parliament's Constitutional Committee.

Several of your recent reports have criticized different officials for failing to comply with laws regarding access to official documents, such as those in the Ministry of Foreign Affairs. Is the Swedish system becoming less transparent?

ELISABET FURA: Yes, there are reasons for our criticisms. But you can reverse this argument and say that in view of the sheer number of decisions that are made every day by government officials, municipalities, and government agencies, perhaps our system isn't so bad. Certainly the ideal would be for my colleagues and I in the Parliamentary Ombudsman's office to be discharged for lack of anything to do.

How can you get closer to this ideal?

ELISABET FURA: We need to be vigilant. Because a lack of transparency breeds a corrupt state, and a corrupt state is a threat to democracy. When the express train linking the international airport to the center of Stockholm was built, for example, the police set up a special anti-corruption unit for the project. Whenever a major infrastructure project is carried out in Sweden, the police create a special anti-corruption unit to monitor the construction work, for we know that there is a large amount of money at stake, a large number of suppliers, contractors, and public officials involved, and therefore huge opportunities for corruption to occur.

Several countries have adopted the Swedish ombudsman model. What is the main lesson of the Swedish experience?

ELISABET FURA: An important aspect is that in Sweden the Ombudsman is elected by a unanimous vote of all 349 parliamentary representatives. The representatives evaluate and vote for just one candidate, who generally is a lawyer, and he or she is elected only if the vote is unanimous. This is important because it confers legitimacy on the Ombudsman. Here's an example: I recently received a visit from the ombudsman for St. Petersburg, Russia, who faces major problems with his credibility. He is also elected by the Russian Parliament, but not unanimously, and he was also previously a member of parliament. In this case, I believe his legitimacy is compromised because people with different political views will have a hard time accepting a former politician, and one who has only a partial mandate from Parliament to carry out the function. We receive a steady stream of visitors with questions like this. More recently, we were visited by several delegations from China, South Africa, and even Turkey, which has just established its first ombudsman. Everyone has encountered various difficulties, and they come here to find out how we deal with our problems. The issue of the ombudsman's credibility is, in my view, an essential point. It is also important that the institution has adequate funding. Because even if the ombudsmen have amazing legislation at their disposal, but lack the resources to apply it, they will not be able to make good and well-informed decisions.

What is your budget?

ELISABET FURA: Our budget is just over 80 million krona per year (about US$9.78 million). It's up to us to oversee everything that is funded by taxpayers' money, such as the 250 government agencies and all the municipalities. It is also my responsibility to supervise the police and the prison system. We receive about 1,000 complaints each year from prisoners about how they are treated, or about restrictions on calling their families. The prison system itself also has a service with legally qualified staff to deal with these issues. So when we receive a complaint and de-cide to conduct a more thorough investigation into the case, we send a report to the prison officials and demand a response.

In cases where there has been a breach in the transparency law, can complaints also be referred to the Chancellor of Justice? Do the two institutions work in parallel?

ELISABET FURA: We try to avoid investigating the same case. We can, but we try to avoid it. First, because it wouldn't be a good use of the taxpayers' money. And also because it wouldn't be a good thing to come to two different conclusions about the same subject.

Who investigates the Parliamentary Ombudsman?

ELISABET FURA: Journalists come to my office and check my own accounts. And I, along with the other lawyers who work here, are very aware of this. We also undergo internal and external audits. We are also supervised by the Swedish National Audit Service (*Riksrevisionen*).

CLAUDIA WALLIN

THE SURVEILLANCE OF GOVERNMENT AUTHORITIES AND AGENCIES

In a quick call to the Swedish Armed Forces headquarters, I ask for the expense reports of the Swedish Supreme Commander, Sverker Göranson. It is my right and that of anyone in Sweden, guaranteed by the law of transparency. The clerk confirms that I do not have to identify myself.

"Any Swedish citizen or journalist can contact our headquarters to anonymously request documents, correspondence, or records received and sent by the Armed Forces. It is part of the Swedish transparency law," says the Armed Forces employee.

"Depending on the request, the processing of the information may take a few days, since in certain cases we need to ensure that sensitive information will not be leaked," she adds.

I make a request for the Swedish Supreme Commander's expense report to be sent to me by mail, and three days later I receive the document. The report lists the commander's spending on domestic and foreign travel, as well as official entertainment costs. The document includes the receipt for a dinner offered by the Commander to foreign defense authorities, totaling 19,268 krona (about US$2,355). The invoice includes the costs of the three-course menu for twenty guests, at 414 krona (about US$50) per person, and food provided for security guards and drivers in the service of the authorities, at 115 krona per person (US$14). The report also details the expenses for the decoration of the tables, the three types of wine served (150 krona per person, or about US$18) and the costs for chefs and waiters.

Swedes do not want their politicians involved in any cover-ups: the accounts of any Swedish authority should be open to public scrutiny.

On the Internet, the official pages of different state agencies show detailed reports of expenditures and activities carried out with funds from the high taxes collected from citizens. The Armed Forces website displays the ratio of its expenses and a detailed description of all operations carried out each year. It shows exactly how the taxpayer's money is spent.

A table shows the officials' names and salaries — the salary of the Supreme Commander of the Armed Forces is also listed. The official page also includes the annual reports of the Swedish military intelligence service (*Militära underrättelse och säkerhetstjänsten*, MUST).

The use of tax revenue is monitored by a group of independent auditors. They act as a lighthouse for taxpayers, in the turbulent sea of the government officials' balance sheets. The auditors' verdicts on the performance of each agency are also regularly published on the Internet.

These independent auditors of the National Audit Service (*Riksrevisionen*) have the responsibility of overseeing the finances and operations of the entire

Swedish power structure — the government, Parliament, and all public authorities, including the police and the armed forces. Their mission is to monitor whether taxpayers' money is being used as it should be.

"If any irregularities are discovered, such as a large amount of money being misdirected, auditors report it to the police," says Pernilla Eldblom, communications director of the National Audit Service.

In addition, it is *Riksrevisionen*'s mission to monitor whether both government and public authorities are implementing the laws and directives decided by Parliament correctly and efficiently. In order to do this, they not only produce financial reports on the public authorities — but also efficiency reports.

"The first question the auditors ask is: 'Is this official complying with and implementing Parliament's decisions?' In other words, the *Riksrevisionen* verifies whether government and public authorities are doing their job. When they observe inaccuracies, auditors make recommendations in order to increase the efficiency of public authorities," says Pernilla Eldblom.

The reports are submitted to Parliament, which in turn sends the documents to the government, which is obliged to comment on the results. If the report recommends course corrections, the authorities have four months to report what measures have already been or are being taken to increase the efficiency of their operations. The appropriate parliamentary committee then reviews the measures reported, and Parliament makes a decision on each case.

The *Riksrevisionen* also oversees companies in which the state holds a minimum 50% share.

In turn, the *Riksrevisionen* itself is monitored by international private audit firms. The internal audit of this Swedish agency is conducted by Price Waterhouse Coopers, while BDO, one of the world's largest auditing corporations, does its financial audit.

"The idea is to ensure society's full confidence in public authorities," says the Auditor General of the Swedish National Audit Service, Claes Norgren.

But Swedish reporter Fredrik Laurin keeps his suspicions on red alert.

According to the journalist Fredrik Laurin, the Swedish government isn't transparent when it doesn't want to be.

A CONVERSATION WITH INVESTIGATIVE REPORTER FREDRIK LAURIN

"When it doesn't wish to be, the Swedish Government is not transparent. Not at all"
— Fredrik Laurin

Fredrik Laurin has a serious, inquisitive, almost fierce look about him. He knows that he lives in one of the most transparent societies in the world. But his vigorous speech, accentuated by forceful gestures, conveys his aversion to the furtive attempts by certain sections of the Swedish system to cover up their actions.

One of Sweden's most respected investigative reporters, Laurin has a collection of awards, including two Stora Journalistpriset, Sweden's most prestigious journalism award. Among several scandals investigated by his team, Fredrik Laurin exposed the role of the government and the Swedish secret service in the handing over of two Egyptians suspected of terror links, who in 2001 were secretly captured by American CIA on Swedish soil.

Since 2006, Laurin has worked as an independent journalist for the prestigious investigative program *Uppdrag granskning* broadcast on SVT, Sweden's public broadcaster.

My first contact with Laurin is tense. We set up a meeting in a discreet cafe on the bustling Södermalm island in Stockholm. After a brief formal greeting, he asks for my identification: his current investigation, he explains, a bit embarrassed but with firm resolve, demands caution.

I show him my press badge, and a suddenly friendly and laid-back Laurin shows me to his table, then sits down across from me. His attentive eyes have already noticed the unopened pack of cigarettes in my half-open bag, and he asks me for one.

After an hour-long conversation, Laurin says goodbye and disappears down the street, in search of the next scandal.

Does the Swedish law of transparency deserve its fame?

FREDRIK LAURIN: It is an extremely important law for democracy, and it is one of the pillars of the Swedish system. Under the official law, full transparency is essential.

Is it, as some say, the most open system in the world?

FREDRIK LAURIN: Now we're starting to read between the lines. Because, in theory, it is one of the best transparency systems in the world. The law states that all official information must be open, except for information protected by the law of secrecy, such as a person's medical records. The problem is that certain government officials have become creative in terms of classifying their information as confidential.

For example?

FREDRIK LAURIN: An example is the *Skatteverket* (Swedish Tax Agency). The agency created a system by which tax information is subject to a special law, the law of tax secrecy. And this law has become a separate statute. It determines that a person's income tax statement is public information, as well as the name, address, and social security number of that person. But any other detail is classified. So you could ask about the Tax Agency director's shoe size, and they would say "Sorry, but this is a secret." With any other Swedish governmental agency, the principle is to respond, "We'll try to discover the size of the director's shoe, and verify if there are restrictions on access to this information. No, there are no restrictions, here is the shoe size." The basic principle of Swedish law that all information must be open is immensely important. But several government authorities have become more secretive.

The Swedish Foreign Ministry has also been the subject of recent criticism by the Ombudsman for failure to record official information.

FREDRIK LAURIN: Yes. The ministry had been ignoring the principle of public access to official information.

How would you compare the Swedish transparency system to that of other countries?

FREDRIK LAURIN: If you compare the Swedish system to that of the European Union in general, Sweden is much more transparent. I have already worked in other EU countries, where it is almost ridiculously impossible to obtain even trivial information. In recent years, the British have finally come to the conclusion that the country needs modernizing, and have adopted certain constitutional principles of transparency similar to those of Sweden. However, if you compare the Swedish system to the United States, this is not necessarily the case. Because in some cases, the transparency of the American authorities is greater than in Sweden.

What sorts of cases?

FREDRIK LAURIN: When my colleagues and I investigated the case of the two Egyptians handed over by the Swedish authorities to American CIA agents, the Swedish transport agency blocked all information about the plane in which they were removed from Stockholm. No information about the flight schedule, the airport, or the plane was available in Sweden. Not even the name of the people working at the airport could be accessed. We had to go to the Bromma airport (in the Swedish capital) and write down the license plate numbers of the vehicles parked in the area reserved for the employees, in order to find out who worked there to be able to contact them.

You used the Swedish law of transparency to identify people through their license plate numbers?

FREDRIK LAURIN: Yes, we did. This is how the Swedish transparency law worked in this case. In the United States, we contacted the aviation authorities and requested all available information about the aircraft we were investigating. I had to send them a check for five dollars, and it cost ten times that amount to transfer the money. But in return, I received a CD on which the complete files on the plane were recorded. In my opinion,

in areas where transparency is really important, such as business and lobbying, the United States is much more open. In Sweden, there is not even a law to regulate lobbyists in Parliament.

Can you cite a case in which the transparency law was instrumental in conducting your investigations?

FREDRIK LAURIN: Several years ago, I did an investigation into Supreme Court justices, and I extensively used the principle of transparency. I contacted the judicial authorities, and got as much information as possible about the judges, what salaries they earned, what kind of property they had, what kind of cars they drove. Basically, what was the financial situation of those men and women. I found that a number of them received income from parallel activities, which is not illegal, but is not regulated. The result was that the rules were changed so that all judges are now required to declare their parallel activities.

Is the Swedish judiciary system actually clean?

FREDRIK LAURIN: In my opinion, it's a clean system. In general, the Swedish judges are very honest.

Are the Swedish courts transparent?

FREDRIK LAURIN: Yes, with very few exceptions. For example, the law of secrecy is used to protect the identity of victims of sexual offenses, and information on such cases is classified as confidential.

In government, is it really possible to have frequent access to even the prime minister's emails, for example?

FREDRIK LAURIN: Yes. The principle is that all emails are public, unless they contain information that can be protected under the law of secrecy. But the main rule dictates that a formal decision should always be open and transparent. Documents sent to a government official should also always be accessible to the public, with the exception of the restrictions provided for in the law of secrecy. But the answer is yes, emails and correspondence sent to the prime minister are documents sent to a government official, and so they are open to the public.

In general, how would you evaluate compliance with the law of transparency?

FREDRIK LAURIN: At the beginning of my career, in the 1980s, the system of transparency worked much better. Everything was more open. Today, I realize that I must become increasingly more like a British journalist. I need to be able to cultivate good sources, instead of having the ability to know where to seek out official information. The Swedish government is moving more in the direction of greater secrecy, and is not transparent when it doesn't want to be. Not at all.

FINANCING OF POLITICAL PARTIES AND ELECTION CAMPAIGNS

"It was an anomaly," notes Swedish political scientist Daniel Tarschys: in this country that created the world's oldest transparency law, public access to the sources of private donations to political parties was off limits until quite recently. Following intense internal and external pressures, Sweden finally approved regulation on this matter in April 2014, legally requiring political parties to publicly disclose both the amount and donor identity of all private donations over 20,000 krona (about US$2,270). Parties who do not comply with the new laws are not entitled to receive public funding.

"This gap in Swedish law was a consequence of the culture of consensus that exists in the country, and of the relatively high degree of trust in political institutions," says Tarschys, of Stockholm University. "But it was an anomaly, and the regulation of campaign accounts is a measure that had been continually recommended by GRECO (Group of States against Corruption), the Council of Europe's anti-corruption body," he adds.

The main source of funding for political parties in Sweden comes from the state, which is estimated to account for about 70% to 80% of the total collected by the parties. On the official website of the Moderate Party, the largest party of the governing alliance, the most recent report by auditors Ernst & Young on the annual accounts of the party states that out of a total of 163.75 million krona (about US$20 million) raised in 2012 by the party, 121.86 million krona (about US$14.9 million) came from public funding received from the government. In other words, public funding accounted for 74% of the total amount raised by the party.

Among the smaller political parties, the story is similar: according to the annual audited report of the Left Party (*Vänsterpartiet*), available on the party's official website, the party raised a total of 34.8 million krona during 2012, of which 30 million (88%) came from public funding to the party.

Public financing of the Swedish political parties totals 438 million krona per year, the equivalent of approximately US$53.5 million. Each party currently receives 333,300 krona annually (about US$40,745) for each seat they hold in Parliament.

Parties that are not represented in Parliament also receive government contributions, provided they obtained at least 2.5% of the votes in the country in one of the two previous elections.

Public funding also covers the parties' administration costs. Each of the eight political parties represented in Parliament receives a basic contribution of 5.8 million krona (about US$709,045). There is also an additional contribution: for government

Moderata Samlingspartiet
Org nr 802001-5452

Resultaträkning

	Not	2012-01-01 -2012-12-31	2011-01-01 - 2011-12-31
Intäkter			
Medlemsavgifter		5 707	5 516
Statligt partistöd		121 865	119 452
Ersättning från länsförbund		16 659	16 716
Hyresintäkter		4 929	5 375
Övriga intäkter	2	14 590	18 090
		163 750	165 149
Kostnader			
Övriga externa kostnader	3, 4	-49 279	-49 778
Personalkostnader	5, 6, 7	-110 797	-100 787
Avskrivningar	8, 9	-1 392	-1 097
		-161 468	-151 662
Verksamhetsresultat		*2 282*	*13 487*
Finansiella intäkter och kostnader			
Återförd nedskrivning aktier i dotterbolag		0	300
Resultat från långfristiga värdepappersinnehav	10	464	-411
Ränteintäkter		1 668	1 504
		2 132	1 393
Resultat efter finansiella poster		*4 414*	*14 880*
Återbetalning aktieägartillskott		0	1 300
Årets resultat		4 414	16 180

Moderate Party report shows that 74% of its donations came from public sources.

parties, the supplementary amount is 16,350 Swedish krona (about US$2,000) per seat in Parliament. For the other parties, the additional contribution is 24,300 krona (approximately US$2,970).

In order to receive government funding, all parties must produce an annual financial report, which must be scrutinized by an authorized audit firm. As in the case of the Moderate Party, the audited reports are available on each party's official website.

Other sources of funding for Swedish political parties come from private donations, membership contributions, and lotteries organized by the parties.

Until 1965, one of the main sources of party income was membership contributions. When public funding of the parties was introduced the following year, government funding then accounted for half of parties' income. According to estimates by Swedish think tank Timbro, in 2010 private donations accounted for between zero and 4.3% of funding for political parties.

In 1980, the parties represented in Parliament reached a sort of voluntary agreement to share their campaign accounts among themselves, but not with the public.

The aim of the new legislation passed in 2014, says the Swedish Ministry of Justice, is to "ensure public control over how parties fund their political activities, and how candidates fund their election campaigns."

With regards to the Swedish powers that be, the light of day is still the best detergent. Everyone knows that transparent government is a powerful force in the crusade against the ever-present enemy: corruption.

"There is an obvious link between public access to official information and low levels of corruption," maintained Jeremy Pope, one of the founders of the global civil society anti-corruption organization Transparency International.

A CONVERSATION WITH THE MINISTER OF JUSTICE

"The transparency of official actions is the reason why Sweden, like other Scandinavian countries, faces fewer problems with corruption" — Beatrice Ask

At four in the afternoon, it is already nighttime in the Stockholm winter. Children play in dark parks with dim lighting, between ornate poles that emit a soothing yellowish glow. In the dark alleys that cut through the beautiful central park of Humlegården, a symphony of intermittent children's cries, heard from the tiny figures that are scarcely distinguishable against the darkness of the lawns, creates a sort of children's opera of terror. The silhouettes of the immense, leafless trees add drama to the scene.

Throughout the city, candles and torches illuminate the entrance to cafés, restaurants, shops, and buildings. When December ushers in the longest night of the year, processions of teenagers parade on the 13th of the month, singing in the country's churches, wearing white robes and crowns of candles on their heads, to ask Saint Lucia to take the darkness away. It is tradition more than faith. But everyone, including the religious minority and the non-believing majority, does their best to exorcise the darkness of winter.

In the Swedish Ministry of Justice, it is the responsibility of a woman to keep the lights shining on the dark corners of power. A woman of no more than five feet, who squeezes my hand tightly when we meet in Parliament.

Is transparency the best antidote to corruption?

BEATRICE ASK: The transparency of official actions is the reason why Sweden, like other Scandinavian countries, faces fewer problems with corruption. When a government eliminates the secrets of the powers that be, it's not as easy to commit corrupt acts. It is important for every citizen to have the means to exercise control over the public administration and to participate in the decision-making process, in order to increase the system's efficiency and prevent corruption. Governments that are open and transparent are accountable to the public and are less corrupt.

The Swedish transparency law is almost 250 years old. In your opinion, has the Swedish system improved or deteriorated in certain respects?

BEATRICE ASK: I would say the system is stable. Sweden faces external pressures from other European Union countries that are still reluctant to adopt a more transparent stance. Since 1995, when Sweden joined the EU, the country has been making efforts to try to make the bloc's decisions more transparent. And, since 2001, there has been progress. Several European countries have adopted rules of transparency, and many are moving in this direction. On our part, we are making constant efforts. Many colleagues in the European Union still prefer to keep documents secret, which is against our principles and our constitutional law. We also face the same problem in our international relations in general when, for example, we sign an agreement and our partner wants to keep certain parts of the documentation closed to public access. We always put our principles of transparency on the table, but it is not always easy to overcome resistance. It's a constant struggle.

Minister of Justice Beatrice Ask: the Brazilian transparency law is good and points to the future.

How do you respond to the criticism by Swedish journalists citing obstructions to access to official documents by certain public agencies in Sweden?

BEATRICE ASK: All administrations make mistakes. But if you look at the system as a whole, the Swedish government significantly enforces transparency legislation. You can access practically any information. Exceptions are limited to matters of national security and other strictly defined aspects of the law of secrecy. Government proposals are presented in public documents, and are available on the official government website. Parliament's decisions are also posted on the Internet. Politicians' expenses and government employees' wages are also open to the public. Of course, there will always be failures, since no system is perfect. We have had some cases where public authorities have unnecessarily delayed requests for access to official documents. This is obviously regrettable. The authorities must handle all requests quickly. But the system as a whole is significantly transparent.

Harsher critics accuse certain authorities of adopting rules of secrecy that are broader than those permitted by law.

BEATRICE ASK: No government authority is authorized to create their own rules of secrecy. Citizens' access to official information is a right guaranteed by the Swedish Constitution. In some cases, interpretation of the law may give rise to doubts as to whether or not a document should be classified as secret. But the decision of any public authority to deny access to a document, or even parts of a particular document, can always be challenged in court. Citizens have the right to appeal to the courts for a fair trial on an application to access official information. The courts must respect the equality of all citizens before the law, and exercise impartiality and objectivity in their judgments. Transparency is what allows citizens to closely participate in government decisions, in addition to overseeing government spending and the efficiency of public institutions.

Could I check your personal expense report?

BEATRICE ASK: Yes. All Swedish ministers and parliamentarians have an obligation to declare their expenses and report their expenditures to citizens.

CHAPTER III

CORRUPTION IN CHECK

*"Beware, the half-wise
are everywhere."*
Hávamál, Viking poem

CORRUPTION MOVES more than a trillion dollars a year on a global scale — in bribes alone. And this is a conservative calculation, according to the World Bank. In politics, it is said that even in Cicero's time the Romans tried to prohibit candidates from sponsoring gladiator fights before an election. Since the first century AD, when buying the votes of ancient Roman citizens became a widespread practice, stealing and plundering have reached monumental proportions.

The Swedes have also had their political scandals. But if Swedish politicians steal, bribe, or abuse their power, they are not protected by virtue of their jobs — for Sweden offers them no immunity. Those accused of corruption do not have the right to be tried in special courts. No politician is above the law. All are subject to the same impartial Justice that judges ordinary citizens.

"Swedish politicians can be prosecuted and tried like any citizen," says Alf Johansson, one of the prosecutors who specializes in corruption cases in Sweden.

The prospect of being unmasked, exposed, detained, and tried causes certain members of this select group of men and women to think twice before committing an illegal act.

More important than the absence of a culture of impunity, however, was the development in Sweden of a culture of honesty and trust in public institutions.

Until the end of the 18th century, one could have said that there was something rotten in the Kingdom of Sweden. But then the time came to uncover the sewers. The process of change that would transform the face of the country was triggered essentially by a revolutionary reform of Sweden's institutions. As an ally of Herculean power, the law of transparency marched alongside the national cleansing that took place.

By the end of the 19th century, political corruption at the national level had practically been swept away. A new moral code, with solid rules of integrity, had emerged in the country. The belief that public funds and assets were at the disposal of those in power had become a thing of the past.

The maneuver was almost perfect. As pointed out by the authors of one of the most recent corruption studies published in Sweden, a society in which no one tries to take advantage of anyone is surely a utopia.

On the national level, everyone agrees that Sweden remains virtually free of political corruption. The Swedes' current dilemma is how to combat the miscreants in the municipal sphere, who feed newspapers with a diet of political scandals. According to Swedish researchers, this strain of twisted morality developed from incestuous relationships between government officials and local businessmen. Some believe this scenario was produced in part as a consequence of the wave of partial privatizations initiated in municipal public services in the 1990s. In a highly decentralized society such as Sweden, the field is also fertile for promiscuous relations at the local level.

In general terms, however, this is a country without major explicit vices in the area of corruption. If the statistics don't lie, there are very few tax predators amidst the official representatives of the people.

"Most Swedish politicians are not corrupt," says political commentator Lena Mellin, of *Aftonbladet* newspaper. "At the municipal level, there are abuses. But at the national level, there aren't any politicians paying for lunches or dinner with public money."

More difficult is to stamp out what the Swedes call *vänskapskorruption* (cronyism) — the infamous exchanges of favors. An extreme example was the controversy involving Prime Minister Olof Palme in the 1980s. A Swedish journalist revealed that when he was invited to lecture at Harvard University, Palme hadn't charge a fee, but had indicated during the visit that his son, Joakim Palme, was interested in studying at the institution.

Shortly thereafter, Joakim Palme received a scholarship to attend the university for free. The Swedish press raised the question: shouldn't the prime minister pay taxes on his son's benefit? Olof Palme had not declared the benefit. But the Swedish tax authorities understood that yes, he should pay taxes on his son's scholarship, and assessed the amount to be paid at 40,000 krona. With the news of Olof Palme's tragic assassination days later, on 28 February 1986, the debate was inconclusive. But the case became known as the Harvard Affair.

Despite any potential stains on its record, Sweden represents an enigma in the debate on corruption. According to the playbook of conventional economic theory, the country possesses all the characteristics that should have transformed it into an irretrievably corrupt society: a broad public sector, an interventionist government, and large bureaucracy with abundant decision-making power over various types of regulations. Yet the world's corruption indicators point precisely to the opposite.

All global indexes indicate that Sweden appears regularly among the least corrupt countries in the world. In Transparency International's annual reports, Sweden has never ranked below sixth place since 1996, when the organization began releasing its list of nations with the lowest perceived levels of corruption. In the World Bank's Worldwide Governance Indicators, Sweden appears among the top countries in the ranking of nations with the best indicators related to rule of law and control of corruption. In 2010 and 2011, the World Justice Project rated Sweden as the nation with the best performance in relation to the effectiveness of justice and respect for the rule of law.

Even so, constant vigilance is needed.

In central Stockholm, the National Anti-Corruption Unit (*Riksenheten mot Korruption*) keeps on the lookout. Even though the country is among the least corrupt in the world, the agency knows that opportunity makes the thief.

The task force of independent prosecutors searches and investigates the main suspected cases of corruption among politicians, business owners, and employees of the administrative machine. The agency is part of a system of integrity that brings together the law of transparency, a robust code of moral conduct, and regular programs of ethical awareness among companies and public agencies.

The strategy seeks to keep fraudsters, cheats and the dishonest in check. The greatest villain to be fought is bribery, which the National Anti-Corruption Unit classifies as a cancer that threatens any system.

In order to contain such a harmful parasite, the government created a code of norms for receiving personal gifts in public agencies and private companies. As the vast majority of Swedes know, receiving gifts worth more than 400 krona (about US$49) in the workplace can be considered a crime.

By law, anyone committing a crime of corruption in Sweden is subject to a fine or penalty of up to six years in prison. However, imprisonment for political crimes is rare in the country.

One of the few known cases occurred in 1995. That year the council president of the small Swedish municipality of Motala found himself sunbathing in a prison courtyard, after using public money to live the *dolce vita* on the beaches of Spain and Portugal.

THE MOTALA CASE

Social Democrat Sölve Conradsson had prepared his way to jail in great style. As president of the Motala town council in southern Sweden, one day he decided it would be a good idea to liven things up for the local politicians and big-wigs with a black-tie dinner. Paid for with taxpayers' money, of course, so that the next morning's hangover might afflict their heads, but not their wallets. It would be a guaranteed good time.

In a probable cerebral lapse caused by the overexcitement of the festivities, Conradsson sent one of the dinner invitations to the editor-in-chief of *Motala Tidning*, the local paper. And she asked herself the obvious question: who is paying the bill for such a regal gala?

Conradsson had barely hung up his dinner-jacket when the editor-in-chief assigned reporter Britt-Marie Citron to turn the host's accounts inside out. With the help of an auditor, she gathered enough material to scandalize a nation unaccustomed to hearing the word corruption on their national news. Heads would roll.

In a series of reports, the newspaper revealed that Conradsson had diverted public money to pay for private travel, dinners, and personal items. The TT news agency emphasized that everything was "at the expense of the taxpayer's money." Swedes had thought that this type of political dishonesty only existed overseas. Police and prosecutors stepped in.

The council president was forced to leave office. Some of his crimes were characterized as "particularly perverse," including the transfer of 140,000 krona from the municipality (about US$17,115) to his personal bank account, and holiday travel to Portugal and Spain, in the company of a merry group of family members.

Conradsson had used public funds for personal consumption "in an exceptionally shameful way," charged the Motala court judge. Sölve Conradsson was handcuffed and sentenced to one year and six months in prison and had to pay a fine of more than 600,000 krona (about US$73,350).

In the 240-page verdict, the judge pointed out that the damage should be measured not only in terms of money:

"The criminal procedure has not only had negative consequences for the municipality of Motala, but has severely damaged citizens' trust in the politicians of this society," the judge wrote. Six of the seven other defendants accused of involvement in Conradsson's schemes were also convicted.

The reporter who broke the case received Sweden's highest journalism award for the indiscretions she found in Motala. She noted that the law of transparency had been her main ally in her investigation of the local administration's mismanagement. In her book about the

Motala case, Britt-Marie Citron wrote that the "municipal law was like a toothless tiger," and the local opposition had a merely "decorative" role. A sort of political class had sprung up there like a predacious weed, far removed from citizens' control or contact with them.

Motala became a symbol in Sweden of all that can go wrong when the political establishment loses touch with its citizens. Sölve Conradsson served his sentence, and was released from prison with his political career buried six feet under.

Perhaps even more emblematic amongst the country's political scandals was the infamous Toblerone affair.

THE TOBLERONE SCANDAL

She bought a bar of chocolate, baby nappies and some other personal items with a government credit card, and paid dearly for it: she lost her job as deputy prime minister. In 1995, the scandal went down in the annals of Swedish politics as the Toblerone Case, and haunted Mona Sahlin until her political demise in 2011.

The drama symbolically brought about by a chocolate bar was unthinkable: Sahlin had scaled the ranks of the Social Democratic Party as a rising star, and her way to the top of the country's leadership seemed as predictable as the freezing of the Baltic Sea each winter.

In 1982, at the age of 25, Mona Sahlin had become the youngest representative ever elected to the Swedish Parliament. With indomitable verve and political talent,

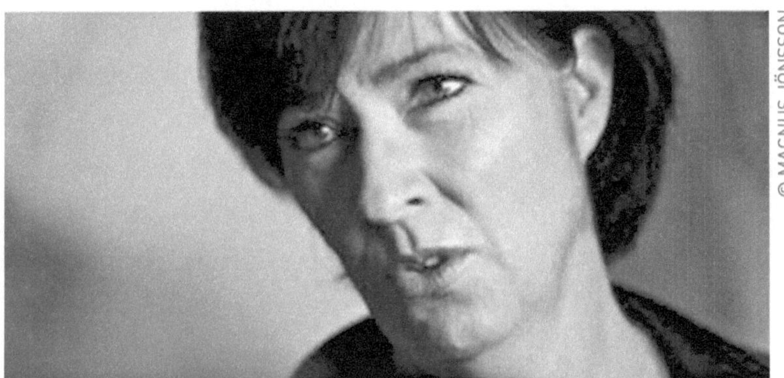

A bar of chocolate and various personal expenses cost former deputy prime minister Sahlin her job.

over the next two decades she secured ministerial posts and positions of power.

"Do not try to hide under my skirts, because they're rather short," she had let fly at Centre Party leader Olof Johansson during the last televised debate for the 1991 election campaign.

Not even the Social Democrat Prime Minister Göran Persson was spared from Sahlin's scorching barbs.

"Do you know the new meaning of the term 'exchanging opinions'? You go into Göran Persson's office with your own opinion, and you come out with his," Sahlin had criticized in 2002, when she was dealing with issues of democracy and integration as minister of Justice.

A year before the Toblerone scandal, and shortly before assuming the post of deputy prime minister, she would coin her most famous quote, an exaltation of the act of paying taxes.

"If you're a Social Democrat, you think it's cool to

pay taxes. For me, taxes are the best expression of what politics really is," declared Sahlin on SVT public television in September 1994.

In October 1995, the *Expressen* newspaper launched the grenade: Mona Sahlin, the natural candidate to succeed Prime Minister Ingvar Carlsson, had used a government card to pay for personal expenses.

"I bought a Toblerone, nappies and cigarettes," admitted Sahlin. The media, which were on the warpath, duly baptized the scandal the Toblerone Case.

In her defense, the deputy prime minister said she had used the government card as a kind of payday advance, which, according to Sahlin, was a common practice at the time. She also said that her private bank card was very similar to that of the government card, and that at no time had she intended to pay for her personal expenses with public money. She also made it clear that the money would be returned to the government coffers. But the damage had been done.

It turned out that it was not only one or two bars of chocolate. In total, the government card had been used to pay 53,174 krona (about US$6,500) for expenses such as car rentals and personal items.

The day after the revelation of the scandal, the Göteborgs-Posten newspaper published an opinion poll indicating that, for 66% of respondents, Mona Sahlin was an inadequate person to lead Sweden.

From the press investigations around the case, revelations arose that she had paid a nanny cash-in-hand without paying taxes and had ceased to pay the TV license, obligatory for everyone who owns a TV set in Sweden. The discovery of a collection of parking tickets also indicated, for Sahlin's detractors, that she was not an appropriate leader to become the country's prime minister.

Sahlin then followed the playbook for all Swedish politicians who find themselves in a tight spot: she immediately announced she was taking 'time-out' — a temporary departure from office. But then she gave her critics even more ammunition when it was discovered that her time out took place in a tropical paradise, Mauritius, accompanied by government-paid bodyguards.

The prosecutor general decided to initiate an investigation against Sahlin. A month later, the deputy prime minister announced her resignation. At the same time, she withdrew her candidacy for the party's leadership and for prime minister. In April 1996, she also left her seat in Parliament.

At the end of the Toblerone affair, the prosecution dismissed the case for lack of evidence, and on the grounds that the rules for using government cards were unclear. As is required of any Swedish politician caught using public monies, whether intentionally or by carelessness, Mona Sahlin had to fully reimburse the public coffers.

But the scandal continued to haunt Sahlin. When she was invited back to the cabinet of ministers in 1998, many felt that her former political authority had been somewhat damaged. In 2007, in light of the hesitancy of several potential candidates to take on the party's leadership, Sahlin's name was once again considered. At the age of 50, and more than a decade after the Toblerone Affair, she finally became the first woman to lead the Swedish Social Democratic party.

On May 9, 2009, as she was delivering a Labor Day speech, someone in the audience threw a Toblerone bar at her.

"It was not the first time," Mona Sahlin later told Swedish TV4. She spoke about the importance of winning back the people's trust. She wanted to show that she was capable of change and deserving of their trust.

"Are people really listening to me, or do they just see a big Toblerone in front of them? I believe they are beginning to listen to me more," Sahlin told TV4.

At the epicenter of the scandal in 1995, Mona Sahlin had said that she felt like she was inside a clothes dryer. Everything was spinning. In the interview with TV4, fourteen years later, she admitted that she still suffered the consequences of having bought the Toblerone with the government card.

"Some people never forget. To them, you will

always be somewhat guilty. I learned a lot and I changed."

I met Mona Sahlin at one of the last rallies of the 2010 election campaign, during coverage for a TV report. It was a sunny Sunday in August at Tantelunden Park in Stockholm, and the crowd settled into the chairs on the lawn. Some displayed the leader's face on their t-shirts. On the platform, Mona Sahlin once again warned against the risk of increasing economic inequality in the country between the richest and the poorest.

"This is not the kind of society we want to build in Sweden," the leader had emphasized.

But the speech did not have, however, the same effect as before. In the midst of the economic crisis plaguing Europe, the Swedes went to the polls that year betting on the security offered by the center-right government and its effective management of the Swedish economy, despite social cuts and unemployment.

Under Sahlin's leadership in the 2010 general election, the Social Democratic party garnered just 30.7 percent of the vote, the party's worst performance since the introduction of the universal vote in 1921. In March 2011, Mona Sahlin was replaced by Håkan Juholt as the party leader. She also went down in the history of the Swedish Social Democratic party as the person who led the party for the shortest amount of time — four years.

A CONVERSATION WITH THE DIRECTOR OF THE NATIONAL ANTI-CORRUPTION UNIT

"If a person has to fight daily for his survival, to have access to food, school, and medical care, the matter of fighting corruption in society will certainly not be among his main interests. But when a person feels part of the society to which he belongs, he does not accept abuses of power" — Gunnar Stetler

Gunnar Stetler frowns, blinks twice and tenses his facial muscles, as if he were working out an extraordinary calculation. He slowly travels through the maze of his memory after a long pause, and finally finds the answer: in the last 30 years, he says, only two cases of corruption have been recorded among parliamentarians and members of the Swedish Government.

"I have just a vague recollection," says Stetler.

"It is very rare to see representatives or members of the government involved in corruption here."

We are in the office of the chief prosecutor of the National Anti-Corruption Unit (*Riksenheten mot Korruption*), stacked high with files and papers. Just a few steps away, on the same Hantverkargatan Street, in the Kungsholmen neighborhood, is the HQ of the dreaded *Ekobrottsmyndigheten*, the Swedish Economic Crime Authority. The April sun has melted off the ice of another winter, and on the other side of the street mothers walk with their prams among the graveyard headstones of the Kungsholms Kyrka church, a common habit in several of the city's cemeteries.

From his small office, Gunnar Stetler heads the specialist prosecutors who investigate the main cases of suspected corruption in the country. Less serious cases are prosecuted at the regional level in the various district offices that comprise the Swedish siege against scams, swindles and frauds in general.

At 1.93 meters, a serious expression and unbribable countenance, Gunnar Stetler is described in the Swedish media as the country's greatest corruption hunter. Among the cases under his watch in 2013 was the allegation that the Swedish telephone operator TeliaSonera had paid bribes amounting to US$ 337 million to establish operations in Uzbekistan.

"Historically, 75 percent of formal bribery charges in Sweden end in convictions," says Stetler.

Born in 1949, Stetler gained fame after leading cases which included that against a former director of the Swedish company ABB, who was sentenced to three years in prison in 2005 for diverting 1.8 million

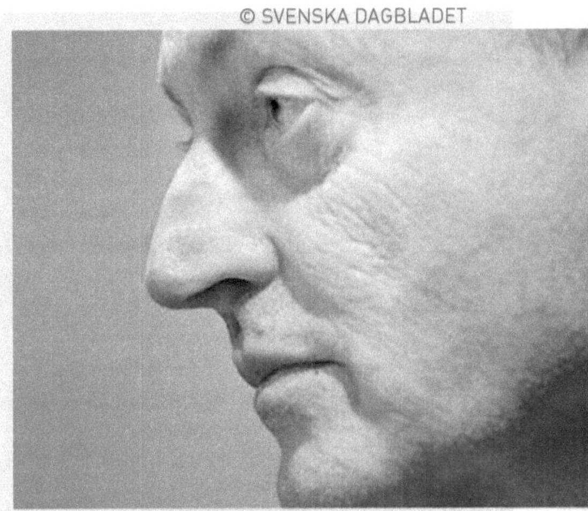

Stetler, corruption hunter: 75% of cases end in convictions.

krona to a company registered in the British Virgin Islands tax haven.

"There comes a time when a person is no longer content with a Volvo V70, and wants to trade it for a Porsche. Greed is part of the human dilemma," reflects Stetler.

For the chief prosecutor, three factors keep Sweden off the list of seriously corrupt countries: the transparency of government actions, the population's high level of education, and social equality.

What makes Sweden one of the least corrupt countries in the world?

GUNNAR STETLER: First, the law of public access to official documents. This law, created in Sweden more than 200 years ago, keeps government abuses at bay. If citizens or the media wish, they can check my salary, my expenditures, and my work-related travel expenses. My files are open to the public. And we believe that by placing official government documents and records within the public reach, we prevent individuals in positions of power from engaging in inappropriate activities. That's the main reason. In second place is the law passed in Sweden (in 1842), which introduced compulsory education in the country and thus raised the population's general level of education.

What is the impact of a more educated population on preventing corruption?

GUNNAR STETLER: If a person does not have access to education, he cannot even understand, much less monitor the system. In Sweden, we believe that you start building a society at the base of the population and not at the top. Thus a good educational system needs to be offered at all levels of society. China has a high level of corruption, but is investing in improving the population's level of education. I believe that this will reduce corruption in the country.

How often does your phone ring with allegations of corruption?

GUNNAR STETLER: I receive about four calls from the public every day. But for every 15 allegations, in general only one of them has any basis for a case. Most cases concern smaller issues, such as when a civil servant agrees to travel to a resort at the invitation of a contractor to facilitate a contract. If you are a civil servant in Sweden, you are absolutely not authorized to accept this type of invitation. We also deal with larger cases. I have just formally accused one of the heads of the *Kriminalvården* (Swedish prison system), who has received bribes of millions of krona from a contractor to build prisons. We work with grievances from the public, the media, and also from national audit systems, such as the *Riksrevisionen* (the independent agency that controls the Swedish government's finances).

What is the level of incidence of corruption cases at the national level involving parliamentarians and other politicians?

GUNNAR STETLER: It is very rare to see representatives or members of government involved in corruption here.

When was the last time this happened in Sweden?

GUNNAR STETLER: If I remember correctly (pause)... maybe there have been a couple of cases (pause)... in the last (pause)... 30 years.

Are you saying that since the 1970s there have only been two cases of political corruption at the national level?

GUNNAR STETLER: Yes.

What were these cases?

GUNNAR STETLER: If I'm not mistaken (pause)... about ten years ago (pause)... a member of parliament representing the western coast made a mistake (pause)... I have a vague recollection.

If you have only a vague recollection of the only two cases of political corruption on the national level in the last 30 years, can we presume that there have not been any major scandals?

GUNNAR STETLER: Yes. In terms of political corruption, more serious cases occur mainly in the municipalities.

But the last time a Swedish politician was sentenced to prison for corruption was apparently in 1995. Does

this mean that the degree of political corruption in Sweden is generally not severe enough to require prison sentences, or is it a sign that the system is lenient with corrupt politicians?

GUNNAR STETLER: In Sweden, in general, every punishment is lenient.

What do you mean?

GUNNAR STETLER: In the Swedish penal system, the basic principle is not punishment, but the reintegration of the individual into society. This is our tradition. The penal code does not hand out harsh punishment for cases of political corruption.

Aren't more severe punishments the answer to fighting political corruption?

GUNNAR STETLER: Public opinion punishes corrupt politicians. If a representative or an official of the state administration commits a corrupt act, they will be punished severely by society, mainly for having made a mistake while occupying a position of power. A representative, for example, may be forced to resign through pressure from public opinion and the media, even when he or she is not formally indicted.

Are there any special rules for investigating and prosecuting politicians for crimes of corruption, such as needing approval from Parliament or a committee?

GUNNAR STETLER: No.

Is it primarily up to the media and Swedish citizens to scrutinise the government, or institutions like the one you lead?

GUNNAR STETLER: It's up to the free press in the first place. If the media has access to legal documents, it can act together with citizens to ensure a more honest society. Of course official organizations, such as the Anti-Corruption Agency, also play an important role. In Sweden most people trust government agencies, and one of the reasons for this is the fact that citizens can oversee what agencies do.

What sort of work does the National Anti-Corruption Unit engage in?

GUNNAR STETLER: Our main focus is bribery. It can be said that bribery, both in the public sphere and in the private sector, is a cancer for any system. Even when the value of the bribe is very low, it may influence a bid of one billion Swedish krona. In the public sector, it is important that purchases of goods and services are carried out correctly. The construction of a new hospital, for example, could cost about 1.7 billion Swedish krona (about US$208 million). When a public sector agency deals with a contract of this magnitude, it is important that there be some distance between the company that will build the hospital and the public servants who approve the contract. From my point of view — and I think that most people in Sweden would agree — it is essential that civil servants do not accept gifts of any kind, even those of low value.

In general, the Swedes really do seem to respect the rule prohibiting accepting gifts worth over 400 krona.

GUNNAR STETLER: In general, no public or private official in Sweden is allowed to accept gifts above 300 or a maximum of 400 krona (US$37-49). In my position, I cannot accept anything.

Nothing?

GUNNAR STETLER: Nothing. Not even a coffee and a *wienerbröd* (a Swedish pastry). And in general, I don't believe that Swedish politicians or public servants ever accept what can be considered as real bribes, namely large-scale bribes.

It doesn't happen?

GUNNAR STETLER: I suppose it could happen, but it isn't likely. The question is what is considered a bribe. For some, accepting an invitation to dinner or spending the weekend at a resort does not imply a bribe. But in Sweden, invitations of this kind actually do characterize a bribe. Especially for those who work in the public sector.

So would it be considered a crime to accept an invitation to dinner?

GUNNAR STETLER: In my opinion, a person or a company cannot invite a public servant to dinner, if there is any kind of business involving both parties.

What would your best advice be for other countries in order to become a more honest society?

GUNNAR STETLER: You have to understand this isn't something than can happen overnight. In order to combat corruption, you need to implement a major system of transparency in government, increase the general population's education levels, and promote social equality. Education is the basic principle that we in Sweden call *jämlikheten* (social equality). And this is also a factor in preventing corruption.

What is the importance of social equality in this process?

GUNNAR STETLER: If a person has to fight for daily survival, having access to food, schools and medical care, the issue of fighting corruption in society will certainly not be among his main interests. But when an individual feels part of the society to which he belongs, he does not accept abuses of power.

Notes:

1. Investment in education represents 42% of the spending in Swedish municipal budgets, according to the Swedish Association of Local and Regional Authorities (*Sveriges Kommuner och Landsting*).

2. Sweden invests 8.62% of its Gross Domestic Product (GDP) in education at all levels, including continuing professional education courses, according to the Swedish Ministry of Education and Research (*Utbildningsdepartementet*).

THE GIFT LAW

Bribery is on the rise globally, but Sweden comes out on top of the list of the least corrupt countries in the world — according to the latest Risk Matrix report of anti-bribery organization TRACE International. The Swedish law keeps an eye on the corrupt and on the friends of the corrupt, and no precaution is too little: any gift given or received in the workplace can be classified as a bribe — both in the public and private sectors.

Those convicted of bribery can be required to pay a fine of up to 180 days' worth of their own salaries, or a penalty of up to two years in prison. And anyone who receives a gift classified as a bribe is subject to a fine equivalent of up to 50% of their annual salary, and a harsher prison sentence: up to six years behind bars.

In order to avoid illegal behavior, Sweden has created a set of rules to specifically regulate the exchange of doubtful gifts and favors in public offices, political offices, courts, and private companies. It is the so-called Code of Conduct Regarding Gifts, Rewards and Other Benefits within the Business Community (*Kod om gåvor, belöningar och andra förmåner*), which contains the rules of conduct to be observed in public and private companies. This is a supplement to the anti-bribery law, which is regulated by the Swedish Penal Code.

Ask specifically any Swedish public servants, and they will know that the kindness of a supplier, contractor or anyone else has a limit. According to the rules, the general principle is that receiving a gift at the workplace worth more than 440 krona (about US$54) can be considered a crime. For this amount, in Sweden you can purchase a dozen roses, a bottle of champagne, or a portion of the unforgettable *Kalix löjrom*, the caviar produced in Kalix, near the Arctic Circle.

But it is more serious than that. Depending on the degree of influence on the person receiving the gift, or on the particular circumstances, any kind of gift can be considered a bribe — regardless of the value.

"When in doubt, it is better to refuse a present and avoid a police report," says Claes Sandgren, president of the Swedish Anti-Corruption Institute (*Institutet Mot Mutor*).

The dilemma regarding whether to accept or refuse a gift in the workplace — or whether or not to give a gift — feeds widespread paranoia. To guide the distressed in the swampy terrain of anti-bribery standards, each institution, company, or public body maintains specific guidelines for its employees.

The questions that public servants must ask themselves when faced with the offer of a gift, for example, are listed as follows on the official website of the municipality of Örebro, in northern Sweden:

"Does this gift represent any kind of advantage? Why are they offering it to you? Is there any relation between this gift and the work that I do? If the answer is yes, the gift is a bribe, and receiving it makes you guilty in the eyes of the law," warn the authorities. And they add:

"Officials are sometimes invited to events or leisure

activities. Regardless of whether it is a trip, a borrowed summer home, or a boat ride, always decline offers like these."

In the Royal Institute of Technology (*Kungliga Tekniska Högskolan*, KTH), the board warns employees: accepting gifts from a person or company related to the institution, under the justification of having friendly relations with the donor, is not a valid argument.

"There are cases where the one who gives the gift and the one who receives it affirm before the judge that they are personal friends. But the courts rarely accept this argument," advises the institution on its official website.

The general reference, in cases of acute doubt, is the Anti-Bribery Institute. The institution's official website offers a wealth of advice for interpreting the Code of Conduct Regarding Gifts, in order to "fight corruption in society" and "maintain a high ethical standard." Gifts of cash or loans are obviously forbidden, and you have to be wary of bonus offers, discounts, meals, conference trips, provisions, and offers to buy goods or services at cost.

Festive occasions are also on the list:

"If it is not possible to refuse a Christmas present, a cautious person should be careful to ensure that its value does not exceed 1% of the *prisbasbelopp* or price base amount, especially if the recipient works in the public sector," notes the Institute. The price base amount (currently 44,400 krona for 2014) is a key component of the Swedish social security system and is used as a base to calculate various social benefits. Thus, according to the Institute's guidelines, any gift whose value exceeds 440% (1% of the *prisbasbelopp*) should not accepted.

"In the case of 50th or 60th birthday parties, the maximum value allowed in the public sector, depending on the circumstances involved, is 3% of the price base amount," according to another rule.

Offering benefits and benefits without economic value is also considered improper, according to the code of regulations. "It could be, for example, offering someone membership of a social club," specifies the Anti-Corruption Institute.

Violating the rules is considered a particularly perverse act in the public sector. "The courts have particularly severe criteria for misdemeanors committed by public officials," the Anti-Corruption Institute says. But the concern about receiving gifts at the office is widespread.

While having dinner at the house of mutual friends, the editorial director of the *Aftonbladet* newspaper, Martin Wåhlstedt, told me that he had to refuse a box of excellent wine sent to him as a gift.

"The value was too high, and so accepting the gift was out of the question. And in any office, an employee who receives a gift valued above the standard of 300 or 400 krona needs to ask their boss's approval in order to accept," said Wåhlstedt. At his side, his wife, an SVT TV journalist, said Swedish reporters are generally barred from accepting invitations to travel from companies or embassies.

Around the same dinner table was doctor and researcher Clara Gumper, from the Karolinska Institute, which annually selects the winner of the Nobel Prize in Medicine. Gumper said that under no circumstances can scientists accept invitations for travel, dinners, or events paid for by companies in the medical sector. Displaying a degree of caution bordering on paranoia, Gumper also said she is afraid to accept even samples and promotional items offered by pharmaceutical companies.

"We always pay our own hotel and ticket costs when we attend seminars and conferences," Gumper said. "I even avoid accepting those pens that are given out as gifts at these events."

In the Anti-Corruption Institute online archives, a selection of court cases confirms that this general fear is well founded. Among them is the case of a doctor and the head of a clinic, who were sentenced by the Jönköping court to pay fines equivalent to 30 days' and 60 days' worth of their wages respectively. They had accepted an invitation from a pharmaceutical company that had paid, in part, for the cost of a visit to a hospital in the Czech Republic.

Shortly before Christmas in the city of Falu, a car dealer handed out bottles of an alcoholic beverage to seven employees of *Svenska Bilprovning*, the body responsible for the annual inspection of vehicles. When the case ended up in court, the judge was categorical: he emphasized that *Svenska Bilprovning* has a duty to be impartial in the treatment of its clients, and that accepting a Christmas gift of that size entailed the risk that employees would give special treatment to the customer who had given the gift. The verdict: each employee was fined the equivalent of 30 days of their wages. The car dealer was sentenced to a fine of 40 days' wages.

In Örebro, in northern Sweden, two municipal officials accepted an invitation from a businessman for a short cruise around the Åland Islands in the Baltic Sea. The court ordered them both to pay a fine equal to 30 days' pay. The businessman was given a higher fine: 50 days' salary. Also in Örebro, a prisoner sentenced to life imprisonment paid for meals and coffee for the guard accompanying him on a series of days of supervised leave. The guard was ordered to pay a fine of 80 days' salary.

In the city of Norrköping, a woman sent a bottle of brandy, a box of chocolates, and a CD as gifts to an official of the Swedish Immigration Authority (*Migrationsverket*) with a request to review a decision that had denied a visa application for her parents. The clerk refused the presents, but the woman was ordered to pay a fine of 30 days' salary.

"Always exercise caution. You will never regret refusing a gift," warns the Ministry of Finance in the document where it points out specific recommendations to the country's public sector employees (*Om Mutor och Jäv — en vägledning för offentliga anställda*).

In politics, even supposed slip-ups can carry heavy penalties.

SOFIA'S CHOICE: TRAVEL AND A BMW

Sofia Arkelsten: in the press's line of fire after taking a trip at Shell's expense.

Member of parliament Sofia Arkelsten's choice would cause her career to flutter in the balance like a Nordic pine leaf in the wind. Arkelsten accepted an invitation from the oil giant Shell to travel free of charge to the south of France, in order to attend a seminar on the environment.

The Shell-sponsored trip had taken place in 2008, when Sofia Arkelsten was the Moderate Party's spokesperson for environmental issues. In 2010, when the revelation came to light, Arkelsten had just been promoted to the position of the party's secretary-general. It was a good target for the public beating that followed.

Smelling blood, the Swedish press investigated further and discovered that Sofia Arkelsten had taken two other sponsored trips.

Even worse: at the same time, the member of parliament had also driven a luxury BMW for several days without paying for it. The German carmaker had contacted celebrities and politicians, inviting them to test its new hydrogen-powered "green" model, the Hydrogen 7. Sofia chose to accept.

"Arkelsten drove a BMW for free," blasted the headline of the *Svenska Dagbladet* newspaper. The revelations ended up on the desk of the director of the National Anti-Corruption Unit, Gunnar Stetler.

"Of course, members of parliament are subject to the rule of law," Stetler told the Swedish press, referring to Swedish legislation against corruption and bribery.

On the Moderate Party's official website, Sofia Arkelsten defended her decision to accept sponsored travel, including attending the seminar held in the city of Pau in southern France:

"My judgment was, and still is, that the trip, the seminar, and the possibility of meeting students, scientists, and politicians from all over the world were relevant to my mission as a parliamentarian," she wrote.

"I apologize if my participation in this seminar gave rise to the interpretation that I may have allowed myself to be influenced in an inappropriate way. It is essential that we, who are elected by the people, act in such a way that our integrity cannot be questioned," she added.

The Swedish media pressed Shell's head of information to find out exactly how Arkelsten had benefited from the oil money.

"We paid for her round trip air ticket, two nights in a hotel, lunch and dinner," the spokesman said, adding that the seminar was attended by a number of organizations and researchers, as well as other politicians involved with environmental issues.

A national debate ensued as to whether the party secretary-general should step down. Arkelsten continued to be pressured for accepting the use of the BMW.

"I drove the car for a few days in order to try out a new technology. I believe this was relevant to the role I played in the environmental sector, and there was nothing unusual about it. I tested the car, and among other activities, I used the vehicle to pick up my grandmother," said Arkelsten.

But for her critics, the member of Parliament should not have accepted a perk from the car maker.

"The carmaker has made efforts to reduce the level of its cars' fuel consumption. But you do not have to drive a BMW to check this out," Social Democrat representative Anders Ygeman contested.

After examining the case, the chief prosecutor concluded that Sofia's choices did not contain the elements of a suspected bribery. According to Gunnar Stetler, the context of her trips was justified.

"Parliamentarians are allowed to accept invitations to certain events as long as their travel is justified," Stetler said, noting that leisure and entertainment travel was not on the list.

The chief prosecutor recommended that Parliament should introduce clearer rules to regulate parliamentary travel.

"It is a simple system to introduce, and in my opinion, it should be done," Stetler said.

With regards to the luxury car, Stetler stated that Arkelsten had tested the BMW but that she had not used the car long enough for it to qualify as an illegal act.

The opposition, however, continued to attack Arkelsten.

"I think she (Sofia Arkelsten) lacked judgment. And, obviously, more than once. Now it's up to the Moderate Party leader to decide whether or not it is reasonable to have a secretary general who has behaved in this manner," attacked the Social Democratic Party leader, Mona Sahlin.

Four days after throwing stones at Arkelsten, Sahlin was sitting in the stand of the Royal Stockholm Tennis Arena, as a non-paying guest of the organizers of the international tennis tournament. As a guest, Sahlin watched five days of play on the courts, including the thrilling victory of Roger Federer in the final. The total value of her entertainment: 7,500 krona (about US$920).

Other guests of the tournament organizers included the Swedish Supreme Commander of the Swedish Armed Forces, Sverker Göransson. But the Commander had paid for the tickets himself.

Mona Sahlin thus justified her decision to accept the courtesy tickets:

"There is a considerable difference between this and the fact that an oil company paid for the travel and hotel of a politician that is responsible for environmental issues, in order to influence a political decision," she said.

Sahlin relied on the support of the president of the Institutet Mot Mutor, Claes Sandgren, who had become one of the loudest critics of Sofia Arkelsten's conduct.

"The benefit (granted to Mona Sahlin) was relatively harmless, since it isn't a situation in which someone is attempting to exert influence," said Sandgren. He did, however, advocate for the introduction by Parliament of clearer rules regarding the types of courtesy tickets that politicians should be allowed to accept.

Sahlin's case was inevitably subjected to the magnifying glass of the chief prosecutor of the National Anti-Corruption Unit.

"In general, in order for a gift to be classified as criminal, there must be a risk that such a gift could be interpreted as personal, thus creating a relationship of dependence between the one who gives and the one who receives," said Gunnar Stetler. The chief prosecutor decided, however, not to open a formal investigation against Mona Sahlin, based on the same argument put forward by Sandgren: there was an extremely small chance that there would be any sort of illegal influence based on Sahlin's acceptance of the free tournament tickets.

"It's not up to the Attorney General's Office to decide what is appropriate or inappropriate, and defensible or indefensible for a party leader or a representative to accept," Gunnar Stetler wrote in his decision.

"It seems clear to me that there is a certain degree of uncertainty in Parliament about what kind of invitation a parliamentarian can accept," the prosecutor general concluded.

Although Sahlin and Arkelsten managed to escape the accusations of their suspected bribery, they walked away from the episodes with charred reputations.

Not even the popular Swedish Royal Family is free from such eternal vigilance. In the eyes of some of the King's subjects, a honeymoon gift that the heir to the Swedish throne received was considered suspicious.

THE HEIR APPARENT'S SUSPICIOUS PRESENT

Princess Victoria's wait for her big day had been as long as the train of her royal wedding dress. Ten years earlier, in 2002, she had fallen in love with her personal trainer, Daniel Westling. Like a fairy-tale princess, she had struggled to obtain the approval of her father, the king, to marry the commoner, who some of the press mockingly referred to as "Daniel of Ockelbo," a reference to the small village where the chosen partner of the heir to the throne had been raised.

The royal blessing was finally granted, after years of exasperating speculation in the Swedish gossip magazines. The day and place of the wedding would be exactly the same as that of her mother, 34 years before, when Silvia, also a commoner — daughter of a Brazilian mother and raised in São Paulo until her teens — had married King Carl Gustaf XVI. After such a long wait, there was no way that the party would be spoiled by minor mishaps, such as a few thousand Swedes joining the *Vägra betala Victorias bröllop* ("Refuse to pay for Victoria's wedding"), a movement created on Facebook in protest against the use of the taxpayers' money to pay for part of Victoria's royal wedding.

"The National Anti-Corruption Agency announced its decision that the honeymoon trip was not a bribe"

Princess Victoria's honeymoon, paid for by a billionaire, was attacked as being a bribe.

On June 19, 2010, a radiant Victoria ascended to the altar of the Stockholm Cathedral next to Daniel, now elevated to nobility and given the title of Duke of Västergötland. Rejoicing, the crowd of royal subjects took to the streets to greet the future queen and her prince consort, and three days of well-deserved celebrations followed.

But when the details of the honeymoon came to light, they left a bitter taste among certain inhabitants of the Kingdom. The trip had been paid for by Swedish magnate Bertil Hult, owner of EF, the mega-agency of language courses. Victoria and Daniel had flown to

Tahiti in the businessman's private jet, cruised the South Seas aboard his luxury yacht, the Erica XII, and had stayed in the billionaire's mansion in the American state of Colorado.

"It's odd that the heir to the Swedish throne would allow a Swedish billionaire to provide transport and accommodation for her honeymoon, when the same person, through his company EF, could potentially have an interest in seeing the favor returned. Everyone in the business world knows that royal glamour can benefit business," criticized Peter Wolodarski, a political commentator for the *Dagens Nyheter* newspaper.

In all, eight Swedish citizens sent complaints about the royal couple and the Swedish billionaire to the National Anti-Corruption Unit (*Riksenheten mot korruption*).

"An ordinary citizen cannot even accept a bottle of champagne as a gift without running the risk of going to court," said one of the complainants, according to the *Expressen* newspaper.

The honeymoon trip had most likely cost more than one million Swedish krona (about US$122,250). After examining the allegations, the chief prosecutor of the Swedish National Anti-Corruption Unit stated that he could not proceed with the investigation against Victoria and Daniel.

"The Princess inherits her job, so she does not fall

into the same category of people defined under anti-corruption legislation," said Chief Prosecutor Gunnar Stetler. Stetler underlined that the current legislation allows "unusual consequences":

"If I try to give an improper gift to the Royal Family, I cannot be penalized, since the Royal Family does not belong to the category of people the anti-corruption law covers," Stetler said.

In other words, the Royal Family is the only group that falls outside the grip of the anti-corruption law. For Stetler, this is an issue to be examined by Parliament.

"I hope that in a future law, trying to bribe a member of the Royal Family is also defined as a crime," he told the *Svenska Dagbladet* newspaper.

The Royal Court issued a statement stating that the honeymoon trip had been a wedding gift from a friend of the couple. The court's chief information officer at the time, Nina Eldh, declined to comment on the prosecutor's decision.

"If the same complaint had been directed at a politician or a judge, the investigation would have been carried out," said Claes Sandgren, the president of the Swedish Anti-Corruption Institute (*Institutet Mot Mutor*).

Princess Madeleine, sister of the Crown Princess, was less fortunate when the Swedish police stopped her in traffic in June 2013.

THE DAY THE POLICE STOPPED THE PRINCESS

Madeleine's marriage to her American commoner fiancé was four days away, and the princess was in a hurry. At the wheel of a royal fleet Volvo XC 60, the sister of the heir to the Swedish crown began driving in the exclusive bus lane in central Stockholm. Soon, she heard a police whistle, and was forced to stop. Facing a fine, Princess Madeleine tried to convince the policeman that she had the right to drive in the bus lane — although avoiding to use the "do-you-know-who-you-are-speaking-to" line of defense. But to no avail.

At first, Madeleine managed to avoid being fined by showing the police officer a document and stating, according to the *Aftonbladet* newspaper, that as a member of the Royal Family she would have immunity in this case.

"The police officer was uncertain about whether the immunity laws applied to all members of the Royal Family, or whether there was some sort of exception for Royal Court cars," said Lars Lindholm, who headed the traffic operation.

Lindholm stated categorically, however, that only the King had immunity in such cases. It was then decided that Princess Madeleine, the fourth in the line of succession to the Swedish throne, would not escape the punishment by the police.

"We're already issuing a fine to the amount of one thousand krona (about US$122)," the police chief said.

But the court's spokesperson stepped in, and sent the police a copy of the special permission that gives the

Princess Madeleine: spotted by police driving in the exclusive bus lane.

royal fleet's cars the right to drive in the exclusive bus lane on special occasions such as days of official visits to the country. And Madeleine's royal wedding, with the arrival of dozens of aristocrats and foreign officials to the Swedish capital, was one of those special occasions.

"The princess was not trying to allege any kind of immunity," pointed out the spokesperson, saying that Madeleine had shown the police officer the special permit.

Thus, at the last minute Madeleine was saved from paying the police fine.

"Due to the special circumstances of this case, the fine will be withdrawn," said police spokesman Hans Brandt.

A CONVERSATION WITH THE PRESIDENT OF THE SWEDISH ANTI-CORRUPTION INSTITUTE

"Politicians should keep in mind their respect for the citizens who elect them"
— Claes Sandgren

Claes Sandgren saves afflicted souls tormented by the fear of bribery. A herd of politicians, businessmen, and public servants seek his good counsel in order to avoid the fire of eternal damnation. Where there is darkness in the law, he brings light. Where there are doubts about whether a gift can be offered or accepted, he brings certainty to doing the right thing. For in Sweden, as is well-known, it is through the act of giving that you might end up receiving a police report.

President of the Anti-Corruption Institute (*Institutet Mot Mutor*) and professor at the University of Stockholm Law School, Claes Sandgren is ever-present in the Swedish media when the subject is suspected bribery or corruption. Since 2008 he chairs the institute, which was founded in 1923.

I walk towards Gamla Stan, Stockholm's Old Town, for my meeting with Sandgren. It's a Friday, and the unfailing shopping bags of Systembolaget, the state-owned company that holds the monopoly on alcohol sales in Sweden, sway in the hands of its many patrons in the city. The purple or green plastic bags stamped with the monopoly's brand expose, to the discomfort of many, the bags' alcoholic content.

The monopoly's mission is to promote the responsible sale of alcohol. Anyone who arrives drunk is prohibited from buying alcohol, as well as those under 20 years of age. For consumers who are more prone to binge drinking, planning is needed: the shops of the popular Systemet, veritable alcohol supermarkets, close their doors at seven o'clock at night, are open just a few hours on Saturdays, and do not open on Sundays. Outside the Systembolaget (literally "company of the system"), only *lättöl* (light beer, 1.8% alcohol) and *folköl* (popular beer, 2.8% alcohol), can be bought.

On the way to Gamla Stan, on this partial holiday, I see more people and bottles than usual in the city's many parks. The thermometers are reading 18 degrees on this late afternoon in May. It's warm enough for a considerable number of Swedes, who are stretched out in the grass in their bikinis.

It will get even better: after months of darkness and cold, June will bring the *Midsommar* (summer solstice) festival, the longest day of the year and the most anticipated holiday of all. It is when the Swedes dance, imitating frogs, around a gigantic pole that symbolizes fertility and harvest. It is thus understandable that it is not possible to be sober on this day of pagan festivities, which has been celebrated since the Viking era.

Gamla Stan is already in party mode, full of tourists and locals that are crowded into the cafés and bars of its old alleys. Situated on Stora Nygatan, one of the main pedestrian streets of the Old Town, the building where Claes Sandgren lives is more than 200 years old and has a privileged view over the hustle and bustle.

Amid a stack of books and reports, the lawyer tells me that the main function of the Anti-Corruption Institute is to guide companies and municipalities on how to maintain ethical standards and keep their distance from any problems with the law. Claes says that in all his 68 years of age, he has never heard of a judge who has accepted bribery in Sweden.

Why is a code needed to regulate the exchange of gifts in public and private companies?

CLAES SANDGREN: The purpose of this code is to establish an ethical standard in order to avoid bribery and corruption in society. Usually, a gift can be accepted up to approximately 440 Swedish krona (about US$54). This represents 1% of the *prisbasbelopp* or price amount used for calculating social benefits in Sweden. People always ask about this amount. But a prosecutor, for example, cannot even accept a gift of 50 krona (US$6.10), and I think a prosecutor would not actually accept even a cup of coffee.

And if a prosecutor accepts a gift, what happens?

CLAES SANDGREN: In principle, he is committing a crime. A prosecutor works in the public sector, where the rules for accepting gifts are much more rigid. Another important point in both the public and private sectors, is that generally the head of a company decides whether or not an employee should receive gifts. If the company head decides that they shouldn't, then employees cannot accept anything.

What, in your opinion, is the best code of conduct to be adopted by politicians?

CLAES SANDGREN: In principle, never accept gifts or invitations for dinners. Politicians should always be mindful of respecting the citizens who elect them. If a salesperson in a private company does something wrong, it matters less to the public. But if a politician commits an act that affects the ordinary citizens' trust in politicians, that is damaging to democracy. And if that trust is broken, citizens may ask themselves: "Why vote? Why pay taxes?" And that undermines democracy.

If a politician accepts a dinner paid for by a businessman, can that be considered a crime?

CLAES SANDGREN: It depends on the circumstances, and the politician's area of responsibility. If, for example, a politician is working on the preparation of a parliamentary proposal related to some business sector, he should not accept anything from any entrepreneur who might have interests in Parliament's decisions. And a businessman should never offer anything. The situation of politicians, therefore, is similar to that of the prosecutors. But there isn't a specific rule that determines that this should never be done. For example, the Minister for Industry should never accept dinners paid for

Jurist Sandgren: "I've never heard of a corrupt judge in Sweden."

by companies. But if a Swedish company is celebrating their 100th anniversary and hosts a huge dinner party for hundreds of people, it may not be a problem to invite some politicians. Every politician must exercise his common sense: what would voters think if I accepted this invitation?

Your phone is constantly busy. Do you get calls from people who are afraid to receive gifts?

CLAES SANDGREN: Afraid to receive, and also to offer gifts. I get daily calls from people asking for advice. In some cases, it is companies that are promoting a product, and they want to know what they can or cannot offer it to an employee in a purchasing department. In the municipalities, the questions are similar. What does or doesn't the law allow? Of course, companies want to offer things to politicians. Not money, but some sort of advantage. The most common questions are: "Can I accept an invitation to dinner? Can I play golf with this person?"

And what is your response?

CLAES SANDGREN: It is not always easy to answer these questions. If a dinner is offered to a politician within the program of a more serious event, such as a seminar to discuss a particular topic, it may be an acceptable invitation.

You were, however, one of the most outspoken critics of the representative Sofia Arkelsten when she accepted an invitation to attend a seminar in the south of France that was paid for by a company.

CLAES SANDGREN: I did not say she committed a crime. But she did, in my opinion, commit an improper act, because parliamentarians have a budget to participate in this type of event. Therefore, Arkelsten had the money to pay for her own trip and her own food, and she should not have allowed a private company to pay her bills. The heir to the Swedish Crown allowed a businessman to pay for the costs of her honeymoon, and I also think that this was an improper act, since the businessman's company could have benefited by it.

Are Swedish judges allowed to accept gifts and invitations for cruises and trips to resorts?

CLAES SANDGREN: I've never heard of a corrupt judge in Sweden. A judge accepting bribes is unheard of here. At least not in recent history. I'm 68 years old, and I've never heard of such a case. The law does not formally prohibit a judge from accepting such things, but in theory he knows he is prohibited. Judges simply do not accept things like trips and gifts.

What makes the Swedish court system corruption-free?

CLAES SANDGREN: Above all, it's a tradition. Moreover, the judges receive good salaries. In the Supreme Court, the highest level, a judge earns the equivalent of 10,000 euros a month (about US$12,450).

Is the court system also transparent?

CLAES SANDGREN: Yes. All documents related to a case are open to the public. You can go to any court and check.

Can I check the documentation on the case of Julian Assange, the founder of Wikileaks who is accused of sexual crimes in Sweden?

CLAES SANDGREN: Assange's case is not in court because he has not yet been formally charged. During an investigation, everything is secret. This rule is intended to protect suspects. Since Assange is currently only suspected of committing a crime, investigations into his case are kept confidential. But if a prosecutor decides to formally charge him, all documents will become open to public access. The law provides only a few exceptions in accessing court documents, for example, to protect the identity of children, or persons with mental disorders.

What kind of work has been developed by the Anti-Corruption Institute since its founding in 1923?

CLAES SANDGREN: The Institute was founded by business organizations. At that time, many businessmen came to the conclusion that it was important to combat corruption in order to avoid unfair competition through dishonest means. Today, the institution's main activity is to advise companies and municipalities, in addition to promoting seminars, lectures, and courses. Among the five organizations currently funding the Anti-Corruption Institute is the Swedish Association of Municipal and Regional Authorities.

What are the most common cases

of corruption listed in the archives of the Anti-Bribery Institute?

CLAES SANDGREN: Bribes paid to municipal officials.

What kind of bribe?

CLAES SANDGREN: Well, all kinds of favors and advantages. It could be a bottle of whiskey offered to try to get a license faster. Some cases are insignificant, such as that of the police officer who asked a driver for a salad in exchange for canceling a traffic ticket. But there are also more important cases.

To the point of being arrested?

CLAES SANDGREN: No, as far as I know, no one has ever been arrested for bribery.

Is it because the crimes have not been serious, or because of the Swedish system is lenient?

CLAES SANDGREN: Both. Our main problem in Sweden, in my opinion, is bribery paid by large companies to establish operations in certain markets. And it is difficult to investigate certain cases. You realize money is flying in many directions,

but it is not easy to gather evidence and make formal accusations. To prevent corruption in the private sector in general, another important issue is the level of competition. We had a bribery case involving Systembolaget employees. I believe the fact that this state-owned company exercises a monopoly on the sale of alcoholic beverages in the country contributed to the fact, since the only way to sell alcohol is through Systembolaget. If anyone could open a store and sell alcohol, there would be no reason to pay bribes. There are, of course, other good reasons to justify the existence of a monopoly, such as the control of alcohol consumption. But from the point of view of fighting corruption, every type of monopoly is bad, for they are an inherent incentive for bribes.

Have you ever feared accepting a gift?

CLAES SANDGREN: I do not think anyone ever offered me anything. Maybe people just realize that I'm not a very influential man.

There are many codes of ethics in the country. But Sweden also has its megalomaniacs:

THE MAYOR AND THE ROMAN LEGIONARY

The controversial mural in Hörby's town hall, adorned with actual people.

In May 2013, with his chest swelling with pride and uncontrollable delight, the mayor of the town of Hörby, in southern Sweden, called together all the local press. The occasion was the ceremonial inauguration of the City Hall's new artistic mural. In this painting of gigantic proportions, one detail caught the crowd's attention: the mayor himself, Lars Ahlkvist, appeared on the canvas portrayed as a Roman soldier, an armed legionary with helmet and armour.

The outlandish work exhibits, at one edge, the mayor-legionary accompanying the procession of Jesus' crucifixion. In the opposite corner, there is a World War II scene, depicting dead British pilots in the area surrounding Hörby. Between the two extremes, another well-known face was identified: one of the city's leading entrepreneurs appears on the mural dressed as Swedish King Karl XI, standing next to his wife, who is depicted as an aristocratic lady.

With attention focused on the aesthetic folly involving the mayor and the businessman, there was little discussion or judgment of the work's artistic merit. The press pointed their guns at the fact that the mayor, when deciding to install a new artistic work in the City Hall, had not called for bids when choosing the artist. The commission had gone directly to painter Johan Falkman, known to the mayor and also a friend of the businessman, the mayor's neighbor. The painting cost the public coffers 600,000 krona (about US$73,350).

The *Skånska Dagbladet* newspaper published the following dialogue with the mayor-legionary:

Reporter: The law clearly states that a committee that is well-versed and specialized in art must be the one to commission a work of art.

Mayor: I come from a family of artists, and I have always devoted a lot of time to art.

Reporter: But do you have any kind of formal art education?

Mayor: I believe that the important thing has always been an aspiration for the knowledge of the arts, and not a formal education in this field *per se*. And in terms of knowledge, I have no doubts concerning my ability.

As they became aware that the mural had made the city famous less for its artistic merits than for the ridicule surrounding the portrayal of the living characters, several local politicians quickly distanced themselves from the work. Some even tried to arrange for the mayor's resignation. But their efforts were in vain.

The municipal administration argued that the commission for the work was given directly to Falkman because it required a specific artistic qualification: a specialization in "monumental art."

The mayor-legionary curtailed the discussion and controversy emphasizing that art should always stimulate debate, and that the painting brought only benefits to the city:

"The mural is drawing attention to Hörby, and that's very good."

THE SECRET POLICE'S SECRET PARTY

Government agencies also step outside the limits of what is tolerated by Swedish taxpayers. One of the most bizarre examples was a big bash held in 2011 and hosted by the Swedish secret police (Säpo), with a hand-picked theme: "Bond, James Bond."

The secret soirée, organized for the 1,000 employees of the Säpo secret police, cost no less than 5.3 million krona (about US$648,000). No amount of money was spared to create the spy-themed environment: the hall was transformed into a casino where Säpo employees circulated among croupiers and played blackjack, making bets with fake money.

On stage, famous artists, dancers, and comedians took turns performing. The Ambassador Orchestra, known for entertaining guests at the annual Nobel Prize party, played hits from Bond films.

"This is where Säpo hosted their James Bond-themed secret party"
Overspending on the secret police's theme party created a scandal.

Among the guests, according to some accounts, was Jonathan Evans, head of MI5, the British secret service. The event's official program exalted the event's source of inspiration, Albert Broccoli, the legendary American producer of the James Bond films.

In 2012, the Dagens Nyheter newspaper exposed and berated Säpo's event.

"Contrary to what the law dictates, there was no call for bids for the event, and the exorbitant contract was offered directly to one agency," the newspaper reported.

The entire cost of the party was reported as an in-house "entertainment" expense, but the newspaper revealed that there was an error in the tax declaration for the amount. The Säpo management admitted to the error.

The head of Säpo at the time, Anders Thornberg, told Dagens Nyheter that the party was meant to be a motivational event for employees after a particularly stressful year that included terrorist threats, a suicide bombing, and a structural reorganization of the agency.

According to the newspaper, however, it was yet another example of a string of abuses in the system.

"Despite a series of revelations about expensive conference trips and staff parties, Prime Minister Fredrik Reinfeldt claims they are isolated cases, and not problems with the system," *Dagens Nyheter* reported.

Also in 2012, the same daily newspaper reported on the splurges of another public agency. According to the accusation, the Swedish Agency for Economic and Regional Growth (*Tillväxtverket*) had spent 25,000 krona (about US$3,050) per employee since January 2010 on staff events such as dinners, ski trips, and spa visits.

In total, during a two-year spending spree, the agency had squandered the equivalent of more than one million dollars. The newspaper revealed that there had been accommodation in castles and extravagant wine and chocolate tastings, luxuries that Swedish taxpayers do not wish to extend to public officials.

At the annual employee dinner party alone, the agency spent 1,476 krona (about US$180) per head, more than double the amount stipulated by the agency's own guidelines. The venue for the party was the luxurious Stockholm Grand Hotel.

"The Grand Hotel was, in fact, the least expensive option," the agency's general director, Christina Calm, said in defense.

"That is enough," decided Swedish Industry Minister Annie Lööf. She fired Christina Calm, and that same week she summoned the heads of all government agencies under her leadership and instructed them to set reasonable and "exemplary" limits on employee event spending.

"The Agency for Economic and Regional Growth needs a general director who has the full confidence of both the citizens and the government of Sweden," said Annie Lööf in an official statement.

During the previous year the agency had received an additional 6 million krona to cover its operating costs. In 2012 the government refused a new request for additional resources. That decision forced the

Tillväxtverket to make economies of 10 million krona (US$1.22 million).

In 2010, Swedish journalist Peter Wolodarski of the *Dagens Nyheter* newspaper had pointed out that "Sweden is not used to dealing with cases of corruption."

"Corruption is an evil that affects much of the world, but the impression we have in Sweden is that this is a problem that occurs only in other countries," Wolodarski wrote in an editorial.

"According to international statistics, we have a relatively low degree of corruption. But we would be deceiving ourselves if we believed that this problem doesn't exist in our country. This year alone we have had reports of bribery in the prison system, in the Gothenburg municipality, and in the plans for the new national football stadium," Wolodarski added, referring to irregularities in the construction of the stadium that replaced the historic Råsunda, the setting in 1958 for the Brazilian national team's first victory in a World Cup.

The editorial also recalled the suspicions — denied by Saab, the Swedish aerospace and defense company — about the payment of bribes for the sale of Gripen fighters abroad. However, there has been no formal allegations directed towards Saab.

The constant stream of unpleasant news, particularly in the municipal political arena, had already begun to disturb the Swedes. It was time to begin to confront the subject of corruption using the Swedes' favorite exercise: the debate.

A TORMENTED KINGDOM

It's nine in the morning on a day in the spring of 2013, and the seats are all taken in the auditorium of the convention center in Rosenbad, the seat of the Swedish government. At the long table on stage, the authors of the latest corruption study on Sweden observe, with some astonishment, the size of the audience that gathers in the amphitheater. In earlier days, a seminar with such an ignoble theme in civilized Sweden would perhaps not have been able to bring together enough people to fill a Scania truck's cargo space.

But today, a crowd of journalists, political scientists, academics and representatives of the police, industry, municipalities, and all government ministries swarm in the room. There are about 200 people gathered to address the question that has been tormenting Swedes in recent years: after all, is there more corruption in this kingdom than their worthy inhabitants had assumed?

"My foreign colleagues are surprised when I say that I study corruption in Sweden," said political scientist Andreas Bergh, one of the authors of the study, in his introductory session. "Why study corruption in Sweden? Actually, the fact that our country is at the top of the list of the least corrupt nations in the world does not mean that corruption does not exist in Sweden."

Anders's speech opened the bowels of a beast that had seemed long dormant in the country. It had been a long time since there had been so much talk of corruption, and the debate had begun just recently: all the nation's alarm bells sounded in 2010 when an unforeseen scandal was revealed. In Gothenburg, the country's second-largest city, local officials had been bribed by a contractor and had diverted public money to pay for personal travel and home renovations.

Other scandals would follow. In one, a politician from the Solna municipality near Stockholm was forced to resign after it was discovered that he was on the payroll of a construction company that had won several lucrative contracts in the region. A perplexed nation began to wonder if Sweden was, in fact, as free of corruption as the global indexes indicated.

That was the question that the seminar in Rosenbad was trying to answer. In the more than two hours of debate that followed the presentation of the report on corruption, one fact is worth noting: no doubt had been cast on the ethical behavior of parliamentarians, judges, and members of central government. All the accusing fingers pointed in one direction: the disturbing occurrences of recent years in the sphere of local municipal government.

The main explanation for the phenomenon, according to the debaters, was the organizational changes implemented in the municipalities at the end of the 1980s. As some of the municipal services began to be outsourced, public resources were used to pay the private companies that provided these services.

Dangerous liaisons between public authorities and local businessmen had led to corrupt practices in some circles, fueling in some municipalities what the director of the Swedish National Anti-Corruption Unit, Gunnar Stetler, described during the debate as an exaggerated dose of "you scratch my back and I'll scratch yours."

"Before, citizens would pay their taxes and the municipality would use the money to provide education, assistance to the elderly, and other social services, and the public had the opportunity to inspect what the local authorities did. But over the last 20 years, various public services have been outsourced to the private sector, "said Stetler, one of the conference speakers in Rosenbad.

"Private companies are running schools and building hospitals. And the point is that the public does not have the same opportunity to oversee these private companies. Thus, opportunities for corruption have increased. This is what happened in Gothenburg. In that city, a number of activities previously provided by the public sector were outsourced to be managed by private companies, and people started acting dishonestly. This is happening in all the Nordic countries," said the prosecutor.

The level of risk in procurement activities at the local level is also considerable, according to the report presented at the seminar:

"The value of public contracts in Sweden is 500 billion krona per year (about US$61.12 billion), of which 100 billion (approximately US$12.2 billion) are purchases conducted in a closed manner, without bidding and without transparency," the authors point out.

Sweden must be extra vigilant to curb potential corruption issues in the municipalities, they say. Activities under municipal responsibility — such as urban planning, the issuing of various types of licenses, procurement, and social services — are particularly vulnerable to improper influences. According to the authors, although exceptions exist, Swedish municipalities are poorly monitored by the media and by the auditors in comparison to how central government functions are scrutinized.

Yet the report says that "nothing indicates" that the size of the Swedish public sector in itself is a factor that causes corruption.

"We ruled out the hypothesis that corruption in Swedish municipalities is due to the relatively ambitious policies of the welfare state, and to the fact that the public sector in Sweden is very large in comparison to international standards," noted the four political scientists who signed the document.

The study acknowledges that a common assumption, especially among economists, is that the size of the public sector is directly related to the degree of a system's corruption. According to this theory, "corruption is an almost inevitable consequence of the existence of the government and the principal agents involved in it." For the Swedish authors, however, this is a "simplistic view":

"An alternative hypothesis is that the larger the size of the public sector, the more likely voters will be to monitor whether resources are being used well. From this point of view, a small public sector could be quite corrupt precisely because it is small, since voters might not perceive that most of their money is possibly being misused. The amounts involved would be too small to arouse the voters' interest in monitoring the government's activities, or to provoke their indignation and revolt."

Whereas a larger public sector, according to this theory, would make voters more critical and engaged in advocating excellence in the management of government resources, thus reducing the problem of corruption.

This Swedish study notes that countries that have succeeded in building and maintaining broad welfare states are also those that historically have low levels of corruption. The report demonstrates, for example, that according to diagrams produced by Transparency International on the relationship between perceived corruption and the size of the state, there are indications that countries with lower corruption rates generally have larger public sectors.

The issue is controversial, and not everyone agrees with the theory put forward in the seminar. But for the political scientists who signed the report presented in Rosenbad, the remedy for Sweden's episodic corruption cases is not to cut public spending.

"When, based on our research, we created an index for quantitatively analyzing cases of corruption in Swedish municipalities, we found that this index had a negative correlation with the size of municipal spending even when a number of other factors were considered.

Thus, we have not identified any element of support for the hypothesis that Sweden could combat corruption by reducing the size of the public sector," say the researchers.

What then would be the solution for rooting out the corruption that emerges especially in the municipal sphere? The participants of the seminar unanimously agreed that the answer for the municipalities is to expand the use of the same tool that proved decisive for sweeping out the excesses of state power: the law of transparency.

"Citizens and the media should have greater opportunities to oversee municipal power. It is necessary to ensure that the control mechanisms work, and it is necessary to broaden the use of the Internet to make public municipal expenditure," said Johan Mörck, a researcher at the Swedish Agency for Public Management (*Statskontoret*).

Another anti-corruption antidote suggested by the study's authors was to strengthen and broaden the auditing of municipal accounts. The prosecutor Gunnar Stetler argued that audits must be carried out in real time.

"Annual audits are not enough," Stetler told the audience. "If I tried to conduct investigations two years after an illegal act has been carried out, I would be lucky to gather enough evidence."

In the last of the 151 pages of the study presented in Rosenbad, Swedish scientists mention, as a positive step, the Brazilian initiative to conduct full audits in municipalities on a lottery-like random-sample basis.

At the end of the debate, the authors of the report failed to produce the answer that everyone was seeking: "We cannot say with certainty whether or not corruption has increased in Sweden," they admitted. Corruption is, after all, a social phenomenon that is extremely difficult to measure, stated the report. But you must keep your guard up. Because "even a low degree of corruption can provoke significant social problems":

"Corruption causes a chain of negative effects in the political and economic system. It distorts competition, reduces the willingness of companies to invest, and weakens entrepreneurship. In addition, corruption threatens the legitimacy of the rule of law and undermines confidence in key social institutions. Consequently, corruption can simultaneously undermine the conditions for economic development and the basis for the functioning of a democratic form of government."

The role of voters in government surveillance is, according to the Swedish political scientists, essential in a representative democracy:

"More highly educated voters are more likely to perceive a problem, be aware of the newspaper reports, identify the responsible politicians, and punish the perpetrators by exercising his or her voting power in elections. Comparative studies also show that countries whose populations have a higher degree of education are associated with lower levels of corruption," the report says.

"Voters must monitor irregularities, connect them with the people and the party that committed them, and punish them at the polls. In this way, politicians will know that reprehensible practices will be punished," the scientists pointed out in the seminar.

On the way out of the convention center, I asked Anders Bergh if Sweden needs tougher laws to punish corrupt politicians.

"I don't think so. When a politician is exposed in Sweden for committing an illegal act, it is virtually impossible for him to be re-elected. Regardless of what the law says."

CREATING A VIRTUOUS CIRCLE

Inscribed on the pavement of Drottningsgatan ("Queen's Street"), the long pedestrian street in the center of Stockholm, are memorable phrases by August Strindberg, the great Swedish writer and playwright who lived on that street. One in particular stands out, since it is so inconsistent with the political realities of present-day Sweden: "Is there a more docile and innocent creature than a former minister?" Strindberg asked in the 19th century.

In 18th and early 19th century Sweden, there were many citizens who were at odds with morality. But by 1840, a process had been set in motion that would lay the foundations for a solid and enduring culture of honesty in the country.

The plan would be executed at breakneck speed. The strategy involved a drastic reform of institutions aimed at establishing good governance in the kingdom. It was a sort of institutional Big Bang, as defined by Swedish political scientist Bo Rothstein. Radical changes would be introduced not only in a few, but in virtually all of the nation's political, social, and economic institutions.

The idea was to create a new virtuous circle. All changes were aimed at the same goal: the creation of an efficient, impartial, and universal state apparatus, intended to guarantee the rights of all citizens, and not just those of a privileged minority.

There was a Herculean task ahead. In the Kingdom of Sweden at that time, bribery was rampant, relationships and privileged contacts with the court of the king were more important than the laws, the nobility took precedence in the allotment of court positions and in the public sector, and military officers and public servants bought and sold positions.

Not even blatant incompetence in office was a valid argument to remove people from positions of authority. It was also common among public servants to receive income from land and property associated with the position they held. In addition, access to universities was largely based on privileged personal contacts. Historians describe the situation in law colleges during this period as "a veritable intellectual

Strindberg's question etched in steel on the street: "Is there a more docile and innocent creature than a former minister?"

and organizational mire," which lasted until the first decades of the 19th century.[2]

The first step was to reform the public sector in order to create a Weberian structure, in which public servants would be recruited based on merit and technical competence, in selection processes that were open and regulated by a set of universal rules. This dramatic reform was implemented between 1860 and 1875.

The new morality required that public officials deal impartially with citizens. Acting in an impartial manner meant treating everyone equally, without distinction, and with respect and consideration. There would be no privileges as in the old order, based on personal relationships or private interests.

The whole concept of what it meant to be a civil servant was transformed. The idea of seeing public office as a fiefdom from which the "owner" could derive benefits would also be abandoned. Corrupt practices continued to occur to a certain degree, but were no longer seen as "standard procedure."

"The old notion that public office was a form of property was beginning to disappear," wrote historian Emil Hildebrand, head of the Swedish National Archives, in 1896. Corrupt practices still occurred to some extent, but corruption was no longer the standard rule.

The old order was simultaneously demolished on several other fronts. In 1842, the school system reform

---

2 According to the Strindberg Museum in Stockholm, the phrase was written by the author in an article on modernity intended for the French public, published by *L'Echo* de Paris in 1894: Strindberg, *"Qu'est-ce que le modern,"* L ' Echo de Paris, 20.12.1894.

created compulsory and free education for all. In 1845, the government's right to confiscate newspapers was abolished, giving rise to a lively debate in the media about government power. In the same year, the supremacy of the aristocracy in occupying high posts of the state bureaucracy was abolished. In 1862, a revitalized criminal code established a new law to punish misconduct in public office. In 1863, reform of the university education system was approved. In 1866, a broad parliamentary reform was introduced. In 1876, a comprehensive reorganization of the national bureaucracy was conducted. The list of reforms was extensive.

It was a metamorphosis of values. Sweden was building a society characterized by the quality of government and trust in democratic institutions. Everyone could see that the old, corrupt system of the past was dying: its days were numbered. Expectations had changed. Citizens now felt certain that they would receive fair, just and appropriate treatment in their dealings with state agencies.

Once they perceived the change, citizens also began to change. They increasingly adjusted their own behavior to the new moral order. It became the rule, therefore, to act honestly and honorably in the public sphere, both in their vertical dealings — between a citizen and the state — and in their horizontal ones — from citizen to citizen.

According to Swedish and foreign scholars, by the end of the 19th century political corruption had been virtually eradicated in Sweden at the national level.

In the municipalities, however, irregularities continued to be detected until around 1950. At the time, a large portion of local government power was concentrated in the hands of the municipal council president, who also managed the municipal finances. The solution was a comprehensive administrative reform throughout the municipalities, which began to employ trained public servants who were untainted by suspicion of corruption. Specialist auditors began controlling the finances.

Gradually, corruption also became rare at the municipal level. For this reason, Swedes are in shock at recent reports of irregularities in the municipalities.

One interesting aspect of the process that cleaned up Sweden at the national level is that only a few of the reforms were aimed at directly attacking corrupt practices. The main tactic was to apply an indirect blow to corruption through an incisive maneuver directed at the central nerve of the country's political institutions. The primary objective was to produce a transformation in the political culture.

"Instead of just attacking corrupt practices directly, this indirect tactic transformed a particularistic political culture into a universal political culture," says Professor Bo Rothstein, of the Department of Political Science at the University of Gothenburg, in his analysis of the evolution of corruption in Sweden.

In a particularistic political culture, the kind of treatment that government agencies give citizens depends on the status and social position of each individual. To be treated better, it is generally better to be well connected, enjoy good social status, and ultimately display a willingness to bribe. According to several scholars on the theme, the root of systemic corruption exists in this type of culture.

As Rothstein says, to be the only honest one in the "rotten game" of a corrupt system does not solve the issue of corruption. In a deeply corrupt system, the study states, the need to offer and demand bribery becomes so impregnated in people's "mental map" that it becomes an informal institution throughout society. Paying bribes or acting illegally when you are stopped by the police, or when you ask for a license to open a restaurant, or when you seek a job in the public sector is standard procedure in a corrupt system.

"Even those who view corruption as morally reprehensible are likely to participate in the scheme, since "all the others" are also a part of it," notes the political scientist. According to him, the solution lies in the establishment of impartial institutions capable of assuring individuals that the majority of "others" will also be honoring their obligations. If most citizens feel that the majority of society behaves honestly, cooperation between individuals who do not share special relationships will become more common, in a society with a greater degree of social trust — which is a fundamental characteristic of the Swedish society.

Rothstein emphasizes an important factor: although corruption has cultural characteristics, it is not culturally determined. As an example, he cites the cases of Hong Kong and Singapore. A study conducted by scientist

Hilton Root shows that a prerequisite for the extraordinary economic growth achieved by these societies was a successful fight against corruption that began in the 1970s. In one of Transparency International's recent lists, Singapore shared fifth place with Sweden in the ranking of least corrupt countries, while Hong Kong reached 14th place.

It is interesting to note that other countries from the same cultural and regional sphere of Singapore and the former British colony of Hong Kong (returned to China in 1997), are considerably more corrupt. In the same ranking of corruption, China was placed 59th and Indonesia 96th.

"We can therefore conclude that the degree of corruption is not culturally determined," the study states. The text cites other sources to assert that ordinary citizens in severely corrupt systems do not normally internalize corrupt practices as morally legitimate acts. If convinced that most people would not participate in corrupt practices, their preference would be to not receive or offer bribes.

According to the research, it is important to change people's beliefs about the honesty of "others." And the institutional reform needed for this purpose must be broad.

"The courts are no more or less important than public service, the integrity of elected political leaders, civil society, or the media," says Rothstein.

According to the Swedish diagnosis, if anti-corruption policies are limited to the introduction of small initiatives, most likely they will have no effect on changing political culture and social order.

"A new kind of equilibrium must be attained," says Rothstein. He concludes his analysis with a quote from Larry Diamond, Professor of Sociology and Political Science at Stanford University:

"Endemic corruption is not a failing that can be corrected with a technical adjustment or political push. It is the way a system works, and it is deeply embedded in the rules and expectations of social and political life. To reduce and maintain corruption at less destructive levels requires a revolutionary reform of the institutions."[3]

---

3 Rothstein, B. (2011). Anti-corruption: the indirect 'big bang' approach', *Review of International Political Economy*, 18: 2, 228-250.

CHAPTER IV

WHAT KIND OF COUNTRY IS THIS?

THE BEGINNING OF TIME

IN THE BEGINNING WAS the ice. It was said that the end of the world was here. In 11000 BC, Sweden was covered by an immense sheet of ice, which in the last ice age was 3,000 meters deep. When the glaciers melted, the first visitors began to discover that this was a strange land. In his wanderings in Scandinavia in 350 BC, Greek explorer Pytheas spoke in horror of an icy place where the sea had become solid, and where for half the year the sun shone, and during the other half there was only night.

Pytheas's story seemed delusional. But the tale was sober in its essence: in the extreme north of Sweden, the sun hardly ever sets in the summer, and all winter the sky is dominated by darkness. One can imagine that any human being exposed to such extremes would become somewhat deranged. Not even in the more favorable latitudes of the capital, Stockholm, could one say that the people live in well balanced conditions. In the ten summers I have witnessed, the sun only goes down very late at night, but never completely, and birds begin to sing at three in the morning, announcing a new day. In the winters, night falls around three in the afternoon.

Stranger than these phenomena of nature, however, is the bizarre, age-old custom of the authorities of this land to consult the people on matters concerning the people themselves. One of the first to observe this apparent aberration was a French Benedictine monk named Ansgar. Around the year 850, Ansgar decided to request an audience with the Viking King Olof in order to obtain royal permission to take the word of God to his pagan subjects. The king answered by saying that the decision would be made through the vote of the people, who would be gathered in the *ting*, the rudimentary assembly of the Viking era.

Surprised by such an earthly revelation, Ansgar noted in his chronicles that it was the custom in these lands to "decide any matter of public nature more by way of the unanimous will of the people than by the orders of the king" [Herman Lindqvist, *Sveriges Historia*, 2002].

In the Middle Ages, this populace remained an unusual people. When Swedish king Magnus Eriksson was elected by the assembly gathered in the outskirts of Uppsala in 1319, four peasants from each district were present. In those days, kings were elected. And the king had to respect the voices of the Swedish common man in matters of taxes. That was the beginnings of a long tradition of popular participation in the country's decision-making.

Next to the king, there was always a Parliament. And when the first structure for the *Riksdag* (Parliament) was created in the fifteenth century, peasants were given a voice. They were one of the four "estates" or classes of the assembly, made up of representatives from the nobility, clergy, bourgeoisie, and the peasantry. This did not occur anywhere else in Europe.

"The popular 'democratic' character was represented by the peasant estate. Throughout its history, Sweden has never experienced periods of clear feudal serfdom, nor periods in which the land-owning peasantry was totally marginalized or excluded by the landed nobility," Swedish political scientist Olof Ruin observes.

Contrary to what happened in other European countries, the king of Sweden never exercised a completely absolute power. The most autocratic period the country went through was at the peak of the Swedish Empire (1561-1721), when warmongering Sweden occupied parts of Germany, Russia, Denmark, Finland, and the Baltic states. It was at this time that one of the most famous European philosophers, the Frenchman René Descartes, succumbed to the cold Swedish climate. Queen Kristina had invited him to visit Sweden, where he was unable to endure the freezing temperatures of Stockholm castle, and is said to have died of pneumonia a few months after his arrival in the country in 1650.

Sweden's time as a superpower came to an end without much to celebrate. The balance of power between the king and Parliament would soon be established by the Constitution of 1809.

But most of the people, including women and low-income workers, remained marginalized from politics. And Sweden was starving.

HUNGER, POVERTY, AND PIGS IN THE STREETS

Cows grazed and pigs grunted in the urban landscape of the Swedish capital, Stockholm, in the first half of the 19th century. The country was poor, hunger was widespread. Around 1860, famished Sweden received voluntary donations from London. The country's economy was agrarian and backward, and nearly 90% of the population lived and worked in the countryside. In the capital, working-class neighborhoods were slum-like places, where workers rented beds in abysmal, overcrowded housing. Until the beginning of the 20th century, Stockholm, which was founded around 1251, was still an insalubrious city. The average life expectancy of the inhabitants of Stockholm was age 39 for men, and 47 for women.

For many, the only escape from despair was via the ports. Between 1851 and 1930, approximately 1.3 million Swedes emigrated in search of a better future — mainly to the United States — a number that corresponded roughly to about 25% of the Swedish population. Thousands of young Swedes abandoned the shortages in the countryside to work as domestic servants in American homes.

But Sweden was beginning to transform its history.

There were valuable natural resources, such as mineral reserves and forests. Industry began to flourish, based on scientific breakthroughs and strong investments in education, technology, and infrastructure. The country was headed toward modernization.

In 1842, free and compulsory primary education was introduced for all. The idea was faced with opposition from both the agrarian sector, which did not wish to bear the costs of the project, and from conservative sectors, which didn't see the sense in educating the poor and risking revolutionary sentiments among the masses who had migrated to the cities. But the decision was implemented, partly as a way to train children to be obedient and socially adjusted citizens. The literacy rate reached increasingly high levels. And working class and lower-middle class children increasingly began to attend universities.

At the same time, trust in institutions was gradually strengthening, due to the structural reforms that would reduce corruption and give rise to an impartial and transparent public administration.

At the end of the 19th century, a series of popular movements for democratic organization would emerge: trade unions and labor movements that fought for better working conditions, temperance movements advocating the prohibition of alcohol, independent religious groups defending the right to religious practices outside of the official Lutheran Church, and cooperatives that organized the distribution of cheaper consumer goods.

"In Sweden, these popular movements constituted veritable democratic training schools, at a time when the parliamentary system as well as universal and equal suffrage were still not fully developed," emphasizes political scientist Olof Ruin. Universal suffrage, for men and women, would only be introduced in 1921.

Until the 19th century, Sweden was one of the poorest countries in Europe. In the 20th century, with a highly educated and skilled population, the country became one of the most prosperous and sophisticated industrialized nations in the world. And many of the immigrants who had left the country in times of uncertainty began to return home.

THE ARRIVAL OF RAILWAYS AND WEALTH

It was with unrestrained horror that the Swedes watched the arrival of the first locomotives. There was talk of the trains' unbelievable speed, which traveled at 40 kilometers per hour. Many feared that, at such a rapid pace, people would not be able to breathe properly and would fall unconscious to the train's floor. To make matters worse, as described by Swedish journalist Herman Lindqvist in his multiple-volume *Historien om Sverige*, a German doctor warned with all his scientific authority during a debate in the Swedish Parliament that a passenger who dared to look out the window at that infernal speed would risk brain damage.

Even more frenetic was the pace of growth of the economy. A series of economic and liberal reforms boosted Swedish expansion, with the approval of the 1864 Free Trade Act and Sweden's adherence to the rules of international free trade the following year.

At that time, previously underdeveloped Sweden experienced an unprecedented technological explosion, with the emergence of a series of inventions and innovations that were patented in the country.

Long before all of this, Swedish astronomer Anders Celsius had already developed the scale used in thermometers. Now Swedish inventions proliferated: Alfred Nobel's invention of dynamite, the first centrifuge and separator of milk and cream, the safety match and the modern Ericsson phone. In 1900, Stockholm had one of the world's greatest number of telephones. Over the years, the advancement of Swedish technology would give rise to innovations such as the zip fastener, ball bearings (which solved one of the biggest industrial problems of the early 20th century), Tetra Pak's long-life packaging, Dr. Rune Elmqvist's pacemaker, and engineer Nils Bohlin's three-point seat belt for Volvo. This innovative and enterprising spirit still survives with Swedish innovations such as Skype, which allows people to communicate freely over the Internet, Håkan Lans' color computer screen, and the Spotify online music streaming service.

At the same pace as the first innovations, Swedish companies — such as Ericsson, SKF, Electrolux, AGA, Saab, Bofors, Scania, and Volvo — have grown and expanded around the world.

The Sweden of peasants and farmers became, in the

few decades between 1900 and 1930, an industrialized nation. Modern Sweden would emerge in the 1930s, and with it was born a new radical concept of urban design and architecture — it was the time of *funkis*, or functionalism.

Sweden's policy of neutrality during the two great world wars would become an advantage in the process of the "economic miracle" that took place: after all, Sweden's industrial capacity was intact.[4] Primarily in the years following World War II, the country was ready to supply the products needed to rebuild Europe, and thus Sweden's economic power expanded even more. The country had become wealthy.

In politics, a radical transformation of the nation's life was under way.

THE SWEDISH MODEL IS BORN

Many now viewed progressive Sweden as the way of the future: in the polarized world scene of the 20th century, the country's radical experiments seemed to offer a middle way between the excesses of capitalism and socialism. The Swedish path was, in fact, what would come

4 Neutral and peaceful Sweden also became one of the world's largest arms manufacturers. Ever since the invention of dynamite by Alfred Nobel in 1865, Swedish innovations have contributed to the art of war. During the Second World War, Sweden's own neutrality was only possible because of particular geopolitical circumstances. Sweden was an important source of iron ore for the Germans, and so it was in their interest to keep the country at peace. Denmark and Norway did not share the same fate: they were invaded precisely to keep the Swedish iron ore route safe. On the other hand, Sweden became a safe haven for Danes and Norwegians fleeing the Germans.. During World War II, Germany was Sweden's main trading partner (Lars Magnusson, Sveriges Economiska Historia, Norstedts, 2010.).

to characterize so-called "Nordic capitalism," a formula which basically combined a vigorous market economy with a substantial welfare state based on equal opportunities, social solidarity, health, education, and culture for all.

At the root of the Swedish welfare state were the popular labor and social movements that emerged at the end of the 19th century. In the spring of 1889, as a consolidating force among those popular movements, the Social Democratic Worker's Party of Sweden was founded. Proposals for social change also came from liberal politicians, and in 1913 Sweden became the first country in the world to create a universal public pension system for all citizens. It was the beginning of the modern Swedish welfare state.

In March 1920, Hjalmar Branting formed Sweden's first Social Democratic government, which would also be the first in Europe.

"Social democracy presented itself as socialist, but at the same time in everyday politics it renounced any concrete ambition in that sense — at least as it is commonly understood by other similar political parties, that is, involving the nationalization of natural resources, industry and banks. Social ownership was not defined as an objective in itself, with industry remaining fundamentally in private hands," explains political scientist Olof Ruin in an article about the development of the Swedish model.

"Nevertheless, there was a willingness to combat capitalist excesses and distortions, and limit profits using various mechanisms," he adds.

The term of the hour was social inclusion. The goal of the welfare state programs, to be implemented from the 1930s onwards, was the establishment of a real safety net for citizens. The expression *Folkhemmet* (Home of the People), coined by Social Democrat leader Per Albin Hansson, symbolized the goal of the initiative: that people could feel as secure in society as they felt inside their own homes.

There would be no more privileges, and no privileged people. This is how Hansson, who would take the train to work when he became Prime Minister in 1932, had explained the vision of a new and more humane society: "A good home has no privileged or rejected members; no favorite or least-favorite children. In such a home, no one looks at anyone with contempt; nobody tries to take advantage of others; in it, the stronger do not oppress or steal from the weaker. In a good home there is equality," Hansson said in a speech to Parliament.

Hansson was also the first Swedish political leader that Swedes referred to and called only by his first name, "Per Albin," without using his last name.

Constructing the new society would involve a historical partnership between capital and labor. As part of the additional set of measures that would shape the so-called Swedish model, the highly organized labor movement and the Swedish industry signed a pact. The flow of industrial production would be threatened by a minimum of strikes, and workers would have better conditions, in a wage system marked by collective bargaining and solidarity.

*Prime Minister Hansson's lesson: in a good home,
the strong do not oppress or steal from the weak.*

This would ensure stable conditions for economic growth, which in turn would support a broad program of social protections. The agreement, signed in 1938, became known as the Saltjöbaden Pact, named after the location of the Stockholm region where negotiations took place.

"Here was the mutual recognition of the roles of the two main agents in the economic process, both motivated by a sense of well-being for a country dependent on its exports to survive," wrote American journalist Marquis Childs.

"As long as the international competitiveness of industry — almost 90-95% of it in private hands — continued to grow, and thus maintain its prosperity, the growing size of the welfare state could be financed through taxes that tended to keep pace with the benefits of the social welfare system."

Sweden had become an example of pragmatism and progress, with a unique model combining a pact between workers and industry, high taxes, generous social policies, and a mixed economy. Under the Social Democratic leadership, the country was ready to build a strong welfare state.

"CRADLE TO GRAVE" SOCIAL SECURITY

In the 1930s, with the Swedish economy in good shape, the gradual construction of a broad and generous social welfare state began. It was carefully worked out to provide coverage for citizens "from the cradle to the grave." The reforms, financed by one of the highest taxes in the world, would be far-reaching.

The first step was the implementation of 32 comprehensive reform packages, which included the introduction of an extensive public health system as well as free maternity hospitals; free and quality education up to university, including school supplies; supplies of vitamins and free dental care for children and adolescents; generous social benefits, maternity leave, unemployment benefits and an increase in public pensions guaranteed by the state.

Sweden was not, evidently, the only nation to discipline capital and develop a new social policy in the 20th century. This was a worldwide trend, driven by Franklin Roosevelt's New Deal after the Great Depression and partly by the British debate around the welfare state, inspired in particular by William Beveridge.

But the Swedish (and Scandinavian) social model contained a distinguishing element in comparison to the other social welfare models: its universality.[5] This was not a policy aimed primarily at the poor, but a set of policies and benefits aimed at the well-being of all — rich, poor, and middle class — regardless of income.

The wealthiest would pay the highest taxes, but they would also receive generous benefits and social services. Redistribution of income would reduce poverty and

____

5 Magnusson, L. (2010). *Sveriges Economiska Historia*, Norstedts.

promote equality, in a society of solidarity where everyone would have equal opportunities.

Investments in public education, as in other Nordic societies, formed one of the central pillars upon which the Swedish system was built.

"This became an historic period of investing in individuals, and provided access to the resources that enabled them to maximize their value in the market. Historically known as the countries with the highest literacy rates, the Nordic countries have long been ranked at the top in terms of basic education and investment in research," wrote Swedish historians Henrik Berggren, political editor of the liberal daily *Dagens Nyheter*, and Lars Trägårdh, a professor at the University of Ersta Sköndal.

The long list of benefits and social services would gradually be expanded throughout the 1940s and 1950s. By the mid 1950s, Sweden had reached the world's highest egalitarian standard of living.

The future had major difficulties in store — especially the profound crisis of the 1990s, which would force the country to make deep cuts in state spending. In the years leading up to this critical point, however, the consolidation of the Swedish social model was still a time of national exhilaration.

In the 1970s, Sweden was the fourth richest country in the world, and the Swedes seemed to have reached the utopia of a just and perfect society.

AN EXTREME NATION

Extreme Sweden also became famous for its unorthodox ideas. The Swedes concluded, for instance, that housewives should have the right to holidays — and why not — paid by the state. This practice was common up until the mid-1970s, when Swedish housewives traveled on well-deserved vacations to hotels and inns across the country.

These were times when Sweden's economy still seemed to allow extravagant spending, and when there were still a large number of housewives in the country. Women entering the workforce would soon be crucial to the expansion of the Swedish economy. Today, approximately 76% of Swedish women are in the workforce, according to *Arbetsmiljöverket*, the Swedish Work Environment Authority.

The Swedish concept of morality was also peculiar. In a famous interview broadcast by the BBC in 1969, a curious dialogue took place between Olof Palme, Swedish Minister of Education at the time, and journalist David Frost. The journalist asked about the notorious subject of Swedish sexual liberality, a subject fueled in part by a series of erotic Swedish films that were making it to international screens.

"Is Sweden really free from censorship ?" asked Frost.

"We still have some censorship for instance of films and of printed material, but it's less strict than in very many countries," Palme said.

Up until the 1970s, Swedish housewives were entitled to state-paid vacation.

"What sorts of things have been censored lately in this country?" asked the journalist.

"We censor violence, especially when it contains elements of sadism. For instance, some Walt Disney films have been banned in Sweden. It's harmful to scare children with violence and sadism," Palme replied, much to the astonishment of the interviewer.

"Morality is not limited to sexual issues. Bad wages and unemployment are also immoral," said Palme, who shortly thereafter would become the prime minister of Sweden.

In 1809, the Swedes had invented the role of the Ombudsman, to deal with the helplessness of the individual in the face of government excesses. Less noble was the idea to create, in 1941, a policy to sterilize physically and mentally disabled persons, which remained in place until the 1970s.

Palme (on the right) with David Frost: Low salaries and unemployment are immoral.

More edifying ideas would arise. In 1979, Sweden was the first country to create a law prohibiting the use of corporal punishment on children. It also completely banned all advertising for children on television. Boys and girls under 12, the Swedes reasoned, are not old enough to be exposed to commercial pressures. In addition, they should not be induced to want toys and clothes that in many cases they cannot afford.

Today, the Swedish advertising industry also reflects the nation's notorious disdain for advertisements that reinforce sexual stereotypes, such as those objectifying women. Billboards featuring half-naked women (or men) are not usually part of the Swedish urban landscape.

"Any advertising executive who tried to sell a car with the aid of nearly naked women would not be hired again," wrote journalist Barbro Hedvall.

In 2008, widespread protests were voiced in Sweden when an Irish airline released an advertising campaign which was considered to be sexist. In the advertisement, a woman in a miniskirt and a tiny top posed as a student next to a blackboard that read "The hottest back-to-school deals."

"The woman's image was used to attract people's attention in a sexual way, which is offensive to women in general," condemned Sweden's Trade Ethical Council against Sexism in Advertising (ERK).

Gender equality is an important feature of this country, where even Finance Minister Anders Borg defines himself as a feminist. In the 1970s, radical experiments were held in schools: girls were given cars to play with, and the boys were given dolls.

To this day, even at the preschool stage Swedish children are freed from expectations related to the roles traditionally imposed on girls and boys. The idea is to ensure that children have equal opportunities and the freedom to make their own choices — regardless of gender.

One night in 2013, TV channels opened their news bulletins with a report that touched off sparks of indignation across the country. A schoolteacher had sent a group of boys to the basketball court, while the girls had been given the task of sprucing up the classroom for a festive event. That was distasteful sex discrimination, accused the media. Several minutes of the TV reports were devoted to the teacher's explanations and apologies, as well as interviews in which the girls said that yes, they would rather have played basketball instead of cutting out paper flowers.

In some spheres, even the pronouns "he" (*han*, in Swedish) and "she" (*hon*) have been abolished: they are being replaced by a neutral pronoun, christened *hen*. This is the case in the Egalia nursery in Stockholm, which adopted the neologism as a way of neutralizing barriers between genders. On the shelves of the school library, in addition to the classic fairy tales, there are also books about single parents and homosexual couples.

The commitment to achieving greater gender equality has gradually created a new reality in the home: household chores are basically divided between men and women, although the workload for women is still greater. The Swedes went so far as to time people's workloads. Daily housework performed by women saw a reduction of fourteen minutes between 2000 and 2010, while the figure for men increased by eleven minutes.

According to statistics from the OECD (Organization for Economic Cooperation and Development), Swedish men spend 177 minutes a day cooking, cleaning, or performing some other type of household task — more than the European average of 131 minutes, but much less than that of Swedish women, who devote an average of 249 minutes daily to household chores.

In the political arena, women are well represented. In the current Parliament, for example, women make up 45% of the total 349 parliamentarians.

The rules for succession to the Swedish throne were also changed in order to allow the crown to be passed on to the oldest child, regardless of sex. The constitutional reform, passed in 1980, made Princess Victoria the heir to the throne instead of her younger brother, Prince Carl Philip.

But the underrepresentation of women in executive positions persists, as well as wage differences between the sexes. On average, Swedish men earn 10-15% more than women.

THE SWEDISH THEORY OF LOVE

The following attitude is one of the main features of the Swedish society: each citizen, male and female, is responsible for their own livelihood.

"Legislation has reflected this approach since the 1970s," writes Kristina Persson, former deputy governor of the Swedish Central Bank and current director of Sweden's Global Utmaning institute, in an article presented at the Davos World Economic Forum: "Taxation is individual, that is, neither the family nor the household is a fiscal unit. Both pensions and sick pay are linked to the individual. Each member of the couple is obliged to care for their children, but none has any obligation to care for each other, whether woman or man."

This is what Swedish historians Henrik Berggren and Lars Trägårdh call the "Swedish theory of love": true relationships of love and friendship in Sweden are only possible between individuals who do not depend on one another.

In 2010, the marriage of the heir to the throne with her former personal trainer delighted the kingdom's subjects. Among commoners, such love stories don't usually end well: Sweden's divorce rate is one of the highest in the world. But when love ends, many men can still live happily ever after alongside their children. And divorce doesn't hurt the wallet as much.

Under Swedish law, since the 1990s men are not obliged to pay maintenance or child support. The one condition for not having to pay child support is to share the custody of the children with their former partner — a condition that actually reflects the desire of many divorced men.

Increasingly, shared custody of children has become the norm in the country. Today, more than 30% of the children of separated couples live part of the time with the mother, and part with the father. Among children of ages six to ten, the percentage is even higher: 50%.

A news story recorded for the Brazilian TV showed how Swede Anders Herlitz lives after divorcing his first wife. Anders told me that he lives with the two children from his previous marriage as part of a shared custody agreement. The children live one week with him, and the next week at their mother's house. Today, he is married to Brazilian Daniela Gradim, with whom he has his youngest child, Maria Isabela. Anders says that in Sweden it is common to share custody of the children — as well as the costs.

During the weeks the children are with him, Anders

takes care of the children and pays the expenses. When the children go to their mother's house, she is the one who bears the cost of food, clothing, and bills. The extra expenses, such as sports classes, are shared between Anders and his ex-wife.

"Everything is divided up, fifty-fifty," says Gradim.

Swedish law is clear: a man is only required to pay child support if the children live with their mother full time. If the children live solely with their father, it is the mother who pays child support. In shared custody, neither the father nor the mother has to pay child support.

According to lawyer Lotta Insulander-Lindh, one of the country's leading divorce specialists, in many cases the system may be unfair. A child may end up eating filet mignon at his father's house and hot dogs at his mother's.

Not everyone agrees. Like so many divorced Swedes, Anna James, the mother of two children, finds it strange to ask her ex-husband for money.

"I do not want anyone to support me. I make my own money and I control my own life," Anna told me. She believes that if a woman doesn't earn enough, "It's her problem and she should strive to get a better job."

"The Swedish way of thinking is different. Independence is very important to them. For me, it would be very difficult," admits Brazilian Daniela Gradim.

These modern Swedish families also spend birthdays and even Christmases together. The festivities bring together former husbands and wives, stepfathers, stepmothers, and half-siblings. All for the sake of the children.

Shared custody of children was approved in Sweden in the 1990s. At the time, many were fearful of this new way of raising children. But a 2012 survey by Sweden's Karolinska Institute suggests that moving from one home to another is more beneficial to children than living with just one parent.

The survey involved more than 170,000 children from separated couples, and found that children who live with both their mothers and their fathers at regular intervals are happier. Research demonstrated that they are healthier psychologically, and adapt better at school than children who live with only one parent.

"Moving from house to house every week is not a problem. For me, the problem would be to have to choose to live with only one of my parents," said Hamilton Lublin, 17, in the report recorded for the Brazilian TV.

As in the other Nordic countries, the role of Swedish men in caring for children is noticeable. In the 1970s, Sweden was the first country to turn maternity leave into parental leave for both mother and father of the child.

Today, fathers claim about 20% of all parental leave, but this number is increasing. According to statistics, on average Swedish men take 93 days off from work to stay home with their babies.

Thirty years ago, the government produced an advertising campaign showing a weightlifting champion with a baby on his lap to convince Swedish fathers that caring for a baby is also a man's job. Today, these signs of modernity are everywhere.

The scene is common in the Swedish capital: every day there are executives in suits pushing baby buggies, while making business calls on their phones. Or fathers jogging behind push-chairs, guiding and maneuvering them through the pathways of the city's parks.

Taking care of household chores and being independent is taught early on, in the very classrooms. In Sweden, learning how to cook, sew, wash, and replace buttons is part of the required curriculum in schools — for both girls and boys.

Poster from the government campaign to encourage fathers to also care for their children.

In school kitchens, students prepare a new recipe each week. That's when they discover the difference between cucumbers and courgettes, and learn the nutritional value of various types of food. The students also have home economics classes.

In laundry class, they are taught to select the correct cycle of the machine for washing different fabrics, such as wool and cotton. In housecleaning classes, students learn what products to use to wash the dishes, the floor, or the refrigerator. Girls and boys also have classes in mechanics and carpentry.

In the sewing studio, the teachers explain how to turn up trousers and make items of clothing. The students even have a knitting class. And the boys' homework might be to knit a scarf.

THE SOCIAL WELFARE SYSTEM

The golden years of the Swedish welfare state system lasted until the mid-1970s, when Sweden enjoyed broad acclaim for having created perhaps the most just and equal society in the world. Soon enough, however, turbulence and crises began to destabilize the seemingly steady ascent of the Swedish economy, resulting in cutbacks in its radically generous social policies.

The oil crisis had profoundly affected Sweden, which in the 1990s would also face a severe recession when the banking-driven housing bubble burst.

In the dilemma of its quest for a more viable welfare state, the Social Democratic government itself had made adjustments and course corrections, such as re-ducing subsidies and partially privatizing public services. Since 2006, new reforms to the system have been intro-duced by the alliance of center-right parties.

Yet despite its imperfections, so far the Swedish so-cial model is still a robust system in a wealthy country that continues to maintain a strong economy and a com-petitive industry.

When a child is born in Sweden, parents are entitled to a paid parental leave of 480 days. Of this total, 60 days must be used exclusively by the father and another 60 days exclusively by the mother. This means that these days cannot be transferred to the other parent.

For the first 390 days, the parent receives an amount corresponding to 80% of his or her income, depending on how much the parent earns. The maximum ceiling for parental allowance is 874 krona (about US$107) per day. For the remaining 90 days of the leave, the amount of the allowance is 180 krona (about US$22) per day. The 480 days of parental leave can be taken over vary-ing periods until the child reaches the age of eight.

The father of a newborn baby can take an extra ten days' leave for the child's birth. If there are twins, the period is doubled: twenty days. Adoptive parents have the same rights to parental leave.

Preschools are highly subsidized by the government, and parents pay only 8% of the monthly cost. There is also a maximum ceiling to be paid per child attending daycare. For the first child of a couple, this limit is 1,260 krona (about US$154). The fee drops gradually until the fourth child of a couple, who can attend the daycare free of charge.

The average Swedish salary is 35,800 krona, according to 2012 statistics. It is also common for parents to join together in cooperatives to create and run their own daycare centers, which are financed by the state to the same degree.

From birth, each child receives a monthly government allowance of 1,050 Swedish krona (approximately US$128) until the child reaches the age of sixteen. The greater the number of children the couple has, the higher the benefit. The allowance increases progressively from the birth of the second child to a maximum of 10,014 krona (about US$1,225) a month for a family with six children.

After reaching sixteen years of age, each child receives a monthly government payment of US$160 per month as financial assistance while completing his or her study period. This is paid ten months out of the year, and does not cover the period of school holidays.

Dental care is free for children and teens up to the age of 18. They may also have regional government-funded braces. When specialists deem it necessary to correct their teeth, patients receive a dental grant from the government to cover the costs of the orthodontist of their choice.

When children have severe vision problems, it is also the regional government that pays for prescription glasses. For families in a difficult financial situation, parents of children with more common vision impairments can contact social services, which then fund the glasses.

The education system is financed primarily through tax collection, and Sweden is one of the countries that spends the most in this sector.[6]

There are no monthly school fees. From six years of age, all children have free access to education, which is compulsory until the last year of high school. Schools also provide all school supplies, including books, handouts, and notebooks. School lunch is also free, and usually consists of a buffet that includes two hot dishes and a vegetarian option, as well as salads, vegetables, bread and fruit. After school hours, daycare centers and supervised activities are provided in schools every afternoon for children between the ages of six and twelve. Beginning at four in the afternoon, parents start arriving from work to pick up their children.

If they decide to attend university, which is also free, Swedish students are entitled to monthly financial assistance until they complete their studies. This assistance consists of an allowance of 3,066 krona (about US$375) a month, plus a loan of 6,710 krona (about US$820) a month. In cases of special need, students can apply for supplemental financial aid. The deadline for repayment of the loan is the day the former student reaches 60 years of age. In my time as a student at Stockholm University, I would automatically receive a monthly check in the amount of the allowance.

---

6 87% of adults in Sweden have a high school diploma, a percentage higher than the average in 74% of other countries of the OECD (Organisation for Economic Cooperation and Development). Source: OECD

The health system is also heavily subsidized, and the hospital stay rate is 80 krona (about US$10) a day. Rates for basic care vary between 100 and 200 krona, depending on the municipality. For specialist consultations, the maximum fee is 300 Swedish krona (US$37).

The system also sets an upper limit on the expenses anyone is required to pay: once a patient's treatment disbursements reach 900 krona over the period of one year, all subsequent medical appointments become free of charge for the next 12 months. A similar ceiling is set for spending on medications. This means that no one spends more than 1,800 krona (about US$220) on health expenses over the period of one year.

In 2005, municipal councils and the central government decided to introduce a new guarantee in the health care system. They decided that no patient should wait more than 90 days, once the type of care the patient needs is determined. If the waiting time is exceeded, patients have the option of receiving the necessary care elsewhere. The municipal government pays the cost, including transport.

The Swedish social security system also includes sick benefit. Employers must pay the benefit to employees for the first 14 days of their sick leave. In cases of longer treatment, the system pays the sick leave allowance for a maximum period of 364 days, with the amount equal to 80% of the employee's income. After this period, patients are entitled to receive the benefit for an additional period of 550 days, at a rate corresponding to 75% of their income.

Calculations are based on annual earnings of up to a maximum of 333,700 krona (about US$40,800). The benefit can be extended in the case of serious illness, and specific rules regulate the granting of sick benefits to students and the unemployed as well. Parents of sick children are also entitled to receive allowances in order to remain at home to care for them.

Disabled people are entitled to free personal assistance, including transportation by taxis or specially adapted vehicles. For the elderly, social assistance is also offered at home, with fees charged according to the ability of each to pay. For seniors with limited resources, the service can be free. In principle, everyone has the choice of receiving care at home or in a nursing home, although the system is far from being perfect.

The Swedish pension system consists of three parts: the income-based pension, the premium pension and the guaranteed pension. A total of 18.5% of the employee's salary and other taxable benefits are earmarked for his or her pension. Of this total, 16% goes to the income-based pension, whose value grows according to income progression and the performance of the Swedish economy. The remaining 2.5% goes to the so-called premium pension, which was created as part of the reform of the Swedish pension system in 1999: the money is deposited in individual investment accounts chosen by the individual, with employees able to choose to have their premiums invested in up to five funds from a wide range of funds. In addition, the government has set up a special investment fund for individuals who do not want to make their own investment decisions; their contributions are automatically invested with the Premium Savings Fund, which is managed by the Seventh National Swedish Pension Fund (AP7). The reason for introducing the premium pension system was that it offers a certain balancing of risk in that the old-age pension will reflect both the rise in society's living standards and the actual return on the invested assets.

For people who have had little or no income in their lives, there is a smaller portion of state pension, called guaranteed pension. The purpose of the benefit is to guarantee those people a basic income every month. Elderly care support provides a final safety net to ensure a decent standard of living.

Everyone working in Sweden is covered by unemployment insurance at a basic level. The Swedish unemployment insurance scheme consists of a universal basic insurance, and an optional loss of income insurance covering both employees and the self-employed. Membership of an unemployment loss of income insurance fund is voluntary. In other words, workers must enroll in specific institutions to be entitled to the benefit and must pay a monthly contribution. These institutions are known as A-Kassa (*Arbetslöshetskassor*). For the basic package, the monthly contribution is 90 krona monthly (about US$11). In order to enjoy an unemployment salary greater than the basic wage, workers must take out supplementary insurance, with monthly contributions proportional to their salary. The payment of unemployment benefits is administered by 36 unemployment insurance funds. Historically these funds have been affiliated with trade unions, but today, the funds are required to be completely independent from other organizations.

When workers lose their jobs, they can receive loss of income insurance benefits for up to 300 business days. The benefits are taxable income. During the first 200 days, the benefit is equivalent to 80% of the amount of the previous income from gainful employment, with a ceiling set at around US$100 per day. For the remaining 100 days, this percentage drops to 70%.

Workers who lose their jobs and are not affiliated with A-Kassa can still obtain benefits, but only at a basic level, and at no more than about US$48 for each work-week day.

For poorer families or families with temporary financial difficulties, municipal governments provide assistance in the form of financial support based on individual assessments. This support includes resources for basic expenditure to ensure a reasonable standard of living.

What is described above is still a largely generous system, although it was once even better. Over the years, the Swedish welfare state has undergone a series of reforms in order to adapt to new economic conditions. Unemployment benefits have been reduced, as has the level of resources for both health and housing. The school system is currently undergoing criticism for its declining student performance and the growing numbers of children in each classroom. The model also faces deficiencies in the number of professionals trained to care for the elderly, and the Swedish press points to public authorities' poor control over the quality of out-sourced services provided by some private companies that are financed with taxpayers' money. Several schools are now run independently, and private management of the health system is a growing trend.

Since 2006, the center-right government has sought to implement its vision for a renewed Swedish model: the idea is that Swedish citizens should be more motivated to work than to live on social benefits. The basic recipe to encourage people into work, given the current formula, is a combination of lower taxes for workers and lower social benefits for those who are out of the labor market. Benefits such as sick pay and disability pensions have become less generous as income tax rates have been reduced.

For the center-right government, it is a matter of modernizing the welfare state and revitalizing the Swedish economy, without alienating the traditional values of the Swedish social model. For the left-wing opposition, this is a death knell for the country's ideals of equality and solidarity.

NEW TIMES

The indexes are enviable: Sweden is among the top-rated countries in global ranking lists such as the UN Human Development Index (HDI), the Prosperity Index of the British Legatum Institute, the Democracy Index prepared by The Economist Intelligence Unit, the

Quality of Life Index and the Global Innovation Index (GII), in addition to being first in the new Social Progress Index (SPI) and the Web Index, which measures the level of connectivity and Internet usage.

But the country's challenges fill the news and worry the population, in a nation that has begun to wonder whether its model of equality and social welfare, which has become a reference to the world, will be sustainable in the future. Economic inequality grows, the continuous and prolonged aging of the population affects the balance of the social security system, and problems with the integration policy for immigrants all lend strength to a new extremist political movement.

Sweden, one of the most egalitarian countries in the world, has become somewhat more unequal. It is the country where the income gap between the richest and the poorest is growing most rapidly among the 34 OECD (Organization for Economic Co-operation and Development) countries, according to a report released in 2013.

"Class safaris," set up to spy on the wealthiest, have become an uncomfortable novelty: in 2012 bus loads of "social tourists" circled through the upscale neighborhoods of Saltsjöbaden, Stockholm's upper-middle class suburb, in outings promoted by the left-wing organization known as *Allt åt Alla* ("All for All"). The rides would inevitably end up with eggs being thrown at the buses by disgruntled residents.

Even greater than the nervous palpitations of the wealthy homeowners, however, were the violent disturbances in immigrant communities in May 2013 that set alight nine Stockholm suburbs and shocked peaceful Sweden. The trigger for the riots was the death of a 69-year-old immigrant, shot in his own home by police officers who said they acted in self-defense when the man confronted them with a machete. But the ensuing battle scenes brought to light the feelings of segregation and exclusion experienced by a considerable proportion of immigrants, who make up 15% of the Swedish population. The epicenter of the rebellion was the district of Husby, where 8% of its 12,000 inhabitants were unemployed.

The most pessimistic have proclaimed the failure of multiculturalism and of the Swedish integration policies. One of the most supportive countries in the world in sheltering refugees who are fleeing conflict zones and political persecution, Sweden has a large contingent of Chilean, Iranian, and Yugoslav immigrants, and is recognized as the nation that received the largest number of Iraqi immigrants after the Iraq war. In August 2013, the Swedish authorities announced the immediate granting of permanent residence visas for refugees from the conflict in Syria, who continue to arrive in Sweden in increasingly greater numbers. Much of the immigrant population lives in communities isolated from contact with Swedish society. And despite having access to free education and other public services, many in these communities have difficulty in finding employment, and do not feel represented by politicians. Tensions have increased.

In 2010, normally cohesive Swedish society watched in surprise and apprehension as the far right entered Parliament. The election of the anti-immigration party, the Sweden Democrats (*Sverigedemokraterna*), with 5.7% of the vote, confirmed the advance of right-wing extremists in Europe, who demand drastic reductions in immigration rates.

"At the time, Swedes were shocked by the election of anti-immigrant extremists. Now, it looks like they've come to stay. One of Sweden's greatest challenges today is the integration of immigrants," says political scientist Jenny Madestam of Stockholm University.

The pace of migration has worried some Swedes. Yet few deny that Sweden seems to increasingly need immigrants due to the challenges imposed by its fast-aging population, and many argue that the question of immigrant integration into the labor force is essential in order to maintain the welfare system.

The country has the highest percentage of people over the age of 80, when compared to other European Union countries. Of Sweden's 9.5 million inhabitants, about 18% are already over retirement age, and it is estimated that by 2030 the number of retirees is expected to rise to 23% of the population.

It's a ticking time-bomb: a smaller economically active population works to sustain a system that has an ever-growing proportion of retirees. Prime Minister Fredrik Reinfeldt warns: Swedes must prepare to work harder. In 2012, Reinfeldt sparked debate by suggesting extending the retirement age to 75 years. In today's flexible Swedish retirement system, citizens can retire at 61 years of age, or work up until age 67.

"The retirement system is not based on some magic formula, but on the work of citizens and the redistribution of resources on a large scale. If people think they can live longer but shorten their time in work, then they will have to accept lower retirement pensions. Are people prepared for that? I don't think so," Reinfeldt told the *Dagens Nyheter* newspaper.

Criticism from opponents of the idea flooded the media.

"For those who live in the political environment, such as the prime minister, working beyond 65 means holding high positions on boards of directors, or working in well-remunerated consulting jobs. But for a factory worker or hospital employee who feels that his knees and back are no longer working as well at this age, it's a different story," the *Aftonbladet* newspaper argued.

More job creation is also needed in Sweden. In July 2013, the level of registered unemployment was 7.2%. Among young people aged 15-24, the rate was higher: 17.3%. Job growth will be one of the main themes for the campaign of the next general elections, which will take place in September 2014.

In 2006, the coalition of center-right parties broke the dominance of the Social Democratic party — which, with the exception of short breaks, had ruled Sweden for seven decades. With less than a year to go until the new elections, the government announced a fifth tax cut for those in work. The reaction was not as celebratory as one might suppose in this unique country: lowering of taxes displeases a significant part of the population and generates intense debate throughout the country.

Taxes in Sweden are comparatively high in relation to other countries. Local municipal taxes range from 29% to 36% of an individual's income, depending on where the person lives. In addition, for those earning over 35,500 krona per month — which is the average salary of a university professor, for example — state taxes of between 20% and 25% are levied, based on certain levels of income. The tax burden is further increased by VAT (value-added tax) of 25% on food items and most other products and services in general.

Even so, about 75% of the Swedes would be willing to pay even higher taxes to fund health, education, and elderly care, according to a 2010 survey by Swedish sociologist Stefan Svallfors. Many Swedes are still suspicious of politicians who promise to lower taxes. They do not want anything to threaten the country's egalitarian values, the welfare state and the quality of public services such as the school system and health care.

"Historically, most Swedes have always paid high taxes willingly because they know the money will come back in the form of quality social benefits and public services," says journalist Sophia Polhammer of the Direkt agency, Sweden's leading financial news agency.

"People are confident that tax money will not be diverted into politicians' pockets, but rather employed in well-defined policies that benefit everyone.

This 'tax morality' survives on a broad scale," she adds.

Sophia Polhammer notes that since 2006 the current administration has supported significant tax reduction for those who work, with the aim of encouraging many who currently live on social benefits to return to the workforce.

"But one of the consequences of this policy has been a deterioration in the living conditions of vulnerable groups such as the unemployed and those unable to work due to illness. This, in turn, has generated a heated political debate about the current policy of reducing taxes," says the journalist.

One of Sweden's dilemmas today is how to minimize the decline in the high standards of the country's welfare state, which is beginning to show cracks in its foundations. On one side of the debate are those who agree with the left-wing opposition, for whom systematic tax cuts and other measures promoted by the government will lead to the worsening of services and the abandonment of the Swedish model of social justice. On the other side are the defenders of the center-right policy, which defines the recent transformations as a necessary adaptation to the new times.

"In the forthcoming elections, one issue will divide voters: is it really possible to maintain the Swedish social welfare model, while continuing to reduce taxes? Right now the Swedish economy is in good shape. It has largely managed to avoid the global recession, and remains one of the most competitive economies in the world.

But that may change in the future," says political scientist Jenny Madestam.

It is not possible to imagine that the Swedes will trust in God to help them overcome the challenges of the future: this is an essentially secular nation, where only one in ten people says religion has any importance in their lives. The Swedish Lutheran Church continues to witness the decline of its flock.

More dominant are the commandments of the *Jantelagen*, or the Law of Jante. It is a "law" created in the 1930s by Danish-Norwegian author Aksel Sandemose, which eventually spread across the Nordic countries. There are ten commandments in all, which revolve around a central message: "Do not consider yourself to be special, and do not think you are better than anyone else."

It's a law that still seems to shape the minds of many Swedes — including the country's politicians.

A COUNTRY AND ITS POLITICIANS

It would be more likely to snow in hell than to see Swedish politicians getting rich in government or parading around in luxury cars, limousines, and private jets. Why is Sweden like this?

The Swedish history tells a story marked by a tradition of democracy and equality between individuals, in a society characterized by fundamental Lutheran values and rigid moral principles that have developed through the ages.

"This is a society with a strong tradition of equality.

And this egalitarian tradition is reflected in the country's political representation," says Swedish political scientist Rune Premförs of Stockholm University. "There is a profound sentiment in Sweden that politicians should be individuals capable of understanding, based on their own lifestyles, the living conditions of the citizens they represent."

This culture of equality is also common to the other Nordic countries, such as Norway and Denmark. In Swedish society, dominated from the earliest times of its development by an agrarian and homogeneous population, with a high degree of democratic participation, the legitimacy of politicians has always been associated with values of frugality and parsimony. In other words, it is associated with the simplicity of the lifestyle chosen by those who are elected to represent the people.

"It's part of our history," says political reporter and commentator Mats Knutson. "Since the Middle Ages, peasants and ordinary people have participated in Parliament and in government, although in certain periods that power was manipulated by the king. I believe this fact is connected to the reality that characterizes political behavior in Sweden: politicians live simple lives. And that's what voters expect from them."

The Swedish political class also seems to generally reflect the values of honesty, frugality, and Lutheran ethics that characterize Swedish society as a whole. Values that author Nima Sanandaji defines as Sweden's strong "moral capital," arduously established through the centuries and which has also sustained the economic success of the country.[7]

"Politicians generally mirror their societies," argues French journalist Jean-Paul Pouron, who has been based in Sweden since 1975. "Sweden has a particular ethical standard. It is a society with its origins in peasantry, and with solid rules of integrity. Swedes may not be the best people in the world, but they do have morals. A politician here has to be clean. Swedish politicians are aware of their role in society. And journalists are always monitoring what they do."

"In my country, we have many divas," Pouron continues. "In France, politicians have countless privileges, and they constitute their own elite. Not here (in Sweden)."

Broad social trust is the Swedish — and Nordic in general — gold: the Nordic region has the highest levels of social trust in the world. This is also reflected in the index of the Swedish people's trust in its political representatives: in the most recent survey, 56% of respondents said they had a high degree of confidence in politicians.[8]

"This is a key element," says political scientist Jenny Madestam of Stockholm University. "Swedish citizens believe that their politicians are not corrupt, and they also trust their public institutions. The high level of social trust in Sweden is the result of the establishment of strong institutions, starting in the 19th century. And that's a central aspect of the system."

7 Sanandaji, N. (2011). *The Swedish Model Reassessed: Affluence Despite the Welfare State*, Libera Institute.
8 Source: Statistiska Centralbyrån, Statistics Sweden.

Each country has its own political culture, which reflects the culture of the society as a whole, says Madestam.

"In Swedish society, the idea of equality between people is a fundamental value. No one should be better than anyone else, everyone should help each other — and that extends to politicians. Political reforms, such as the creation of the Swedish welfare state, reflect this basic societal value."

"So Swedes do not want to see politicians leading a life of luxury. We want them to be normal people, without luxury cars, without mansions, without expensive clothes, and without spending too much public money. Because it's about our money, and our money must be directed to the welfare of society as a whole," she points out.

Madestam acknowledges that the values of Sweden's political culture cannot be mechanically transposed to other societies. But she says the Swedish experience may serve as a wake-up call to some nations:

"I am not familiar with the circumstances of the reality of other countries. But in many societies, the population's perception regarding the privileges of politicians has been changing. In Italy, people are already questioning the extravagant lifestyle of their representatives, and are wondering whether a politician should really have perks, such as riding in luxury cars and buying whatever he wants. It's a similar story in Greece, partly due to the economic crisis. Increasingly, people view politicians' privileges and perks with a critical eye, and say to themselves: "It doesn't have to be this way.""

On the other hand, Sweden seems to have been influenced by other cultures.

"The salary of parliamentarians, for example, has undergone a series of increases in recent times, despite still being comparatively lower than in other countries," says Jenny Madestam.

Right now, at the end of this August afternoon that the sun insists on illuminating, the Swedish Finance Minister will be returning to his small studio flat, and the Speaker of Parliament will probably be on the underground on his way home. On TV, the nightly news of this unique land reports that five drunken moose invaded a house on the island of Varmdö, after getting drunk by eating fermented apples in someone's back garden.

In the corridors of power, there is another victim.

In the main headlines of the evening news bulletins, the minister of Labour announces the immediate resignation of the director-general of the Swedish Public Employment Service (*Arbetsförmedlingen*), Angeles Bermudez-Svankvist. She has been forced to resign following two media reports. The first: Bermudez-Svankvist took a cab home, for which she paid 575 krona (about US$70) after her 50th birthday party — "and the bill was paid with taxpayers' money," the *Aftonbladet* newspaper reported. The second revelation: Angeles Bermudez-Svankvist's mobile phone bill had been hitting the mark of approximately 15,000 krona per month (about US$1,830), due to the fact that she had neglected to block the device's roaming services during her trips abroad.

"This is unacceptable," the labor minister said to the TV cameras.

The stories continue.

In this orderly country where everything is organized to the point of despair, and where people even count each week of the year by number, I make a final call to try to get the views of yet another political scientist.

"Could we schedule it for Week 36?," says the voice on the other end of the line.

CLAUDIA WALLIN is a Brazilian journalist and author based in Sweden since 2003. Prior to moving to Stockholm, she worked for ten years in London as the bureau chief of TV Globo in Europe, director at International Herald Tribune TV and producer at the BBC World Service, for whom she still contributes as a permanent stringer correspondent. She holds a bachelor´s degree in Journalism from the Federal University of Rio de Janeiro (UFRJ), a masters degree in Russian and Eastern European Studies from the University of Birmingham in the United Kingdom, where she held a Chevening Foreign and Commonwealth Office scholarship, and a certificate in Swedish language from the University of Stockholm.

www.claudia-wallin.com